The Age of Hot Rods

The Age of Hot Rods

*Essays on Rods, Custom Cars
and Their Drivers from
the 1950s to Today*

ALBERT DRAKE

McFarland & Company, Inc., Publishers
Jefferson, North Carolina, and London

All photographs and illustrations are from the Albert Drake collection unless noted.

LIBRARY OF CONGRESS CATALOGUING-IN-PUBLICATION DATA

Drake, Albert.
The age of hot rods : essays on rods, custom cars, and their drivers from the 1950s to today / Albert Drake.
    p.   cm.
Includes index.

ISBN 978-0-7864-3404-6
softcover : 50# alkaline paper ∞

1. Hot rods—United States—History. 2. Automobiles—United States—Social aspects. I. Title.
TL236.3.D73 2008   629.228'6—dc22   2008013232

British Library cataloguing data are available

©2008 Albert Drake. All rights reserved

No part of this book may be reproduced or transmitted in any form or by any means, electronic or mechanical, including photocopying or recording, or by any information storage and retrieval system, without permission in writing from the publisher.

On the cover: The 1937 Ford coupe that appeared on the cover of the April 1952 issue of *Hot Rod Magazine* in present day Las Vegas (Photograph by Glenn Johnson)

Manufactured in the United States of America

McFarland & Company, Inc., Publishers
Box 611, Jefferson, North Carolina 28640
www.mcfarlandpub.com

For Linda and Moss,
riding mechanics

Acknowledgments

Some of these essays first appeared in the following publications, and are used by permission:

American Scooterist: "Cruising on a Vespa at Midcentury."

CruZin' Magazine: "The Spirits of Hot Rodding."

Goodguys Gazette: "American Gothic," "Bonneville Speed Week, 1955," "Bruce Geisler and the Chipmunks," "Bud's Beanee-Weenee," "Car Pooling," "Class Angle," "A Classic Memory," "CTA Reunion," "Dale Moreau: Ace Photographer," "Ed Almquist," "False Memory," "The Genuine Artificial Zebra Skin Interior," "The Glenn Johnson Coupe Revisited," "Growing Up," "Henry Gregor Felsen," "In the Garage," "Incident," "Les Amis de Route 66," "Let Us Now Praise Famous Men," "Linda Vaughn: First Lady of Motorsports," "Love of a Fine Car," "Luke the Drifter: Hot Rodders' Troubadour," "The Minister's Sons," "Mystery," "My Brush with Greatness," "1956: The First Portland Roadster Show," "Odd Balls," "Old Customs Never Die," "Old Dogs and New Tricks," "Oregon Original," "The Pacific Gunsight Special," "Racing the Reaper," "A la Recherche du Temps Perdu," "Records," "Roots," "The Service Station," "Simple," "Small Wonders," "Street Scene, Los Angeles," "Summer, 1955, A Sunday," "Synesthesia," "Thanks, Tex," "The First Ticket," "The Slo Poks Celebrate 50 Years," "The Suicidals Car Club," "Traffic Court," "The True Meaning of Christmas," "The War Effort," "War Surplus," "What's in a Name Anyway?" "Zen of Nostalgia."

Kickstart: "Scooters on Campus."

Old Cars Weekly: "The Amazing Story of Tad Winiecki's Safercycle," "Aussie Rodder Finds Good Tin," "Hot Rodding 101: Back to Basics," "Stan Mott and the Cyclops Saga."

Street Rod Action: "Celebrating the Low Buck and Beater," "Bridge to the Fifties," "Coming Home," "Cruising the Neighborhood," "Cruising with the NW Speedsters," "Dave's '37," "George Riley," "Girls and Rods," "Going, Going, Gone!," "Gordon M. Buehrig, 1904–1990," "The Great Unwashed Deuce," "Haney's Hot Rod," "Hill Autotorium," "Hot Rod Citroën," "Hot Rodding Down Under," "Hot Rods as a Belief System," "Iggy," "In Praise of Originality," "James Dean Run," "A Letter to a Young Hot Rodder," "Living the Fabulous Fifties—Again!," "Mr. Motor Manners," "The Mild Custom," "1932 Lincoln," "The Original Fonz," "Our '40," "The Outsiders," "The Pan Draggers Reunion," "Road Angels Redux," "The Search for Truth," "Sunraycers," "Swap Meets," "Trophies," "Tyler's Tales," "Watching Traffic," "Wendover," "X-51," "The XM-800 Dream Car," "Yard Art."

Woodie Times: "Iron Mountain Meal."

Contents

Acknowledgments vii
Introduction 1
Prologue: Watching Traffic 3

Roots: Exhaust Cutouts and Wire Wheels 5
1932 Lincoln 5
George Riley 7
Car Pooling 9
The War Effort 11
Street Scene, Los Angeles 13
Gordon M. Buehrig, 1904–1990 14
War Surplus 16
Roots 18
Growing Up 19
The Service Station 20
Ed Almquist 21
Hot Rod Citroën 23
Iron Mountain Meal 26

American Gothic: Hollywood Hubcaps and Duals 28
The Search for Truth 28
What's in a Name Anyway? 29
Synesthesia 30
American Gothic 32
Old Customs Never Die 33
Henry Gregor Felsen 35
Let Us Now Praise Famous Men 37
Love of a Fine Car 39
Racing the Reaper 42
Simple 44
Yard Art 45
Small Wonders 46
Girls and Rods 47
Haney's Hot Rod 49
Our '40 51

The Fabulous Fifties: Chopped and Channeled 54
In the Garage 54
Luke the Drifter: Hot Rodders' Troubadour 55
Oregon Original 57
The First Ticket 59
Traffic Court 62
The Minister's Sons 65
The Original Fonz 67
Bonneville Speed Week, 1955 69
Summer 1955: A Sunday 74
1956: The First Portland Roadster Show 76
Cruising on a Vespa at Midcentury 78
Scooters on Campus 82
Records 83
Bud's Beanee-Weenee 85
Class Angle 86
The Genuine Artificial Zebra Skin Interior 88
Odd Balls 90
Incident 91
The Mild Custom 93
X-51 94
The XM-800 Dream Car 99
Trophies 102

The Zen of Nostalgia: Reflections in a Bullnose Strip 104
Hot Rodding 101: Back to Basics 104
The Slo Poks Celebrate 50 Years 105
Stan Mott and the Cyclops Saga 107
Dave's '37 109

Celebrating the Low Buck and Beater	111
Thanks, Tex	113
The Pacific Gunsight Special	115
Mystery	116
A la Recherche du Temps Perdu	118
Hot Rodding Down Under	119
In Praise of Originality	122
Bruce Geisler and the Chipmunks	123
The Zen of Nostalgia	125
A Classic Memory	126
False Memory	127
The Glenn Johnson Coupe Revisited	129
Bridge to the Fifties	132
The Great Unwashed Deuce	139
James Dean Run	140
The Pan Draggers Reunion	142
Coming Home: Back to the Fifties	145
Coming Home	145
Les Amis de Route 66	146
Dale Moreau: Ace Photographer	149
The Amazing Story of Tad Winiecki's Safercycle	152
CTA Reunion	154
Going, Going, Gone!	155
Mr. Motor Manners	157
The True Meaning of Christmas	159
Aussie Hot Rodder Finds Good Tin	161
Hot Rods as a Belief System	163
Old Dogs and New Tricks	164
The Suicidals Car Club	166
Wendover	168
Tyler's Tales	170
Swap Meets	172
Road Angels Redux	175
The Outsiders	177
A Letter to a Young Hot Rodder	178
Hill Autotorium	179
Iggy	180
Living the Fabulous Fifties—Again!	182
Linda Vaughn: First Lady of Motorsports	184
My Brush with Greatness	186
Cruisin' the Neighborhood	187
Cruising with the NW Speedsters	188
The Spirits of Hot Rodding	191
Sunraycers	192
Index 195	

Introduction

By dint of the year and place of my birth, I was able to participate not only in the Golden Age of rods and customs, but also, decades later, in the wave of nostalgia for those good old days.

I was born in the middle of the Depression, when people kept the family car running well after it should have been junked. I grew up during World War II, when gas and tires were severely rationed, and no new cars were being made. Older cars were treated with care, or put on blocks for the duration. In 1950, when I was 15, I cruised the neighborhood and beyond on my bicycle, looking in yards and open garages for a car that had survived hard times and a world war. There was no shortage of them. Durant, Essex, Oakland, Studebaker, Hudson and other now-forgotten makes were everywhere, in addition to a wide range of Buicks, Chevrolets and Chrysler products. There were more Model A Fords than any of us can remember, some in excellent condition while others were battered wrecks; many were still being driven.

I wanted them all. Cars were available from ten dollars up and although I had my paper route money, I had to settle for one. What a decision! It was a wonderful time to be a young kid nuts about cars. I thought I wanted the '39 Crosley convertible parked near my house, powered by a two-cylinder air-cooled engine, small enough that I could drive it on the sidewalk and deliver papers from it. My father pointed out that there were no sidewalks in our neighborhood and, anyway, I was too young to get a driver's license or insurance.

I kept looking until I found a Model A Ford roadster that I knew I wanted. It was parked across the street from the theater where I worked. Although I was still too young to drive, my father looked it over and said okay. Years later I realized that he had a plan: He and I would take the car apart and put it back together again, so that when I did drive it I'd have some idea of how a car worked. He was a competent mechanic, and I learned a lot; some of what he taught me I've used all my life. He wasn't afraid to tackle any job, and he was willing to use baling wire or tape, to shim a bearing or file the ring land on a cast-off piston, to use a piece of rope in place of a fan belt or to put heavy grease in a noisy rear end, if that's what it took to make the car run. He'd grown up with tractors, threshing machines and Model T Fords, at a time when the nearest parts house might be a day's journey away. Also, he couldn't afford to pay someone else to do the work so he had to do it himself. In summer he'd paint a car with a brush, and it looked good. He could strip an engine and install new rings and bearings in a weekend, so he could get to work Monday morning. He'd lap the valves in the driveway, as the men in the neighborhood gathered around to offer advice and encouragement.

Something amazing happened during those postwar years: There was not one publication aimed at car nuts, and then several appeared to fill the void. *Road and Track* started in 1947, *Hot Rod Magazine* was first published in January 1948 and *Motor Trend* a year later. Those magazines offered information about how to hop up an engine or restyle a body, and the examples shown on their pages created enthusiasm. I learned more from their display ads than I did from my school books. Soon the only thing I could think about was a hopped-up car. As I learned, I knew what I wanted: a fenderless roadster with chromed, hopped-up Ford V-8 engine, just like the cars I'd seen in magazines. My father and I worked on the engine in the garage, on weekends and evenings, like Druids performing some ritual. We did not hand lap those valves, but sent the block to a machine shop, where things were done right.

I was not alone. A generation of young men suddenly wanted their car lowered, fitted with dual pipes and fancy hubcaps. They wanted an old car to look newer, and a newer car to look different. They wanted to have something to talk about when they went to the barber shop on Saturday to get a crew cut or a Princeton, and they wanted a smooth ride when they cruised through the drive-in restaurant with a date on Saturday night. This sudden desire for automania led to the founding of a bevy of new businesses. Body shops became customizing shops. Muffler shops sprang up to accommodate the need for dual exhausts. Certain garages became speed shops, for drivers primarily interested in performance. Auto parts stores began to expand their inventory, to include aluminum heads, dual intake manifolds and chrome accessories.

Things were happening quickly. The clunky old square cars of the Thirties were soon sharing the road with sleek cars of the Fifties. The new Kettering OHV V-8 was introduced in the 1949 Cadillacs and Oldsmobiles. In 1951 the new 180 hp Chrysler Hemi came out. By 1953 Dodge, DeSoto, Studebaker and Buick had OHV V-8s. As soon as these engines showed up in wrecking yards they got swapped for the old flathead V-8 in Fords and Mercuries. Instant horsepower! When the Chevrolet V-8 appeared in 1955 it was a lightweight, compact engine that fit nicely in a Model A or a '32 Ford, almost as if that was what the designers had in mind.

As a hot rodder during the Fifties, I was both participant and observer to all this activity. In 1951 I joined the Road Angels, a hot rod club, and the Columbia Timing Association (C.T.A.). I attended the first hot rod show held in Portland, Oregon, was at the early drag races in Eugene and the first drag races at the Scappoose strip, was present at the first timed runs at Madras, attended circle track races, had a car in the first two Portland Roadster Shows, went to the early Oakland Roadster Shows, spent a week on the salt at the 1955 Bonneville meet and so on. I looked and listened, made mental notes and took photos, although far fewer than I wish I had taken.

Decades passed, and I did other things, but I never forgot about the wonderful rods and customs I had seen as a teenager. Sometimes those photos were all I had to look at; rods and customs became rare. The custom car craze ended by 1960. Hot rods went into a steep decline during the Sixties and Seventies, and when they began to emerge they were called street rods. There was little or no nostalgia for the good old days.

In 1982 I wrote a book called *Street Was Fun in '51*, the first book on historical hot rodding, and it met with success; it's still in print and has a cult following. That same year I began writing a monthly column for *Rod Action* called "Fifties Flashback," which examined the cars, people and trends of a decade that made such an impression on me. Later others wrote books about historical hot rodding, but if one were to make a grid chart showing the rise of rodding nostalgia it would have to begin in 1982.

I wrote that monthly column in *Rod Action* for 17 years, until the magazine ceased publication. For a time I also wrote columns about the Fifties for *Street Rodding Illustrated* and *Rodder's Digest*, both defunct. For the past eight years I've enjoyed writing a monthly column for *Goodguys Gazette*, called "Flashing Back," where I continue to mine this rich ore. There seems to be a great deal of interest in what went on 50 years ago, not only by the graybeards who lived it but also by their grandkids. For those who want to know what a Frazer was, what a genuine trophy was like or what life was like before the federal government imposed EPA standards, I'm happy to offer the following material to new readers.

Prologue

WATCHING TRAFFIC

So I'm back in Portland again, the town where I grew up and where I keep returning. Where there is no road salt, and where cars grow old gracefully.

Occasionally, in the evening I like to drive to the local Safeway to buy a maple bar, unavailable in the Midwest, then to the Plaid Pantry for a take-out cup of coffee, and then to the Fred Meyer store at 82nd and Foster where I park, sip hot coffee, savor the maple-sweet bar and watch the traffic on 82nd.

Tonight a bunch of boxes on wheels parade past — Toyotas, Datsuns, Hyundais (would *you* buy a car made in Korea?) and Yugos. Also look-alike Plymouth Colts, Reliants, Chevettes. Then a raked 1950s Willys station wagon scoots past. Nothing wild, but fun to see, mainly because I haven't seen one for a while. It's someone's idea of a neat machine. And that's the point of sitting here: to see the odd, the interesting, the everyday driver that's been reworked a bit.

Another bevy of boxes, but among them a Datsun roadster from the early Sixties with mag wheels and a nutty exhaust. A couple more changes of the traffic light and a VW notchback rumbles quickly past, winding through the gears; it, too, is raked, with bright blue paint, graphics and a bra. Beside it, a whale among minnows, is an early Sixties Pontiac — a big one, a Catalina, I guess, with whites, chrome wheels and baby moon caps. It looks tough, but it lets the VW motor past as if it is beyond being threatened into a race.

There is something fascinating about this traffic watching. You can go to a car show and see dozens of immaculate machines, or to a rod run and see hundreds, thousands of high-buck rods, but here I'm seeing the odd and interesting everyday drivers in their natural environment.

A '49 Ford pulls into the service station across the street; it's lowered, with whites, skirts, Fiesta hub caps on the front, dual spots and lake pipes. Behind it is a '47 Chevy coupe; it has been lowered, with no door handles, but it's two-tone, with brown fenders and a tan body. It is also heavily pinstriped. The Chevy gets gas while the Ford waits near the driveway Soon they leave together, leaving the echo of V-8 and in-line six dual pipes hanging in the air.

For a minute things feel like the Fifties — I can imagine sitting on this corner on a particular night, which I did many, many times, and seeing a pair of mild customs pass. Or many — in those days one saw a plethora of '40 Fords with big 'n' little whites, '49 Fords with primer spots covering what had been leaded in, a newish Chevy or Olds with lowering blocks and pipes, and any number of young kids in Model A Fords, from stock to slick.

A new Jap bike burns away from the light, hitting double the legal speed limit within a block. Traffic has decreased during the past hour, and now it's possible to crank it on between lights.

That, too, reminds me of the Fifties: there was almost *no* traffic after 8:00 P.M. Most people came home from work, ate dinner, watched TV if they had one, and went to bed. This left the streets more or less empty. You could pull up to a light and not see another car ahead. If the car that pulled up beside you was ready and willing, you'd probably go through the gears until one of you backed off. Driving was fun!

That's what I yearn for — streets nearly empty except for rods and customs. And two-bit a gallon gas!

Then I recall a letter I got from a car nut in Glasgow, Scotland. He was ordering some books and enclosed a color photo of his daily driver. It was a 1958 Rover four-door sedan that had been lowered with door handles removed, whitewalls and dual spots. Painted yellow, it looked like a neat car. He was, I'm sure, proud of his ride, but kept apologizing for it, saying it wasn't as good as what we have in the States. He said there were no other custom cars around, or anyone really to talk customs with, but he has a good friend in Sweden who's really into customizing!

I'm thinking about his letter as I watch a '65 Chevy low-rider slouch past, red lights under the fenderwells and tassels bouncing in the rear window. I'm wondering what it would be like to live where the car culture did not exist — where you had absolutely no interesting machines to observe and no car nuts to talk with. And I suddenly realize that in many ways this really is the Golden Age of rodding. There have never been so many neat cars, so many events to drive them to, or so many people to talk cars with.

My maple bar gone, the dregs in the cup cold, I fire up my truck and head home, thinking how lucky I am to be in this time and place. I have to wait for the light at the intersection, and then I realize that the road ahead is barren of cars. When the light changes to green I get on the gas and goose it up to 45, just enough to hear the duals rumble past a shift point.

Roots: Exhaust Cutouts and Wire Wheels

1932 LINCOLN

Jim Griffin has a very specialized interest in cars: he's nuts about 1932 Lincolns. His tastes haven't always centered on this particular year and make; in fact, there was a time, before he got into classics, when he was a hot rodder. A charter member of the National Hot Rod Association, back in the Fifties he ran a couple of roadsters at Half Day drag strip outside Chicago. One had a full race V8-60, the other had a fuel-burning Riley OHV four-banger that turned a fast 86 mph in the quarter.

But over the years he's mellowed, and has focused attention on the stately '32 Lincoln — he owns five, including a roadster that is one of two known to have survived the years. He's become an authority on this make and model, and has done a great deal of research on the car. His idea of a fun vacation is to travel around the U.S. taking pictures and talking to people who are fortunate enough to own one of these cars.

Within every special interest there is a special-special interest, one that borders on the arcane. For 1932 Lincoln fans it's the roadster body built by Murphy. Only five were built, and one was the pace car for the 1932 Indy 500. Jim has a photograph of Edsel Ford sitting in it at the Brickyard. Edsel was interested in speed and styling, and although Henry kept him on a tight rein Edsel is generally credited with the Lincoln program. The Murphy-bodied roadster he's in looks a great deal like an over-size '32 Ford roadster, down to the tri-fluted bumper. But Jim is quick to rattle off figures to show what kind of car this is: 145-inch wheelbase, a V-12 engine with a 3-¼-inch bore and a 4-½-inch stroke, resulting in 448 cubes. Even with a compression ratio of only 5.25:1 the engine is powerful enough to go from zero to 60 mph in 26 seconds using only *third gear!* It could pull a three-ton limousine to a true 95 mph, and lighter-bodied cars to well over 100 mph, which was really cooking in those days.

Jim will also tell you what history is known of the five cars. Three were painted Laurel Green with polished aluminum belt moldings; the first one (KB 11) was built for the New York Auto Show, and it still exists. The Indy pace car was painted Gaya Red and was given to the race winner; the remains of this car were found in a junkyard many years ago, and it no longer exists. The fifth car was painted light and dark pearlessence.

Recently Jim ran an ad for KB Lincoln parts in *Antique Automobile*. A fellow out in Long Island responded that he had a chassis whose ancestry he was unsure of but that it had an engine with a KB number (KB 1281). Jim sent him a photograph of a Lincoln V-12 engine and the fellow said, "That's it!"

Jim traveled halfway across the U.S., to Long Island, N.Y., to get his purchase. It was only a chassis, but the engine was the original 448 ci Lincoln V-12, one of 1,600 made in 1932. Jim noticed in a flash that the engine had been modified. It had dual exhausts, Mallory coils and the fan had been removed. A temperature probe and brass cooling strips had been welded to the pan. The carb was missing, and the intake manifold had been butchered. Jim was puzzled why

The license plate identifies the place as California and the year as 1950. The Lincoln has been stripped for speed and runs big blower on engine.

anyone would try to hop up a brute of an engine like the Lincoln, and this was the beginning of a series of questions.

Jim has copies of the Lincoln factory records, and after getting the chassis back to Wisconsin he began to research his purchase. He learned that he now owned the remains of the fifth and last Murphy-bodied 1932 Lincoln roadster. He also learned that it had been purchased new by Mrs. Katherine Holden-Higbee of Cleveland. In that one year, at the height of the Great Depression, she had purchased two new cars, the 1932 Murphy-bodied Lincoln roadster (cost: $7,200) and a Judkins-bodied Belline (cost: $6,800)! Jim made contact with Mrs. Holden-Higbee, now 86, and she confirmed that she had owned the '32 Lincoln roadster from 1932 until several years later. She wasn't certain of the date, but recalled that she had driven the car from Cleveland, Ohio, to her winter home in Santa Barbara, California, on three separate occasions.

Later Jim bought a collection of photographs from a man in New Jersey. Two of the photographs surprised him: they showed the fifth Lincoln roadster, the one he now owned the chassis of, in modified condition. One, dated May 12, 1945, shows the car with bobbed front fenders and with the headlights and bumper removed — someone's attempt, no doubt, to make a sports car sportier. The second photograph shows the car greatly modified: all four fenders have been removed, as have the running boards, hood and the top of the windshield. The most dramatic change is the huge Rootes-type blower atop the Lincoln V-12 engine. A note on the back says: "This one is blown with a 6–71 G.M.C. blower. Custom wheels 7:00x20. Dual (sic) transmissions. Top speed is 150 at 3000 R.P.M." The car has lights and license, so it was apparently driven on the street. The date on the California plate is 1950.

Jim was scratching his head at the sight of these photographs. He knew that Mrs. Holden-Higbee had a winter home in Santa Barbara, so that could explain how the car got from Ohio to California. But who had modified it into a hot rod? Why would anyone choose to soup up a heavy engine like the V-12? Who had engineered the mating of the blower to the V-12? Was the car actually timed at the lakes, or was the speed indicated someone's fantasy?

And the big questions in Jim's mind remain: how did the car get from California to Long Island, NY? And what happened to that lovely body?

The Murphy-bodied 1932 Lincoln roadster is a rare and historically interesting car. That one of five should, almost twenty years later, become a hot rod is somewhat bizarre. That such a unique machine should not have received notice in the very early rod magazines, or even later, is strange. If there's a reader out there who knows anything about this car, please let me know.

GEORGE RILEY

The Ford four-barrel was the fast engine of the Thirties, even years after the Ford V-8 came out. In 1938 Ernie McAfee set a record of 132 mph with his Winfield flathead four in a modified; he had a one-way speed of 137 mph, which was really cooking in those days. The flathead Ford V-8 began to catch up around 1939, seven years after it came out, but even then the four-barrels were making it work. At the end of the 1939 season the roadster record was held by Eddie Meyer's rear-engine Ford V-8 at 114.285 mph, but close behind was Arnold Birner's four-port Riley which turned 113.49 mph and the same day Bob Rufi's little Chev four streamliner turned 124.13 mph.

There were rods at the lakes in the early Thirties that were running between 108 mph and 118 mph, and they were generally four-barrel Fords equipped with a Riley OHV head. They might have also been running Riley carburetors and a Riley cam. The head came in either two-port or four-port configuration, and properly installed it gave a light roadster terrific acceleration and a decent top end speed.

George Gibb's 1930 Model A roadster was nearly new when it ran over 100 mph on a Missouri ½-mile track in 1931. Credit was given to the Riley two-port head (courtesy Dan Iandola).

Top: A nutty "tear drop car" built by Libby Body Works of Kansas City, Missouri. The Model A engine was in the rear and had Riley two-port head. Where is it today? (courtesy Dan Iandola). *Bottom:* I love Eugene Von Arx's sports special, with its Chrysler Royal front end, DuVall-style windshield, front and rear stepped frame and neat hood. The engine was Ford V8 with rare Riley OHV conversion (courtesy Dan Iandola).

This line of speed equipment was designed, produced and marketed by George Riley (1885–1964). Although Riley went to school only through fourth grade, he was a self-taught automotive genius in the manner of Henry Ford. While working as a miner in Arizona, he got a patent for an expanding mandrel. The following year, 1919, he invented the Multi-Lift, a device to increase the valve lift on the Model T Ford and other cars. In the late Twenties he developed a high-compression flathead for the Model A; this was followed by his OHV racing heads.

Dan Iandola, who has built and raced fast Ford four-barrels for 40 years, has compiled what he describes as an unauthorized biography of George Riley in the *George Riley Racing Scrapbook*. This isn't the kind of biography where we learn what Riley had for breakfast, or if he enjoyed going to the movies, or if he had a dark side, although glimpses of the man emerge. We learn, for example, that Riley's first experience with airplanes was in 1911 when he was in the cavalry and met a young woman whose rich father had given her a plane. Later, when he was working on an experimental airplane engine, he stuck his hand into an unguarded propeller and lost the tips of several fingers. Worried that he would lose dexterity in those fingers, he invented a contraption that used rods and clamps and a windshield wiper motor to exercise the fingers while he slept. I'm sure that Iandola, who knew Riley, could have told us more anecdotes like that to round out the person.

The man emerges primarily through his inventions, and Iandola has done us all a service by obtaining rare documents that illustrate Riley's mechanical thinking. Most rodders are unaware of Riley's involvement with boats and airplanes. He developed a unique hydroplane hull, built the boat and broke the old record the first time out. He built the Riley Stern Drive, a power drive attachment that provided inboard power to run through an outboard drive; it worked beautifully, and required almost no maintenance. He also invented and marketed the Riley 74 outboard motor, a powerful motor almost as tall as the builder. Less successful were his midget auto engine, a two-cylinder opposed unit, and his twelve-cylinder airplane engine.

Iandola has dug up extensive information on the Riley carburetor, including Riley's own notes and photographs of the wooden patterns used to produce the original small Riley carburetor. This information should be of genuine interest to anyone owning a Riley carburetor or anyone seeking information on vintage speed equipment. There are also chapters on the Riley OHV heads for the 1932–37 Ford engines and the DOHC V-8 engine that used Ford parts and would fit in a Ford V-8 chassis.

This 260-page book has over 140 black and white photographs, plus pages of charts, blueprints, drawings, correspondence, notes taken by a Riley employee, patent applications, Riley's article on how to build a race car, a parts list for Riley racing equipment, etc.

Car Pooling

My old friend Bill Zerbach sent a pair of photographs that I had never seen. During World War II many families had to double up, and Bill's family lived in his grandmother's house down the street. Not only did Bill and I play together, our parents did whatever young adults did when there was a war on. In the early 1950s, Bill got a slick '40 Ford coupe and built a fast flathead for it. Around 1954 Bill and his parents moved to another city, but we've kept in touch, and I always enjoy talking with him.

His mother and mine were dear friends for years, and as Bill was going through her things he found these photographs, which she must have taken. The print is minuscule, about two-inches square, and since there are two photographs on the print, each is about the size of a postage stamp. I had them enlarged, and was pleasantly surprised. I felt a sense of the familiar as I saw things long

The 1930 Hudson sedan in 1942, with Billy Zerbach's grandmother's house looming in the background, in the left photograph, and the author's mother and a 1941 Chevrolet coupe, right.

forgotten: the road in front of our house was tarred gravel, one car wide; the lack of curbs and sidewalks; the tall telephone poles; the twin paths of the driveway, worn smooth by use, with grass in the center; several unpainted buildings; a sapling that later grew large and was cut down years ago; the rocks my mother placed before our yard, then painted white, indicating a boundary; a length of sidewalk, recently made, that extended from the cement front steps—my father's work.

That piece of sidewalk dates the photographs as being taken in 1942. In one photograph my mother appears younger and slimmer than I remember: she is either ducking to avoid having her photograph taken, or is puzzled by something on the ground. Behind her is a lovely 1941 Chevrolet coupe, the only new car my father ever owned.

Beyond that is our old garage, unpainted, and to one side the slanting roof of our chicken house, later my chemistry laboratory. Beside the house are the stubs of rose bushes and laurel, recently planted, and still there, nearly 65 years later.

The other photograph, taken in the opposite direction, shows our front yard and the street, and a car I have not seen since those bushes were twigs. It's a 1930 Hudson four door sedan, a seven-passenger model, and although it's only twelve years old it appears primitive compared to the new Chevy in the driveway. My father always had one or two old cars or motorcycles around, and this Hudson helped him during the war when new cars were not being built and used cars were expensive and hard to find. I don't know when he got the Hudson, but I seem to remember an occasion when he traded a bunch of stuff—a pocket watch, some jack knives, perhaps a motorcycle, perhaps a car, and perhaps some cash—for a car. Nor do I remember when he got rid of it, although I know it was still around after the war. I loved to play in it, a room on wheels, with dusty upholstery and a huge wooden steering wheel. I could not reach the pedals, but once I got on the floor and pushed the starter; the car was in gear and moved forward a couple of inches. I was surprised, and when I looked up I saw my sister in front of the radiator; although there was little danger, I felt much guilt.

My mother never learned to drive a car, but on several occasions, around the end of the war, she took lessons. My father was the teacher, the Hudson the classroom; why she didn't learn in the '41 Chevrolet I have no idea, but perhaps my father feared it would get wrecked. That Hudson must've been a bear to steer, and it took force to depress the clutch. The final lesson involved downshifting. The car went up a hill, stalled, and my mother became hysterical as she tried to keep it from rolling back while trying to work four pedals—starter, gas, brake and clutch—to get it to move forward while my father, also out of control, laughed.

During World War II my father was 4-F and unfit to serve in the military for health reasons. So he did defense work, working at both Swan Island and Oregon shipyards. He drove a "whirley crane," where each day he climbed a ladder a hundred feet high, and sat in a cab, guiding the crane along tracks while lifting huge loads into the Liberty ships that were being built. It was no doubt the best job he ever had.

It was also the only time in his life when he made decent money. It's sad that it took a war to bring workers a sense of prosperity, and ironic that there was little to spend the money on. Meat, butter, eggs, sugar and other foods were rationed, and things like clothing, hot water bottles, rubber boots and raincoats were in short supply. It was difficult to find certain candy bars, and impossible to get bubble gum. Manufacturers came up with substitutes, which were not always satisfying; once when there were no peanuts I bought a bag of roasted soybeans—they were awful!

Gasoline and tires were also rationed. The average car owner got a Class A sticker for his windshield, and rationing stamps that allowed him to buy no more than five gallons of gasoline a week. But a driver who was doing "essential war work" got a Class B sticker and stamps, and doctors and politicians got Class C stickers and stamps for an unlimited supply of gasoline. The shortage of rubber was the real problem, and it was impossible to buy new tires. By limiting driving, the amount of gasoline available, and by imposing a wartime speed limit of 35 miles per hour, it was hoped that tires would last for the duration.

Under those conditions, people began to share rides. There were few women drivers then, and men who did not own a car; they needed to get to work. My father may have begun driving the new Chevrolet to the shipyard, but, seeing an opportunity, he switched to the old Hudson and began a carpool. The Hudson had huge front and rear seats, and between them a pair of jump seats that folded into the floor. He put a padded ironing board on the jump seats, and that Hudson could carry at least nine people. It was no problem to find people who wanted a ride to and from the shipyard, and they were willing to pay four-bits, or a buck a week.

The philosopher George Santayana is often quoted when things get chaotic: "Those who forget history are condemned to relive it." Usually it's hard to know how to apply that advice. Today, in the face of escalating gasoline prices, a declining oil supply, and too many cars on the road, the answer should be easy. Remembering history, we should be able to carpool as easily today as we did during the crucial years of the war. It seems so simple, and it should not require legislation, just the personal initiative shown by my father and his old Hudson.

That was the Hudson's finest hour! My father got a Class B sticker, additional ration stamps and money to put aside. At the end of the war he had saved enough from the carpool money to buy my mother the wedding rings he had not been able to afford ten years earlier, when they got married.

THE WAR EFFORT

Either Wes has become a better storyteller or I've become a better listener. We worked together in a garage 50 years ago, and we're the last of all the guys who were connected to that place. A good deal of interesting history is gone and so I listen hard, trying to grab onto any piece of the past that drifts by.

Recently Wes told a story that I thought was really funny. I told it to two or three guys, but I must have told it badly because I didn't get a reaction. Maybe I can tell it better on paper. Part of the story's appeal for me is that it predates my experience with cars or almost anything else. It took place in 1943, during the middle of World War II, so the context of the story is totally different from anything I might have experienced when I was a similar age, in the 1950s, or from anything a kid might experience today. It was a dark time, with war raging over half the world, but it was also an innocent time, especially on the streets of Portland, Oregon. Gas was rationed. Driving was limited to essential trips, and because tires were impossible to get many owners put their cars on blocks for the duration. It was a patriotic duty. People collected waste paper, tin cans and kitchen fat for the war effort. Everyone knew someone in uniform. Everyone believed in being patriotic, pledging allegiance to America, saluting the flag, practicing civic duties, not wasting things, going to church and obeying the laws of man and God.

"For most, getting gas was a problem," Wes said. "The average Joe only got five gallons a week. I got my first car, a Model A tudor. I was in high school, and I bought it with paper route and berry picking money. I was sixteen, my dad didn't like it, but what the hell." Wes laughed, thinking back 60-some years. "I got gas at Bud's station. He'd slip me extra ration stamps so I could get all I wanted. He did that for all the guys at Franklin High. When the war ended we kept buying gas from him; I got all my gas from Bud for years. Of course the problem when I was sixteen was getting money—I could get the gas!"

Every sharp edge of the story caught my attention. Bud's gas station was at 59th and Foster, and in 1937 or '38 my dad worked there. I have a photograph of the two of us beside the big gravity feed pumps. Years later Bud moved across Foster and it became Bud's Auto Supply. In the old station I found my first car, a Model A roadster. The smallness of this world, with all the connections, interested me greatly.

"Three or four of us would be driving around at night, goofing off. That car would only do forty, tops, so we couldn't get in too much trouble. But we tried," he said, laughing. I was laughing too, thinking of that Model A bouncing around on Foster Road in 1943, at night, the street empty of traffic. Oh, maybe there were a pair of headlights far off, the lenses partly painted black as required during the war, but essentially the street was empty. No pedestrians either. Every decent person was in bed by eight, or perhaps the family was up late, grouped around the Philco in the front room, listening to "Singing Sam, The Barbasol Man" or "Lum and Abner."

"We were kids looking for something to do. Too young for taverns, too broke to hit the drive-in, no girls around, so we'd bug these guys. Air raid wardens, or auxiliary cops—too old for the army or 4-F, mainly trying to get away from their wives. We'd drive down Foster, then slow down when we got to the branch, which was in Mt. Scott Fuel yard. We'd go slow and count how many guys were in the branch playing cards."

That got me. I was in that *Oregonian* branch a few years later. Today the branch is gone, but Mt. Scott Fuel is still there. I can see that street in my mind, and the branch, and the Model A tudor with Wes and his chums, like four duplicates of Mickey Rooney, jazzed up ready for action.

"We drove past real slow, and counted the guys. We had to know how many there were. Then we made a big loop around a couple blocks and came down Foster again. Doing 30, maybe 35 miles an hour, and as we got close to the branch I flipped the ignition off, then back on. There was a helluva backfire!"

Wes doubled over with laughter, thinking of that noise, like a Japanese bomb had been dropped in that sleepy neighborhood, and the flash that lit up houses for a long second. "I jammed it into second and was going full speed before the first guy wheels out. I turned right onto 72nd, cut my lights, slammed on the brakes, put it in reverse and backed up into that trolley cut behind the buildings."

I have been past that corner a million times, but didn't know about the trolley cut until ten years ago. In the old days the trolley tracks came down Foster, but at 72nd the turn was too sharp, so someone trimmed off the backs of the buildings and laid the tracks in a slow curve that the trolley could negotiate. The tracks were gone by World War II, but the cut remained. Wes backed the Model A into the space behind the buildings and waited for his pursuers to pass by.

"The first guy would come around that corner, hell bent for leather. Then the second pair of headlights, and then a third. That's why we had to know how many guys were in the building. If there were four, I'd wait until the fourth car went by and then I'd fall in behind, headlights out. I'd follow the cars around, us guys laughing like hell. Then pretty soon they'd get tired and go back to the branch and their cards. We'd wait a while and hit 'em again!"

We were laughing. It was like a Norman Rockwell painting, this old Model A tudor with four whipper-snappers laughing their heads off. I thought it was funny, that Model A going past a second time, then a third, each time there was the crack and flash of that backfire in a silent neighborhood. Then a race for the corner and swinging in backward between the buildings, lights out, the four young miscreants trying to stifle their laughter. Then again, the trick and the chase, until the novelty wore off and they finally went home. The next day, in math or English class or gym, they'd repeatedly tell the story of the night before, and a year later, facing combat, they'd tell it again, to break the tension.

"And what if you'd been caught?" I asked.

STREET SCENE, LOS ANGELES

I love this photograph taken by Robert "Flash" Beston in Los Angeles at the end of World War II. I think I know why Beston took it: he was a noted automotive artist and illustrator, and the neat coupe could serve as a model. But he was also a hot rodder, according to his life long friend, Robert Hammel. They grew up together in Sacramento, California, built fast cars, belonged to the Sirocco Club in the 1930s, hung out with guys like the Barris brothers, Joe Bailon, Harry Westergard, Norm Milne and others. They were also attracted to airplanes and flying, and both worked at McClelland Field before World War II where, Hammel said, "Beston got the nickname 'Flash' because he was always moving ... which drove his supervisor crazy!" During the war Beston joined the Army Air Corps, and he saw combat in Europe as a navigator on B-24 bombers. He later became Supervisor of Support Engineering at McClelland Air Force base. He passed away recently at age 79.

But during the 1940s and 1950s he was also doing illustrations of vintage aerial combat for pulp magazines such as *Wings*, and cutaway, technically perfect drawings of exotic sports and race cars for *Road & Track*. As an artist, he'd be attracted by the clean lines of this 1936 Ford 3-window coupe, which is period perfect: the spare tire has been removed and the license plate and light put it in its place; solid side panels and a bull-nose strip contribute to the car's uncluttered appearance. There are subtle touches, such as the removal of the original taillight and the use of a flush-mounted light, or lights, such as 1939 or 1940 Ford, although I can't tell from the photograph.

Those changes, which seem minor today, would have excited young hearts then, and would have been enough to set this car apart from most of the other ten year old Fords that filled the city. Imagine, then, the excitement removal of the running boards generated! Nothing dated a

Robert "Flash" Beston snapped this photograph in L.A. in the mid–1940s. It must have been a fun car to drive on those empty streets!

car like running boards, and one way to make an old car appear modern was to get rid of them. But if one simply removed the running boards one was left with an ugly gap. The owner of this Ford removed the boards, then formed a piece of sheet metal to cover that gap. But he also had to reshape the lower sections of the fenders, getting rid of the flat areas where they bolt to the boards. The rear part of the front fenders required extensive reshaping, with the flattened area pulled to a point. Three chrome rub strips, perhaps taken from the hood of, say, a 1941 Ford, and a handmade, chromed rear fender stone guard are perfect, practical, finishing touches.

So little has been done. The coupe is not chopped, channeled or sectioned; in fact, it looks nearly stock height. It has stock bumpers, headlights and possibly stock grille. It might have a stock interior, even a stock engine as it doesn't appear to have dual pipes. The later wheels hint at juice brakes, but that seems optimistic. It has aftermarket hubcaps but it doesn't even have whitewalls (because of wartime rationing, no doubt). And yet this coupe, with only minor changes, stands out — look at the reflections in the paint!

This is a car that looks to the future and the glories of the expansive post-war years. Perhaps that's what Beston saw when he took this photograph. My reaction is purely romantic: no one will ever build a car like this again. But my reaction includes the wide street without traffic, empty curbs that allow you to park darn near anywhere, wide sidewalks with a single pedestrian, the smooth architecture of the building in the background which offers cocktails and nightly entertainment with four star girls and even paper racks, which might hold copies of the edition with the headline announcing V-J Day. I love this photograph because it captures what we have lost, and will never again see.

Gordon M. Buehrig, 1904–1990

Gordon Buehrig, who passed away at age 85, was an automotive design genius who became a legend before his death.

He was a man of intelligence and vision who was born at the right time to enter the automotive design field. Cars were still fairly new, companies were still fairly small, and it was possible for one man to design a car. All the cars that Gordon Buehrig designed are of interest, and several are considered aesthetic wonders.

By age 24, he was chief designer for Stutz; this was in 1928, shortly after Stutz placed second in the LeMans 24-hour race, and that year he designed the Stutz Blackhawk boattail speedster. The following year, at age 25, he became chief designer for Duesenberg, the most prestigious automobile ever built in the United States. He designed the J Models, including the 1930 Model J Derham Tourster and the 1933 Duesenberg J513, the Rollston-bodied machine that was displayed at that year's World's Fair. In 1934 he worked at Auburn, where he designed the boattail speedster. In 1936, in the space of four months, he designed a car that most auto buffs consider the epitome of automotive design, the Cord 810, which featured front-wheel drive, concealed headlights and a supercharged V-8 engine. At the end of World War II, he went to work for Raymond Loewy Studios where several of his ideas turned up on the 1947 Studebaker, the first of the restyled postwar cars. From 1949 until his retirement in 1965, he worked at Ford, where he designed the 1951 Victoria, Ford's first hardtop convertible; the 1952 station wagon, a model that took Ford from the bottom of the list of wagon makers to the top; and the 1956 Lincoln Continental Mark II.

For his own use, Buehrig built a Model A roadster that resembled the Duesenbergs he designed. He bought a new Model A cabriolet in 1930, drove it four miles to Augie Duesenberg's race car shop, and had the body removed. The top was chopped, the body moved back several inches, a new, longer hood was made and a new rear section of the body made of aluminum. The finished car resembled a short-coupled tudor convertible. He made other changes, including hopping up the engine with a Miller OHV conversion. He drove the car until 1934, and he said later that he had never owned anything that gave him as much pleasure as did that car. "Its quality in every respect was equal to a Duesenberg and that was pretty good!"

He was far less excited in retrospect about a sports car project he got involved in after World War II. It was called the Tasco, which stood for The American Sports Car Company. This was years before the Corvette and Thunderbird were developed, and the group of men who contacted Buehrig felt that America should have a sports car. Buehrig designed the car using a brand new 1948 Mercury as a basis. The body was removed and discarded. The frame was shortened, engine moved back and fitted with speed equipment, and a new body designed. Buehrig drove the stripped car from Indiana to Pennsylvania, to the Derham Body Company, where a futuristic body was hammered from aluminum. It was a closed coupe, with aircraft styling, using pontoon fenders made of fiberglass, a new material at the time. The front fenders turned with the wheels, and the rear fenders moved independent of the body. Buehrig designed a set of magnesium wheels made by Dow Chemical Company, which were "well machined, beautiful and strong, but very expensive."

Buehrig said that the car handled very well, but that the project exceeded its budget. He later felt that if he had designed a simple roadster-style body "we would have had a fine sports car on our hands instead of a disaster." The car went back to the Derham Body Company, and was apparently sold; what, I wonder, happened to it?

The Tasco was designed with a top that had removable panels, and although only one Tasco was built, the top lives on in the T-Top-popular today. To recoup his losses, Buehrig got permission to patent the top design. When he went to work for Ford in 1949, he repeatedly tried to interest the company in his "Buehrig top," but to no avail.

In 1955 he bought one of the first Thunderbirds and built a top with removable panels in his garage for the car. Unable to interest Ford in using the top, he got permission to try to sell the idea to General Motors, but GM was not interested either. He eventually tried Chrysler, and even Mercedes-Benz, without luck.

Seventeen years later, in October 1967, he picked up a copy of *Road & Track* and saw on the cover a new Corvette using his top. Since the patent would not expire for another year, Buehrig contacted GM about this infringement. Eventually they offered him a sum of money for the rights to the T-Top, and since he knew he would not be able to sue GM, he accepted the offer.

I met Gordon Buehrig several times at the St. Ignace Auto Show. He was incredibly calm, courteous, witty and articulate. He was also modest about his accomplishments, which spanned 60 years of auto design. I searched hard for two years to find a copy of his book, *Rolling Sculpture;* I finally found a copy, and got it to him to have it personalized about four months before he passed away. I treasure that copy of the book, as I treasure my memories of Mr. Buehrig.

WAR SURPLUS

There's a great deal of interest in building a hot rod that resembles one built during the late 1940's or 1950's but rods back then used parts that came primarily from wrecking yards, and few yards have parts that old anymore. Another source, largely forgotten today, was the local Army surplus store, where all kinds of neat things could be had for little money; most of that stuff is also gone. A test of America's greatness was the way it met the challenge of World War II. The country had been in a severe economic depression during the 1930's, with millions of men out of work, but even before Pearl Harbor, with war clouds on the horizon, those men were soon busy building planes, ships and tanks. An incredible amount of materials were produced, and at war's end much of that stuff was offered to the public at low prices.

There were two "Army Surplus" stores not far from my house and the one I remember best was simply a huge tent permanently pitched beside a busy street. I was not yet old enough to drive, but I was an avid hunter and fisherman and that canvas tent was filled with what I wanted: machetes, bayonets, web belts, canteens, steel ammo boxes, water purification tablets, etc. A transparent plastic rain shelter made to be used once or twice was in a small, sealed package. A yellow plastic container held a survival kit. When I began riding my bicycle on the motorcycle trails, I bought an Army Surplus "Ike" jacket, leather flying helmet, gloves and pilot's goggles, which made me feel like a real racer.

There was still an abundance of surplus in 1950, five years after World War II ended, which was when I got interested in cars. I bought toggle switches, electrical wire, a large compass and a real pith helmet, which I painted white with red lettering, like the examples I'd seen in the photographs of rodders at Bonneville.

There were older rodders who were able to buy more surplus items and use them. I recall a couple nice rods with lots of gauges, which I'm sure were from airplanes. For example, Mid Barbour's 1936 Ford phaeton had numerous gauges—including air speed, with Pitot tubes from an airplane beside the cowl. A guy could also buy everything he needed for his home shop, from hand tools to a compressor, and the prices were right!

Surplus stores were everywhere, and available to rodders across the nation. "California Bill" Fisher told me where he got many of the parts for the Chevrolets he raced at El Mirage in the late 1940's. "In the Los Angeles area was Palleys in Glendale on Colorado Boulevard. We got a lot of hose fittings, hose clamps, tubing, and Adel clamps. Also gasoline tanks, oxygen tanks that ended up on small compressors or got used as fuel or oil tanks, pumps that we used for fuel injection, aluminum boxes that we used to hold small parts (they were probably aircraft junction boxes originally). We also got fuel shutoff valves, great fuel filters, swivel-ball ends for linkage and suspension, tie-downs, clamps of all sizes, scrap aluminum — and the list goes on and on. The prices were so reasonable we tried to figure out how to use more of it."

Bob Hammel remembers using military surplus when building cars. "I got all kinds of nuts, bolts, nut plates, etc. I made an oil reserve tank from a military squirt gun with a check

War Surplus

valve in it. And when I was converting my 1939 Citroën roadster to rear wheel drive I wanted to get rid of that cable actuated clutch arm, so I used a couple cowl-actuating flap (mechanisms) from a DC-2 or DC-3 as slave and master cylinders.

"The guy who had a shop next to me was rebuilding a 1936 Cord using a flathead Cadillac V-8 that came from a tank. And of course belly tanks were great for streamliners, and the bubble canopies."

Hammel was an aircraft mechanic, so he was surrounded by military surplus, but I think anyone could buy it. When seat belts became necessary for drag racing, a member from my club went to the Troutdale, Oregon airport and returned with a bunch of wide seat belts from military aircraft. I bought one, and I think it cost a buck or so. Also available were several kinds of aluminum bucket seats, including the one with the smooth curved back. They were a little uncomfortable, but they were lightweight, attractive and easily mounted in a hot rod (They were popular for a time; where did they all go?).

Several kinds of military jackets were available at surplus stores, including leather flying jackets, which were great for roadster drivers in nippy weather. The prices were really low, which makes me wonder why I didn't buy a bunch of those jackets and stick them in the closet, where they would eventually appreciate faster than a retirement fund. The answer, of course, is that I didn't have any money, nor did most of my fellow rodders, which was one reason we were buying surplus stuff to begin with!

Roots

The photograph of Bob Knowles' first hot rod gives testimony to the simplicity of both rods and life 50 years ago in America. The story about this car also says something about hard work, initiative and American ingenuity, all requisites for being a hot rodder back then.

Bob began working when he was eight, and by age twelve he was working in a service station. His first wages bought him a 1927 Model T coupe, which of course, he was too young to drive. Two years later, in 1946, he moved to Portland, Oregon to live with his mother and attend high school. Too young to get a regular job, he created a position as apprentice window washer. He worked with an older man, who showed him the ropes, and within a short time Bob bought the business! Bob was not yet 15, and did not have a driver's license, but he was able to borrow his mother's 1938 Buick sedan and clean windows every morning before school.

Bob coveted an older friend's Model A roadster. Well, it wasn't actually a roadster — it was a 1929 Ford coupe that had been rolled and was now topless. Bob traded his Model T coupe and $25 cash for the A-bone and he thought he was in heaven. He had plans to make it into a hot rod. Bob removed the body, cleaned the chassis and painted it black. Then he bought a 1930 Model A roadster body for next-to-nothing, and mounted it on the chassis. Because the car would not have fenders, he had a friend weld a bar and mounts for two small headlights, which had been fog lights on his mother's 1938 Buick. When the Buick got a new set of tires, Bob got the old tires, which he mounted on 1940 Ford wheels. They were big, front and rear, but at least he had tires. That windshield is a mystery; he simply went to a wrecking yard, found a windshield that was the right width, then made mounting brackets on the Model A cowl. Finally he painted the car gray, using a brush. Except for the welding, and some help in lifting the body, Bob did all the work himself.

It was a tall, bone stocker, but to a fifteen-year-old kid it was a hot rod. Bob used it as a work car and figured out new ways to make money with it. He leased the roadster to Lynd

Bob Knowles' first roadster was a coupe with the top cut off.

Pomeroy Florists to use as the basis for the Hood River float in the 1948 Rose Festival Parade. Then he insisted that he drive the float, for which he was paid $15, while traveling in the company of seven beautiful Hood River girls who graced the float in the parade.

That rod was the first of a long string of rods and customs that Bob has built over the years. He'll never quit being a rodder, which should be an inspiration to other rodders. But the message I hope this story sends to young rodders is this: There are more windows than ever in this country, and they all need washing, sooner or later.

Growing Up

A recent phenomenon are the commercials on radio and television that portray the male as a blithering idiot. There are a plethora of these commercials, and what surprises me about them is not just that they cost millions of dollars to produce and present, but that the sponsor expects me to buy their product. I'm not that big of a blithering idiot!

There was a time when someone had something to sell and their product, whether hair oil or engine oil, was simply presented to the public. Then, a few years ago, conflict was introduced. I don't know why it's necessary to show conflict to sell a product, but perhaps it reflects the nature of the world in which we live. So if two people are in a commercial, one has to be wise, informed, level-headed, practical, instructive and attractive; the other has to be uninformed. That is to say, in advertising lingo, a "jerk." This conflict is "gender specific," and it seems that in committee rooms at the ad agency it was decided that the latter should be male.

You only have to turn on the TV and within a few minutes you'll see examples of what I mean. You might see the advertisement for a certain brand of "wonderful" bread. In it, the wife asks her husband to pick up some groceries and adds, "Don't forget the 'wonderful' bread." The husband, who has to be talked to as if he were a child, regresses, remembering the bread he grew up with. As soon as he gets outside he begins to zoom around the yard, arms extended like the wings of a plane. Then he stops, looks at the back steps, where his wife stands dangling the car keys, an authoritarian figure. She has to puncture his fantasy and bring him back to the present with a practical gesture. Oddly, the focus of the commercial does not make me want to buy their bread, but it does make me "wonder" what kind of work the guy does and how he manages to get through the day without his wife's help.

That commercial, like a million others, presents the wife as an adult and the husband as a child. Psychologists call that the Peter Pan syndrome. In 1904 James M. Barrie wrote a play called "Peter Pan" about a boy who refused to grow up. The play was a great success, and is still being presented 100 years later. The epithet, however, is a pejorative when applied to men where it covers a multitude of alleged faults. Variations on this theme include the idea that a guy is still a mama's boy, that he lacks commitment and so on. If you haven't heard the charge in real life, you've heard it in the other life, self-help talk-shows. A seemingly infinite number of women complain about the man in their life and often the commentator, a woman, will explain that the guy has not grown up.

Every guy who messes around with cars is vulnerable to the charge that he's still a kid playing with toy cars, or a teenager reliving the past with the car he had or wanted to have. It may be valid, but two things bother me about the charge. One, there is no similar epithet for women, where playing with dolls and toy dishes is seen as a practical activity that prepares them for the role of mother and wife. Two, there is no useful defense against being told that one has not grown up.

After years of thinking about my maturity and trying to be a full-time adult, I find myself accepting the notion that I have not grown up. There, it feels good to admit that in print. But I'm not satisfied just talking about whether cars are for kids, I want to enter my second childhood full bore! I want to wake up in the morning with a sense of excitement, the feeling that something. is going to happen! I want to slip into a pair of clean Levi's with a 28" waist and a clean T-shirt and walk barefoot on the porch looking across the vacant fields of the neighborhood. I want to see two quarts of milk in glass bottles on the steps, with the upper part pure cream. Every day is Saturday, but on this Saturday, as I eat breakfast, I listen to "Let's Pretend" and "Grand Central Station" on the radio. I'll lie in the hammock and read *Boy* comics and *Jingle-Jangle Tales*. Toward noon I'll jump on my Western Flyer and pedal to the Aero Theater, where, for a dime, Ican see a full-length feature starring Sunset Carson or Wild Bill Elliott, plus a couple of cartoons and another episode of "The Masked Marvel" starring Tom Steele. Maybe I'll ride my bike to a friend's house, where two or three of the gang are examining parts removed from his car. Perhaps it's a stripped-down Ford, or a shark-nose Graham, or a Terraplane; the mystery of oily parts is the same. We clean parts, exchange ideas and opinions, or simply sit on the front tire in the warm sun, unaware of time, living in the immediate present, knowing that somehow all of this will go on forever. When the sun drops below the rooftop and my stomach cries for food I'll reluctantly head for home.

What guy wouldn't give a wad of dough to ride his fat tired bike through the old neighborhood, pedaling lazily, knowing the odors of freshly cut grass and frying meat and the sound of a distant radio? What guy wouldn't give everything he owns to toss his bike on the lawn, rub Fido's head and bound up the front steps, throwing open the screen door? To stand there for a minute, smelling dinner on the stove, hearing familiar voices and to say: "Mom! Dad! I'm home!"

THE SERVICE STATION

I'm looking for a service station where the people speak my language. I don't mean English necessarily, although that would be convenient. No, I'm thinking of a guy named Gus, a grumpy guy with a greasy skull cap and the stump of a dead cigar at the corner of his mouth, who checks my oil and water while the gas is flowing into my tank. And as he's collecting my money he offers advice, such as, it looks like my front tires are wearing unevenly and maybe I ought to go to the line-up shop down the street. Or maybe a slick young guy in a white shirt and a clip-on black plastic bow tie who washes not only the windshield, but the rear window and cheerfully asks if he can check under the hood and mentions that there is a special price on new tires.

Once the service station was an American institution. It actually offered services that people needed. A buck's worth of gas, check what needs checking, maybe replace a tire, or a battery, or a fan belt. Most did minor repair work, such as brake jobs. Many did major repairs on up to an engine overhaul. It was also a meeting place where teenage kids could gather, drink a Coke, talk about cars and learn about them. They'd gather most nights just to gab. For the owner, it was a profession. If he sold enough gas, tires and batteries he could buy a decent house, maybe a new car and pay his bills. Perhaps not enough to send his kids to college, but it seemed that few people went to college in those days, and no trips to Europe.

I always thought I could work in a station, and maybe own one. When career day came around in high school, I'd put down gas station attendant, hoping some guy would speak to us and tell us what to do with our lives. I did work in a bunch of service stations. My father owned one — well, leased it — and I worked there often, especially when my father became sick. I took home what he got, $50 a week, and gave it to my mother. Later I worked in various service stations part-time and occasionally full time. It was not unpleasant. After eight o'clock at night there was almost no traffic, and guys, sometimes girls, would drop in to chat. Sometimes I'd pull my own car onto the rack and lube it, maybe change the oil or check things that needed checking. The neighborhood would shut down early, lights would go out and the streets would be empty. I'd read the pumps, lock them, put the money in the safe, turn out the lights and jump in my car and fire it up. It was a happy sound in that dark, lonely neighborhood.

When I was in college I got a job in a new type of station, a Regal station, part of a chain. I wore a white shirt and pants with a black bow tie; all I did was pump gas. No tire repairs, no lubes or oil changes and no battery replacements. Even though I was required to wash windshields, rear windows, headlights and taillights, and ask to check their water, oil and tires—even if the guy only bought a buck's worth of regular—it was gravy. I figured I could do this all my life, but when they offered me a manager's position, forcing me to make a decision, I said no because I did not want to quit college. I felt I was making a mistake because this station was clearly the future.

An obituary in today's paper describes the life of Mike Morelli, a Portland service station owner. It notes that Mike had spent 50 years, "his entire working life," in a gas station. We're told that for years the station was open seven days a week and Mike worked 16 hours a day; doing everything a good attendant did, and found time to fix kids' bicycle tires for free. He told his attendants to run, not walk, to the car. "You treat every customer like they're the most important person in the world." The customers treated Mike well too, because every Christmas the station was packed with gifts.

That was the Golden Age of the service station, and I suspect that 50 percent of today's drivers never experienced it. Then something happened, and service stations quickly disappeared. I talked with Mike Morelli once and he recalled when there were over 50 stations in a 50-block area of a main street; today there are three! In 1971–72 I worked half-time at a high school on a federal study administered through a university and the technical area of the study bought a service station that the students could use to learn how to run a business. That year the Arab embargo hit and gas stations became donut shops, restaurants, dog grooming salons, etc. I don't know what happened to that service station that the school bought, but it became clear that service station attendants were not needed.

Today I filled up my truck to the tune of $50, and the attendant didn't offer any services. I walked into the office area to pay and it was clear that the big business was selling hot dogs and heated food wrapped in foil, cigarettes, chips and huge pop containers. Three young women were behind the counter, chattering in a foreign language. They looked at me, laughed, and one said something to the others. I don't think they were saying my front end needed alignment.

Ed Almquist

As I get older, wiser to the ways of the world, I am seldom surprised. But I'm astonished, or is that astounded, when I call a number in Milford, PA, and Ed Almquist himself answers! He strikes me as a kind man, and still sharp at 81; he relates information with great patience, as if I were ordering an Almquist Y manifold, a set of Sparkomatic plugs or one of the floor-mounted shift levers he designed. He's friendly, he's informative, but I know he'd like to move some products and make some money, because he's a born salesman.

I'd like to think that Ed Almquist's name looms as large today as it did 55 years ago when I got into hot rodding. In those days Eastern magazines carried full-page ads for his products, including Almquist heads and dual intake manifolds, Hollywood mufflers and complete dual exhaust systems for Ford and Mercury flathead V-8s as well as for many other cars. He wrote articles for magazines like *Best Hot Rods*, such as how to build a '32 Ford roadster for $300, and "Soup's On For Auto Bugs," which showed him bolting his own heads and dual intakes onto a Mercury block. In the mid–1950s he manufactured some of the earliest fiberglass bodies, including a 1932 Ford roadster body.

The Almquist story is the American dream fulfilled, and although I'd like to think that it could be duplicated today, by a sharp, hard-working businessman, it might have been the times. Ed was born in Zim, Minnesota and worked on machines as a kid; in 1936, when he was 14, he reworked a Model A Ford, and in 1941 he customized a 1935 Buick convertible.

Most of Ed's knowledge of mechanics was self-taught, although he did take two grade school courses and an extension course in diesel engineering given by the University of Minnesota. This background was useful when World War II broke out and Ed became a junior officer in the Merchant Marines.

When the war ended, Ed was still in uniform, with time on his hands. He began drawing customized cars as he'd like to see them. His shipmates approved of his drawings, and because of their enthusiasm Ed decided to compile a small book, which he titled *How To Restyle Any Car*. Ed told me, "I didn't have the good sense to go to a publisher, so I decided to print the book myself by renting a used mimeograph machine and typewriter, and consequently placing a $12 ad in *Popular Mechanics*. The ad pulled in orders like crazy, bringing me a pile of orders at $1.98 each." It's important to note that there were no rodding or customizing magazines being published in 1946, and obviously people were hungry for this kind of information.

In 1946 Ed moved to Milford, Pennsylvania, and in a year his mail-order business grew so much that the post office was changed from second-class to first-class. That year he wrote and published a second book, *Speed and Mileage Manual*. Both books sold well, and anticipated the advent of high-performance magazines by two to three years. Ed is a dreamer and a doer; ideas come fast, and he has the gumption to see them through to reality.

Ed Almquist and a racing engine with Almquist heads and dual intake manifold, circa 1950 (courtesy Ed Almquist).

He began to see a need for specialty automotive products. He designed and manufactured a water and alcohol injector for production engines, and a Stromberg 97 with bigger jets that were adjustable from the dashboard. Then he began making aluminum adapters so that a carburetor could be used on any manifold with two, three or four bolt flanges.

The step to a more full line of speed equipment was a big one, and required a big cash payment. Ed worked out a deal with a foundry and they cast his aluminum V-type manifold that adapted two carbs to virtually any manifold. By 1949 he realized that modified stock-car racing was becoming popular in the Midwest and South, so he began developing more speed equipment for flathead Fords. He made high-compression heads for these engines, and a low-profile 180-degree dual intake manifold. He also designed and sold the Hollywood muffler, and dual pipe set-ups; he said he sold "thousands" of these conversions. He began grinding racing cams, and then worked with California cam-grinder Harry Weber.

He also sold "compression riser gaskets," a thin head gasket, and a mini-supercharger, a best seller for which be received a patent. He also got a patent on his traction bars, which could be adjusted to equalize traction at the rear wheels. Another product that Ed should have patented was a cool-air induction kit that he called Air Ram. This concept was borrowed about ten years later by Pontiac; they called it Ram Air!

Ed made and marketed many other items, including various styles of fiberglass bodies that would fit stock chassis, and a multiple electrode sparkplug called Sparkomatic. His company made numerous bolt-on accessories, such as bubble skirts, rear fender fins, dual headlights, special grilles and interior consoles. He developed an interest in ways to better lubricate an engine, and found an English firm to grind moly (MoS2) to an extremely fine size. The product was called Presto-Moly. He sold lots of this in the late 1950s, and notes that he used similar technology in the 1980's making new lubricants. Ever the salesman, Ed has made numerous trips to China, where he has found a huge market for his lubricant. Ed found time to compile an impressive book, *Hot Rod Pioneers*; it runs 378 pages, is hardbound and includes lots of black and white and color photographs. The price is $39.00, plus postage. Ed will even sign the book, if requested. Send to 115 Norman Hills Rd., Milford, PA 18337. If there's a delay, it's probably because he's on a trip to China!

HOT ROD CITROËN

When Bob Hammel returned to Los Angeles at the end of World War II, he was eager to buy a sports car. During the war he had rebuilt and customized a 1935/36 Ford roadster while stationed in Pensacola, Fla., and had built a 1927 Chevrolet coupe into a hot rod sports car while stationed in Barbers Point, Hawaii.

Before the war Bob had been an airplane mechanic at McClellan Air Force Base in Sacramento, Calif., and his daily transportation had been a 1930 Ford roadster with a hopped-up flathead V-8. He worked with and became friends with another airplane mechanic/hot rodder, Leonard Talboy, of La Jolla, whose reading interests included the British periodical *Motor Sport*.

Bob recalled, "It was through his hoard of English car magazines that I became acquainted with such marques as Alfa-Romeo, Bugatti, Aston Martin, and MG. It was a whole new world to a guy who thought a hot rod was the ultimate in automotive art."

Eventually Bob owned examples of those marques, but in 1946, when he again became a civilian, such cars were scarce. "I began to look for a sports car that I could afford and use," Bob recalled. "I had been impressed with the Citroëns that had been racing on the stock car cir-

Bob Hammel, the Citroën roadster and his dog, Wolfgang, in 1947. The front end has been reworked but the car still has the original engine and front-wheel drive.

cuit in the Los Angeles area before the war. I liked their technical features such as front-wheel drive, torsion-bar suspension and rack-and-pinion steering."

He found the Citroën dealer, Charlie Druchell, and saw that he had a nice little 1939 convertible for sale. Bob wanted it, "So I sold my motorcycle (which was my postwar transportation), took my mustering out pay, went into hock, and bought the car."

Bob loved the car, but as an ex-hot rodder he needed to modify it! He began by making subtle body changes that he felt improved the car's graceful lines, He cut the fronts of the front fenders upward at an angle, so they resembled an Auburn or Brewster, and changed the front end. For a radiator shell he used a cut-down Studebaker President; the mesh of the grille and

Bob Hammel sweeps through a curve on a Little Tujunga Canyon hill climb.

the chevron-shaped V s came from an Auburn. He added 1939 Ford taillights, a 1935 Ford front bumper, Hollywood single-bar hubcaps, and then had the car painted black.

It was a sweet little streetster, but Bob sometimes hoped that people would think it was a 1934 Ford, which it resembled. He said, "At that time the hot rodders would gather at the drive-ins in Culver City and other places, and the big deal was to 'burn out' as you left. My little Citroën would pass pretty well as a '34 Ford, but when I left, with my front tires burning rubber, it got their attention!"

Bob noted that such driving was hard on ring and pinion gears. "After I used up the stock of ring and pinions that the Citroën dealer had, including a set of straight-cut gears that we had made locally, and which howled like a Mercedes blower, I finally decided to convert the car to rear-wheel drive. Quite a number of Cords were undergoing this treatment at that time, so it was not that drastic a decision."

His choice of engine, drivetrain and hop-up equipment is interesting and makes a comment about what was available during the mid–1940s. "I ended up using a Willys Jeep engine, mated to a transmission made up of a Jeep transmission housing (to get a top-shifter), using Studebaker Champion gears and overdrive and a Champion rear axle. I kept the Citroën front end with torsion bars and fitted Champion wheels."

That Jeep engine was readily available and inexpensive after the war, a workhorse that had proved itself, but Bob improved it until it was a performer. He rebuilt the engine, then fitted it with a rare Alexander OHV conversion — at least rare to this author, since I had never even seen a photograph of one. I knew that DuVall, the fellow who designed and built the boat-style windshields before the war, had also made an OHV conversion for the Willys, but that windshield was also a rare item.

Bob added a pair of Winfield SR down-draft carburetors and built a neat exhaust header. He also built the clutch release system, converting it to hydraulic action using a pair of B-25 cowl flap actuation cylinders. Bob noted that this system worked well.

He used the roadster as his daily driver, and during the evenings he cruised the drive-ins along the Pacific Coast. Within a short time Bob met other aficionados, and became part of the fledgling sports car scene.

"The sports car movement in Los Angeles was just getting started and the nucleus was Roger Barlow's International Motors, where Phil Hill worked as a mechanic. We organized a couple of 'outlaw' events. One was a hill climb in Little Tujunga Canyon above the San Fernando Valley; another was a race around some unused roads in Palos Verde.

"Some names that later became famous were there: Phil Hill, John Von Neuman, Roger Barlow, Louis Van Dyck, Donald O'Connor in his Bugatti/Ford, and Phil Payne in his Baldwin Special, and others that I cannot recall right now. I ran the Citroën/Willys there, but had more fun than I did success."

Bob said that he kept the Citroën for only a short time, not because he found fault with it but because he found a 1939 Jaguar SS 100 "that had been liberated from China. So once again I sold everything, went into hock, and got the SS 100, which I restored and kept for a number of years. All I can say is, once you are hooked, you are hooked forever!"

Iron Mountain Meal

I was curious about this interesting bread wrapper, which shows a huge redwood tree, notched out for automobiles, with a 1940 American Bantam woodie driving through the opening. That image piqued my interest. To understand this Ripley's Believe-It-Or-Not oddity I had to do considerable research; it led to quirks of automobile construction, a better understanding of the stuff in our diet, a public furor that brought about a HUAC (House UnAmerican Activities Committee) hearing and inspired Congressional legislation unheard of since Upton Sinclair's book *The Jungle* revamped the meat industry nearly a century ago.

This current wrapper recalls a bread produced during World War II, which used a food substance called Iron Mountain Meal. The meal was a substitute for flax, an ingredient in bread since Babylonian times, or roughly 3,000 B.C. Historians have noted that leaders such as Eric the Red, Attila the Hun and Charlemagne championed the use of flax, and the latter believed in the nutritional value of flax so strongly that he passed laws requiring his subjects to eat it.

Flaxseed contains both soluble and insoluble fiber. When America entered World War II, flax went too; in addition to C-rations, it was used in items as diverse as munitions containers and Mae West life vests. With flaxseed unavailable for civilian use, a substitute had to be found. The answer, after considerable experimentation, was Iron Mountain Meal.

Iron Mountain in the Upper Peninsula of Michigan is where Henry Ford had thousands of acres of forest. Most of the wood, used extensively in most cars built before World War II, came from Iron Mountain. The lumber milled here was also used in such woodie wagons as that American Bantam shown on the bread wrapper. Henry Ford hated to waste anything; it is well known that he turned scrap wood from Iron Mountain into charcoal briquettes that could be used in portable barbecue grills, which he also made.

The automakers had not found a profitable use for one by-product of the mills—the sawdust. While extensive experiments were run, the sawdust piles grew. One experiment that worked was refining the sawdust repeatedly until it was digestible; the fine dust was called Iron Mountain Meal.

While the experiments were done in the name of capitalism and profits, the bread baked with the meal was consumed as an act of patriotism. In addition to gasoline and rubber, wartime rationing included butter, margarine, eggs and sugar. Iron Mountain Meal was heavy on fiber, but had a bland quality, so consuming it was considered a contribution to the war effort. "Eat Iron Mountain Meal, send the Axis real steel!" went the wartime jingle.

When the world got back to normal and our boys returned home victorious, bakeries went back to baking those two staples, fluffy white bread and fluffy brown bread. Cut off from Iron Mountain Meal, large numbers of the population began acting strangely. At first the authorities thought people were "shell-shocked," en mass, but they soon realized that those afflicted were not veterans and never had been. Tests soon showed that many people had become addicted to Iron Mountain Meal! Further tests indicated that the addictive element in the meal was something akin to hemp (aka marijuana, pot, pod, junk, stuff, wacky weed, etc.).

The meal had none of the qualities of stronger drugs, and the rehabilitation sessions lasted only a few weeks. However, the large number of people involved did tax local economies. Oddly, or perhaps not so oddly, the main tool in getting the addicts back on their feet was large doses of fluffy white bread, sometimes buttered, sometimes soaked in a white milk gravy.

The crisis had not ended, however. As the older workers, those who had been employed in shipyards and airplane plants, died, rumors spread that the meal had killed them. The rumors seemed to originate in the Iron Mountain area, where numerous mill workers were struck down with a strange illness. Autopsies were performed, and it was clear that there was damage done to the stomach and the gastro-intestinal system, possibly by splinters, but the damage was not severe enough to cause death. The public outcry would not be stilled, however, and things got so bad that in 1947–48 the House UnAmerican Activities Committee, chaired by Senator McCarthy, held extensive hearings. Although no direct cause and effect could be proven between the sawdust-laced bread and subsequent health problems, the committee did recommend that Congress pass legislation to omit this source of fiber from the American diet. But, of course, the bakeries had already stopped using the stuff.

Perhaps not coincidentally, American automakers began phasing out their woodie models in 1948, and within five years station wagons would be all steel.

American Gothic: Hollywood Hubcaps and Duals

THE SEARCH FOR TRUTH

From the time I first got interested in hot rods, I was interested in whatever had happened years before. I knew almost nothing about rods or customs, but sometimes I sensed a car had a past and I wanted to know about it. The problem was that in the limited text the writer (and editor) treated every car as if it were a new creation. It was implied that hot rodding was so new it had no past, no roots, no traditions: it was the rare editor who wanted to look backward.

A good example of that kind of thinking was when a seafoam green '29 A V-8 roadster was featured on the cover of *Hot Rod Magazine* in 1953, and it was mentioned that the car had been built from a "mediocre" rod. The car had been built by Don Ferrera, and had appeared on the cover of *HRM* only two years earlier, in August 1951—and it was an outstanding car, one that everyone should have remembered. As I recall, only the paint and the taillights had been changed, and these minor changes could not disguise the car. To the magazine's credit, in the next issue an apology appeared, and an acknowledgment of Ferrera's skills.

It is precisely that kind of distortion of fact that I have become obsessive about. The year when a car was built, who built it, what changes were made, what kind of speed equipment did it have, etc. I mean, I want to know exactly, and, if possible, I'd like some proof. On the one hand, it's tiny thinking that interests almost no one and doesn't matter very much. On the other hand, if it *is* of interest, the information had better be secured now or it'll largely be lost forever. Time moves on, memory fades, people die, and what was known becomes hopelessly lost. And worse than no information at all is misinformation: the misremembered stuff that is passed on as fact, and the fabricated stuff that comes from some guy's weird imagination. It's also true that some car guys are given to BS a bit, for whatever reason.

I'm guilty of errors, no matter how hard I try to get things right. Sometimes the truth emerges only after lots of thought. Recently I was rewriting a column I'd written about a dozen years ago, one that developed from a race I'd had in 1953 on a local main street. I mentioned that I was ahead in my '37 Ford coupe and that I tried to stop with those old mechanical brakes when I saw the flashing stop light overhead.

As I was rewriting it, I visualized that same intersection and realized that in 1953 it did not have a single flashing light but rather stop signs on each corner. It's a small detail, but true to the period. And what that detail implied was that the street did not have enough traffic to require a single flashing light, much less the four-way signals that are common today. And that's one reason we were racing on it—there was no one else around! That reminded me of other streets where stop signs controlled traffic. Then I realized how many more traffic lights are on those streets today than were there, say, 30 or 40 years ago. Now drivers have to stop often, where at one time you could go 20 or 30 blocks without having to stop. Just that one detail reminded me of the lights that control how we drive, how fast we drive and how, in my opinion anyway, driving with fewer lights was more fun. That alone was reason enough to have a hot rod!

I imagine that I could document the number of traffic lights then versus now, if someone called me on it. Memory is so tricky, it's good to have proof. Almost every week I read or hear about a rod or custom that was built in the 1930s, 1940s or 1950s, but the details are so vague there's almost no way to confirm the car's origins or history. One would like to see old photographs of the car, or get DMV documentation, or racing history, if any. Sometimes I suspect it's a matter of not wanting to go to the trouble of tracing a car, because that kind of research can be a lot of work.

Perhaps carbon-14 dating would indicate whether this plaque does indeed date from 1946.

Recently I saw an old car with an unusual club plaque. It was a "Kustom Klub" plaque from Seattle, and so I asked the driver about it. He said that it was the second oldest club in the Northwest. Well, that piqued my interest, and so I asked some questions, such as what was the oldest club, in his opinion; he didn't know, he just knew that this was the second oldest.

When was it formed? I wondered, and he said 1946. That was early. To the best of my knowledge, and I've tried hard to learn what I can, there was only one club in Portland in 1946, a track roadster club. I'm always curious about how the first of anything came about, and although there were car clubs in So-Cal at least as early as 1932, they didn't get going in Oregon until around 1950. So the question I ask myself is, why would someone decide to start a club if none existed? The answer isn't as simple as it might seem.

I asked this fellow if any documentation were available—a club charter, incorporation papers, even a membership card, something with the 1946 date. He didn't think so. Well, I'm not doubting his word, but a number of clubs have surfaced in recent years, with fuzzy backgrounds, claiming to have been formed 50 or 60 years ago. But until the mid–1950s there weren't many clubs outside of So-Cal. and even in So-Cal there are only a very few clubs that existed in the late 1930s. On the other hand, this plaque had some things going for it. The size was larger than plaques made in the 1950s, the casting was pretty simple and even crude, as if it'd been whittled from aluminum. Since it lacked a timing association acronym, it may have pre-dated such a group.

But what about the "K" in "Kustom"? I pointed out that Barris popularized that spelling in 1951.

"We were ahead of him," the guy said, and he could be right. Who knows?

What's in a Name Anyway?

Some of the boys were sitting around grousing about how dull their lives had become: how they drive to a local rod run park themselves in lawn chairs and nurse their diet pops through a long, hot afternoon. "Somewhere," they say, back in their collective memory, "life used to be more fun."

I suggested they reinvent themselves by changing their names. A new name means a new identity, and if a guy chooses an interesting name he may automatically become a more interesting and fun guy!

The idea springs from memories of my childhood. When I was growing up, it seemed like everyone had a nickname, and in some cases I never did know the person's real name.

Sometimes the name was earned because of a physical characteristic, so a guy was called Shorty, Lefty or Red. People of my parents' generation were often called by the name of the place from which they had migrated: with names like Tex, Jersey, Dakota, etc. My ex-father-in-law was called Kansas by a small group of friends who had known him from the 1940s. When I was introduced to Bill Fisher I called him California Bill, the name I remembered from his ads for hot rod books published 50 years earlier.

Some names came from popular culture. I have known two guys named Duck; they were actually named Donald, and it took a while before the names clicked — Donald Duck! Other names are harder to figure. Recently I spoke with an old rodder, and we realized that we have a mutual friend, Ray Van Dorn, whom he kept calling Crazy Ray. I mentioned that to Ray, and he called the other guy Limber Louie ("he walked like Jim Nabors"), adding that everyone had a nickname in the old days.

For example, look at an old racing program and you'll see names like Sailor, Crash, Rajo and Racer. Once a guy earned a nickname, it usually stayed with him for life. In Portland there was Suicide Bob Dillon, a county sheriff and motorcycle racer who got his name by driving his motorcycle through a burning wall in thrill shows. I never heard anyone call him Bob — it was always Suicide Bob Dillon.

Another old racer was Wild Bill Hyde, who always got the full treatment to separate himself from the other Bills. If you wanted to be called Wild Bill, it would, I assume, affect the way you lived your life. I doubt that you could be called Wild Bill, or Suicide Bob, or Crash Corrigan and also be, say, a minister or an undertaker. People expect you to behave in certain ways. If you called yourself Wild Bill, you'd probably be a little wild — though not so wild as to be killed as this Wild Bill was: in a Porsche on a city street.

Now that I've grown older, I find it fascinating to look back at guys I knew when I was young; and who insisted on being called Speed or Killer or Ace. I try to imagine a morning when a guy decides he wants others to call him Bulldog or Sailor, and wonder what he was thinking! These guys usually rounded out their image by having long hair combed into a DA, a leather jacket, a dangling cigarette and a car with a raucous exhaust.

All those things are obtainable today, and if you're tired of the way your life is going, it's maybe time to make some changes! Start with a name that you want to live up to. At the very least, it'll confuse the bean counters with computers, who not only want to know who you are, but where you are at all times. To set things in motion, I'll make them puzzle over my new nickname: "Frisco Al."

SYNESTHESIA

I recently read of the hardships faced by young Hispanics who work in Oregon's berry fields. The story told of long hours, the heat, the dirt, the strain on the backs and knees and the low pay. I felt a great deal of compassion, because I remembered that as a kid I did the same work for the same reason: money! In my last two years of grade school I had a paper route, or routes, for one extended into another, and in the summer I also picked berries. I hated picking berries, but jobs were hard to find if you were younger than sixteen, and I needed the money. The only way I could get anything was by working. I tried to keep that in mind when my mother woke me at 4:30 A.M. and a half an hour later when I was standing on Foster Road waiting for a beat-up old bus to take us to the fields. Of course, work would have been easier if my mother had been prepared. Instead of a baloney sandwich and pop, or even Kool-Aid for lunch, we had crackers, cheese and a jar of water. That was not a satisfying prospect after hours of kneeling in the dirt under an intense sun with indelibly red fingers. My throat was dry with dust and the thought of even an ice cube popsicle seemed like heaven.

In eighth grade I became aware of clothes, and as I prepared for high school I knew I wanted what the older kids had: a pair of incredibly white pegged Day's cords and English brogues dyed oxblood and given a high polish. I wanted a couple dress shirts with muted thin stripes of pink or grey. Even socks were important: argyles with an infinite variety of colors in broad diamonds, the fuzz remaining even after many washings. I calculated how many strawberries I'd have to pick at a nickel a pound to get the ultimate shirt, a Stradivari, which cost $9.95. Once I earned ten bucks there was the terribly difficult decision of choosing a color: cherry red, lilac, chartreuse, or any of two dozen other colors, each beautiful. The decision was difficult because I knew I could only get one and only if I worked hard.

The only good thing about picking berries were the girls who sat next to me on that beat-up bus. Girls with berry stained lips and exotic names like Yvonne, Lavonne and Laverne. Even in the oppressive heat they were animated and chatty. I longed to enter their dialogue, and while I was afraid to look I couldn't take my eyes off of them.

When we got home I escaped from my dirty clothes and put on a pair of cut-off jeans. Our house never had a shower, and my mother, who grew up on a farm without indoor plumbing, thought it was a waste of water to take a bath every day. So I sat in a galvanized washtub in the yard or stood under the garden hose until the dust was gone and I felt reasonably cool. My mother might make a pitcher of red Kool-Aid, rich with ice cubes, or bring out a tray of home-made popsicles. We never had soda pop but occasionally I'd walk to the neighborhood grocery store where the bottles sat in slightly cool water, the tops like wee lily pads: Hires, Squirt, Shasta. Usually on really hot days I'd stop at the halfway point on my paper route at a modern gas station and buy a Coke. A nickel was a lot — a pound of berries — but in this machine, where the bottles rotated horizontally, the pop was wonderfully cold. I had to force myself to drink it slowly to make it last.

A real treat was to go to the fountain in the Mt. Scott Drugstore where a Coke with ice or flavored phosphate cost a nickel. Sometimes, after much debate, I'd buy a root beer float for fifteen cents. That was a goodly sum and not spent casually. I don't think you can compare that float with anything you can get today: two scoops of ice cream, the root beer shot into the glass under pressure to create frothy bubbles. A milkshake cost two bits but was rich and cold and served in a metal container that held two and a half glasses. Usually I got a milkshake only after getting a haircut and to make it last I took a couple comic books from the rack to read at the counter.

At some point all those thoughts and more merge until one recalls another. When I bite into a ripe strawberry there's the odor of diesel, those girls' bright lips, a song called "The Hucklebuck," a red Stradivari shirt and a cherry phosphate. The checkered pattern of a Dan River sport shirt echoes the floor tiles of the drugstore, a cherry Mountain Bar and waffles on a December morning.

From clothes to cars the sensations are similar. Chrome acorn nuts, velocity stacks, air cleaners, bright, shiny and cold, were like ice cubes. Often I was less interested in how a part functioned than in its appearance. The shape of a Stromberg 97, a '40 Ford dash and a '39 Ford taillight that suggested, in some way, lovely female curves. The richness of rolled and pleated Naugahyde upholstery also triggers that spot in my brain where images and sensations flash like nano-blips: strawberry milkshake, pegged cords, dickey collar, a boy and a girl parked in a '40 Ford convertible with the top down under a whitewall-like full moon. The sensations and their echoes are endless.

American Gothic

In addition to my work to end world hunger, I volunteer a fair amount of my time advising young rodders. As the lads gather about my feet they ask questions, wondering what rodding was really like in the good old days. "Oldtimer, you were there — was rodding different back then?" I mention that coffee cost a nickel a cup and gas cost 20 cents a gallon; they laugh, thinking I've entered an old guy's fantasy. I say that often there was absolutely no traffic, that you could (illegally) drag race on city streets in a rod that cost maybe $50. Again they express incredulity; the trip into the Fifties is too fantastic.

I debate whether to tell them about paint, which is a clear distinction between then and now. Nine years ago a friend had his '32 highboy roadster painted red and the cost, including materials, was $4,000! I was incredulous; in the world where I live, one ought to be able to buy at least four complete cars for that price. In recent years I've heard of a couple paint jobs that cost around twelve grand, and I photographed a '36 Ford coupe whose proud owner reportedly paid $61,000 for a paint job. It was gorgeous, but what a price!

In the Fifties, lots of cars ran primer forever; there were various reasons they never got painted but cost was not a factor. But some guys wanted color, and there were various ways to do it. In 1951 my friend Larry Deyoe drove his 1937 Chevrolet sedan over to my house to show the new paint he'd applied with a powder puff. I thought it looked, well, crappy, and memory has not improved the car's appearance. Recently I asked Larry how he applied the paint and what was it called, but he said he couldn't remember. (I think he's repressing the memory.) Another friend, Don "Duck" Collins, said he painted his A-V-8 roadster in the 1940s using a similar method. He said the paint went on like a paste wax, and dried fairly quickly. (Later he had the car painted black by a professional, and it was beautiful.) An old friend from Michigan, Roy Petersen, said that in 1941 his father bought a new Chevrolet limousine — very rare car! — and after a few years he got tired of the maroon and cream two-tone paint. He repainted it, and Roy remembers the event clearly: "This (the painting) was done in the driveway ... in bright sunlight. He used Jac-O-Lac paint, and because he was afraid of brush marks he used a powder puff. Somehow the theory was flawed. While it didn't have brush marks, I guess we would have to call them puff marks. No one ever got blinded by the shine, though."

Longtime rodder and ace photographer Dale Moreau remembers his early paint jobs. In 1958 Dale and his buddy painted a 1938 Ford coupe by hand. His buddy's father worked in a lumberyard and was able to get the paint for the boys. Dale thinks they might have got it

Al Drake in 1951 sprays a cycle fender for his roadster.

for nothing, but he clearly remembers that that paint was the only option they had. The father brought home a gross of 1¾ ounce jars of black enamel, each with its own brush. "It covered the car — after a week and a half of painting; two guys, 144 bottles! We thought it looked good. It was green when we started, and black when we got done! We painted the fender skirts and whitewalls with white house paint. They turned yellow after a week and had to be repainted. It must've looked awful, but we were fifteen years old."

Next Dale and his buddy removed the rear door handles on a 1952 Ford four door — to make it look like a tudor! — and painted the car using a Flit gun. (I should explain to younger readers that a Flit gun was pumped by hand to spray insecticide.) Dale said, "We put paint in a Flit gun and sprayed the car. That took a long time and broke your arm!" The third car the boys painted was a 1951 Ford convertible, "We turned professional, and used my buddy's mother's Electrolux vacuum cleaner, with the hose on the opposite end. That really threw the old red lacquer on, and then you'd have to sand for a week to get it smooth!" Dale mentioned that they painted a red racing stripe, about 12" wide, on the convertible top.

In 1951 my father and I painted my roadster in the driveway. He tried to dissuade me from painting it red, saying that every cop would be on my tail, but I was adamant. We did some sanding and masking, wet down the dirt and grass around the car and shot it red enamel using a constant flow gun that we'd rented or borrowed. Yes, there were some runs over some imperfect bodywork, but it was red! Moreover, the whole job couldn't have cost us over $10.00. In those days, that was important.

OLD CUSTOMS NEVER DIE

Hot rodders are not big on writing things down, but they love to tell stories. They'll talk at length about a certain race, the sound of an engine, a car they once owned or almost owned. As such, they're in an oral tradition that goes back to the cave men, the early tribes, and includes post–Guttenberg groups of oral storytellers such as cowboys and sailors. When Joseph Conrad quit the sea at age forty and began writing fiction, he considered himself a storyteller in the tradition of sailors. His American counterpart, Henry James, described Conrad as "that artful mariner" because of his techniques in telling a seemingly simple story.

But sometimes a simple story is enough. We delight in hearing the twists and turns of real life and discovering the unexpected. My friend, Bob Hammel, told me such a story the other day and I knew I needed to write it down. Bob, and his wife, Gina, are real car nuts and have owned and restored numerous cars over the past 50 years, including Bugattis, a hot rodded 1939 Citroën roadster, a 1929 1750 Alfa-Romeo which was Gina's grocery getter, Porsches, an early Austin-Healey, an HRG race car, a sprint car with a two-port Riley, etc. In spite of his background, Bob is a modest fellow and not given to long-winded narratives. This story was brief, and I thought of considerable interest. But let Bob tell it:

"Early in 1983, my old friend Bill Binney and I were attending an auto show in Palm Springs. We began talking with a guy and we could tell that he was a real enthusiast. He lived out in the desert, where he had an extensive collection of sports cars. He also mentioned that he had an old custom car which got my heart beating because I thought I knew which one it was. It was a car that interested me greatly.

"Later Bill and I went over to his house in Yucca Valley, about 30 miles from where I lived. This guy was single, lived alone with his collection, and he collected all kinds of things; in fact, there was barely room to move inside his house. His collection turned out to be mostly Triumph TR-2s and TR-3s, which did not raise my blood pressure much.

After a quick wash job, the car appeared as it had on the cover of *Custom Cars* (Trend #101) in 1951. The body was power-hammered from sheet steel, and no aluminum or fiberglass was used.

"But the custom car was, as I had suspected, the 'Coachcraft Special,' a car that had been a favorite of mine for years. It had been built in 1940 by Coachcraft of Los Angeles on a Ford chassis shortened to a 91-inch wheel base. The entire body, which resembled a 1940 Ford, was built of sheet steel and power-hammered to get the right shape and finish. It used a DuVall windshield and '40 Ford headlights.

"The original upholstery was pigskin, but that was now a mess. There was also a large dent in back, as if someone had tried to push it. Otherwise the car was complete and original.

"Bill and I saw this fellow several times. He was in very bad health. Then we invited him to Bill Binney's house one time when the gang of us were having a party-dinner, dancing and stuff. He came over. He was really ill, but he had a very good time. A few days after that he died. That party probably didn't help him much, but he had enjoyed himself.

"Then, I'll be damned, we found out that he had left all his cars to Bill and me. The Triumphs were basically okay, but they weren't something I wanted. Bill liked them — he probably had 20 cars in his backyard — and he towed 6 or 7 of them home. I trailered the Coachcraft Special home and cleaned it up. I loved that car. I wanted to restore it, but I just had too many projects going at the moment to undertake another restoration.

"I contacted Strother MacMinn, who was a friend and who knew the car well. With his help, I contacted the original builder, Rudi Stoiesser, who was still with Coachcraft. Rudi contacted the person for whom the car was originally constructed in 1940, Mr. Ted Johnson. Forty-three years had passed, and Johnson was pretty excited about getting the car back but only if Rudi would restore it for him. Rudi agreed to do the restoration, and came to Palm Springs with a trailer and took the car back to Los Angeles. I looked in on the car several times when I went to LA, and the restoration was going well. Then I lost track of the car after some time had passed."

I started to tell Bob that I thought that the car was now in Texas, but that seemed beyond the point of this story. I tried to see whether Bob had regrets about this car that got away, but he was launching into another tale, this one about the time he and Gina drove a Ferrari from Latrode, Pennsylvania, to Los Angeles for his friend Joe Lubin in the middle of winter.

HENRY GREGOR FELSEN

I can't think of Henry Gregor Felsen without a sense of regret.

I knew Henry, or Hank, as he insisted on being called, well enough to consider him a friend, as he did me, but in the end how good a friend was I? After someone dies we all say we could have done more, but in this case it's true, and it would not have cost me anything.

Like millions of high school boys, I met Felsen long ago when I read his early novel, *Hot Rod*. A decade later, in 1961, I began work on a novel that also involves hot rods, *Beyond the Pavement*. My debt to Felsen's work wasn't clear to me until around 1982, when I went back and re-read four of Felsen's novels about cars. I didn't plagiarize, I had simply been looking for models, something that would show me how to write a novel, and years later I realized that I had absorbed Felsen's work and had it in mind as I did my own writing.

At the time I assumed that Felsen was dead. I had poked around Des Moines, Iowa, the locale of some of his work, but

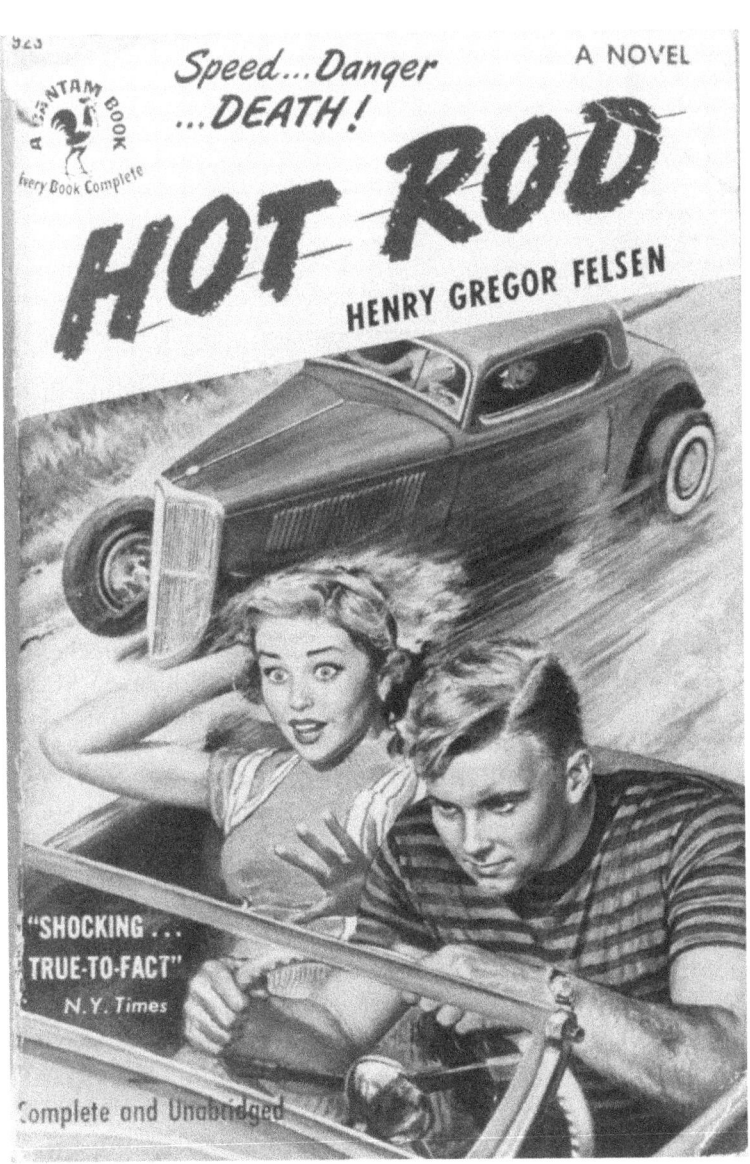

Hot Rod (the first edition paperback).

Henry Gregor Felsen (left) and Albert Drake in 1990.

found nothing. Then, in 1984 my friend, Ed Reavie, told me that Felsen was living in Vermont.

I called Felsen several times from Oregon and interviewed him for my book, *Hot Rodder!*

Months later I returned to Michigan and, by an odd chance, Felsen moved there also. We exchanged letters, made phone calls and eventually met at the KKOA Nationals.

Felsen was a writer all his life. He was born in Brooklyn, NY in 1916, the son of Jewish immigrant parents, and grew up in a family that valued learning. He attended the University of Iowa in the 1930s, and although he never told me when he decided to become a writer, it might have been during college, because in those tough times he traded stories and essays for food and drink. After two years, he dropped out of school, hitchhiked around the country and sailed the seas as a mess-boy. All this activity was the typical training for writers, and Felsen wrote fiction and non-fiction for the pulp magazines as well as *Look*. Then he began writing for magazines aimed at young people. This led to a series of nine books for juveniles. Felsen learned how to put together a story and how to write quickly; the nine books were written in eighteen months.

When World War II broke out, Felsen joined the Marines, and while he was being trained for combat he spent most of his time writing for *Leatherneck* magazine. In 1946, again a citizen, he returned to Iowa and wrote books for young people, with an occasional humorous adult story published in the mass-market magazines. As he told me, he had to write quickly and often, because his work didn't earn much money, and he had a wife and family to support. But he was earning a living from his writing, and he estimated that only about 100 people were able to do that after the war.

In 1948 his office was across the hall from the Des Moines Safety Council, and he was approached by the director about writing a book about driver training for teenagers. Felsen was reluctant, but he wrote the book in 14 days, and titled it *Hot Rod*. The book was in print for thirty-two years and sold around two million copies. It changed Felsen's status with the publishers, and he began getting advances of $5,000 and up. His other books— *Street Rod, Crash Club, Road Rocket*—quickly followed. There was talk of movie deals. He was a writer who had found success.

When I met him he proved to be a sweet old man who loved to talk about books; I do not remember that we ever talked about cars. People who met him only through his books assumed that he knew all about hot rods, but he pointed out that all one needed to do was to give the reader the impression of the car and car activity.

Felsen considered himself a teacher, which was, he said, the highest calling. And that's why I have a sense of regret. He came to my town one day with his wife, and while she worked, we hung out. It was a delightful time. We sat in a booth in a cafe, drinking coffee, munching on doughnuts, and Felsen apologized for not wearing his dentures while he gummed a fat cigar to death. He talked about Plato, Homer, *Crime and Punishment*, Dickens, books and authors he greatly admired. We talked as two writers, about sitting in a chair for hours, alone, writing. Felsen complained, but without malice, about editors and publishers, small advances, late royalties. He was still writing, he said, although he'd had some health problems, and he looked forward to a comeback. The problem was he had no contacts in the business anymore; the editor at the paperback house that had sold over two million of his books would not return his calls or reply to his letters.

That's when I feel regret. That was the last time I saw Felsen, although we enjoyed a solid correspondence for several years, until his death. After that meeting it occurred to me I should have invited him to my house where we could have kicked off our shoes, gotten down on the floor and looked at the books we'd been discussing. Felsen could've lit that cigar, and had a shot of bourbon, if he wanted. And my other regret, realized much later, was that I should have invited him to my writing class and just let him talk about books and writing. It would not have cost me anything to do that, and in fact we all would have been richer for it.

LET US NOW PRAISE FAMOUS MEN

So many men have worked with skill for a lifetime, building neat machines, and too many risk being forgotten. They bent metal, fabricated, built hot engines, sewed leather, shot paint and had an unerring eye for design. The guys I'm thinking of were incapable of doing faulty work. They sought perfection, sometimes at the expense of wife and family. They were more than folk artists; some ought to be named along with Calder and Brancusi.

Such a man was Vern Houle. Who? you ask. Houle began hot rodding in Wisconsin, then came to California in 1936 in a new Ford topped with Federal-Mogul heads and a McCullough supercharger. Almost immediately he collaborated with Jack Henry and they built an unusual dry lakes car that was unusually fast. After World War II he wrenched at Indy, Bonneville, oval tracks and sports car circuits. All that, and yet I've found only a single recent reference to his achievements: in a book on the Mexican Road Race the author calls Houle (in 1954) the world authority on setting up an automatic transmission for racing!

I know Houle's name because he's mentioned in a caption in Veda Orr's *Dry Lakes Pictorial*; the photograph shows him sitting in a pre–World War II lakes machine that he owned with Jack Henry. But his name was not on the list of So-Cal rodders I wanted to talk with when I traveled the area in the 1970s and 1980s, nor was Dick Ford's name. Ford was recommended by another sterling fellow, Strother MacMinn. Thirty years ago it was difficult to locate people, especially if you lived in the Midwest, as I did, and the people you wanted to locate lived in So-Cal—if they hadn't moved or died. I wrote numerous letters; few were answered. There was little interest in nostalgia. Moreover, who was I? I had no reputation as an automotive writer, and my letters were vague. I had no plan. I was a guy obsessed with really old hot rods, the dry lakes, and I wanted to identify some old photographs. My motives were pure, my intentions honorable, but as for a goal I was fuzzy.

About the only one who responded was Strother MacMinn. He was a prince of a fellow, and I could not have connected with a better person at that point. Totally out of the blue, he also sent some photographs. Today we're all familiar with the old rods, due to a number of books and articles that have been published in recent years, but thirty years ago they were a mystery. MacMinn could have sent thousand dollar bills, or pieces of the Dead Sea Scrolls, that's how rare the photographs were. MacMinn could have written me off as a crank, one of an army of people who must have bugged him every day for information, but he apparently saw some promise in me; he had a generous spirit and in addition to the photographs he offered encouragement, advice and several addresses. Talk with Dick Ford, he said.

The next summer I went to El Mirage, and when I eventually got to Newport Beach I called Dick Ford. He was polite but evasive. I'm not a pushy guy, but I'd traveled 3,000 miles and I needed to talk with him. Finally he told me that he had cancer and wasn't up to talking, which made me feel guilty, but if I'd go to the Briggs Cunningham Museum the next day we could talk over lunch. I arrived early, saw Ford working on a big classic car in the shop, then I got distracted by all the neat machines on display. Suddenly it was past noon, and Ford had gone to lunch. When he returned we had only 20 minutes before he had to go back to work. So our meeting was brief, but I liked him immensely. He was tall, lean, with blonde hair; his voice was soft, and he spoke with the same precision with which he worked. He told me about growing up near Pomona in the 1930s, owning rods and cycles; he was in the Army Air Force during World War II, had his B-24 shot down and was interned in Sweden until the war ended. I was impressed with his story about reaching London and visiting the Temple Press, where he spent an hour talking with Lawrence Pomeroy, who was working on his landmark Grand Prix book. Back in California, he built an A-V8 roadster with a supercharged flathead in 75 days, and went street racing. His competition was future Indy racers like Manuel Ayulo and Jack McGrath, all kids then. He showed me pictures of a slick '27 Chevy roadster he'd owned a couple of times, before and after the war, and of a recent project, where he'd adapted a small supercharger intended for a Fiat to his 750 Honda motorcycle. All of his work was impressive.

Although the time we had together was brief, everything he told me was simply great! It was what I wanted to hear. As I drove away I knew I would not need to change a word. In fact, I was so impressed with his oral history that I read it to a literary group a couple years later when I was Writer-in-Residence at an Oregon university; I have no idea what the audience made of it.

Since I was heading north Ford said to visit Vern Houle, who lived "in the middle of nowhere." I found Houle's All-American Garage, and found that Houle had a visitor, Jack Henry, a name I recognized. Houle and Henry had belonged to the Road Runners club before the war; fellow members included Wally Parks, Eldon Snapp, Dean Batchelor, Vic Edelbrock and other go-fast boys. As I listened, they invoked the names of the greats: Johnny Junkins, Pete Bertrand, Clay Smith, Ed Iskenderian, Bill Stroppe, Connie Weidell, Bud Hare and many others. It wasn't bragging, it wasn't name dropping — they were simply talking about guys they'd worked with or raced against.

Two quick examples that sum up their abilities; in 1936 Jack Henry saw a need for an inexpensive dual manifold for the Ford V-8, and he made one out of a '32 Ford intake manifold; it worked, and he said "I sold hundreds of them." A couple years later, Houle realized that Lincoln gears would fit in a Ford case, and he came up with the first set of Zephyr gears. "Man, I used to suck those roadsters up ... they'd say, how can he wind that flathead so far?"

Henry was thoughtful, introspective, liked to discuss theory, while Houle was more demonstrative, a hands-on guy. They talked, I listened, and after a while it was lunchtime. They ran the car hoist up to hip level, placed a sheet of plywood on it and got out the makings for sandwiches and coffee; 1 was invited, even though Houle was ready to throw me out a time or two. He kept saying that they had to get to work, although I never saw a car being worked on.

I was fortunate to meet these guys, especially since Henry would die the following year. I stopped to see Houle a couple more times, he alternated between welcoming me and threatening to throw me out. I stayed simply because Houle had a rich way of speaking, and I could listen to him all day. "I'm still a hard-charger!" he said, showing me the engine in his Ranchero. "I was smokin', baby," he'd say of a fast run. One year he ran a 1957 T-Bird at Bonneville and turned 212 mph on gas. "I had the antenna and the wind wings and bath in it and everything." He ran 181 and they put him in the streamliner line. "I went in the streamliner line and all those boxes were about two feet high, and here's this big old Mack truck. The guy says, 'What are you doing here?' I showed him the sticker ... he says, 'What?' The next day, I blew her down the course to over 200 mph." He told me about being a member of the Lincoln team in the Mexican Road Race; he drove with Billy Vukovich. "Vukovich couldn't drive a stock car worth a damn," Houle said. In a treacherous area Vukovich spun out, and the big Lincoln went over a cliff. The right side door flew off and Houle could look down a long ways. He and Vukovich were trying to figure out how badly they were hurt when the car shifted a bit, threatening to fall. "Hold it," Houle told Vukovich, "she's still pissing!"

I got in touch with Houle several years later, when I was finally finishing the book *Hot Rodder!* He'd mellowed some, I thought, or maybe not. He was 80, had gotten a divorce, and was racing his motorcycle on the freeway. The bet was a C-note, and the race started at 85 mph! They don't make guys like that anymore!

LOVE OF A FINE CAR

Long before there were gala gatherings of the Goodguys, owners of interesting cars were loners, or banded together in small groups of like-minded enthusiasts. For example, the Bugatti bunch. Although the Bugatti Owners Club (of England) was formed in 1929, in all of recorded automotive history there have never been more than a handful of Bugattis gathered together in one place. And even then the owners had only each other to talk to. The general public did not know, nor care, that Bugatti's first name was Ettore and that his favorite food was truffles, let alone know the difference between a Type 35B and a Type 35C, or appreciate the sound of that gear-driven Roots blower at 5,000 rpm.

My friend, Bob Hammel, owned a Bugatti around 1958–62, and recently he showed me photographs of a group event. I was impressed! Sure, it was a small gathering, fewer than a dozen cars, but there was variety—everything from open-wheel Grand Prix-type cars to a Bugatti Royale, which has been called the biggest automobile ever made. Bugattis have always been rare—I think I've seen three in my entire life—and exotic. I also consider them expensive: any one of the cars in the photographs would sell for a cool million and up today.

I had to revise my thinking when Bob told me that if could have found a Bugatti, in good shape, in 1960, it would have only brought a couple thousand bucks. So these Bugatti owners didn't buy a Bugatti as an investment; they simply loved fine machinery. That certainly describes Bob Hammel. He is a real car nut who over the past 60 years has owned some rare and exotic cars. He was born and grew up in the Sacramento area, and before World War II his daily driver was a 1930 Ford A-V8 roadster; it featured a DuVall windshield, Federal-Mogul heads and an

Edelbrock slingshot manifold, all rare items even back then. During World War II he was in the Navy but managed to build two cars, under adverse conditions, on Naval Air Stations: a customized 1935/36 Ford roadster in Florida, and a Chevy four roadster in Hawaii. When he got out of the service he moved to Los Angeles and bought an Army surplus Harley-Davidson, with horizontal opposed cylinders and shaft drive. He traded that for a rare 1937 Citroën front wheel drive convertible, a car that resembles a customized '34 Ford. He amazed guys by burning the front tires whenever he left a drive-in, but soon found out that was hard on gears. After using up all the Citroën rings and pinions in Los Angeles, and cutting a few new sets himself, Bob converted the car to rear wheel drive. He built up a Willys Jeep engine topped with an Alexander OHV conversion and a pair of Winfield carbs; a Willys transmission using Studebaker gears and overdrive got power to the Studebaker rear end.

Bob drove the Citroën in some of the first So-Cal sports car events. He also became a charter member of the California Sports Car Club, a club that included a very young Phil Hill and the actor Donald O'Connor as members. He drove his Citroën in the 1947 Tujunga Hill Climb, and the next year he owned a 1937 Jaguar SS100, which he drove in the time trials at the Davis Car Company test track. Between 1947 and 1995 Bob owned two dozen exotic cars, including a 1934 Singer LeMans model, a 1951 Porsche 356 coupe which he bought in Germany, a 1929 Brooklands Riley that Whitney Straight once owned, a 1952 Aston-Martin DB 2 Vantage, a 1952 Frazer-Nash LeMans once owned and raced in England by Bob Gerard, a 1934 Morgan three-wheeler with a JAP engine, a 1939 HRG roadster and a 1947 HRG roadster. Gina, his wife of 50 years, owned a 1929 Alfa-Romeo supercharged Zagato roadster, which was her daily driver in the 1960s.

This list, while terribly impressive, is inadequate in describing the cars. Every one was in concours condition, and Bob did all the work. Part of his interest in sports cars is, I think, the challenge of working on engines with one or two overhead cams and superchargers. Bob is modest about his abilities and knowledge, but over a period of years I've asked him about a car or airplane or engine that I've only read about, and without fail, in an un-pedantic manner, he's been able to discuss the subject at length. His knowledge is encyclopedic.

That's no doubt a prerequisite for owning a Bugatti. That is, if you want to keep it running without depending on others. Bob owned a 1929 Bugatti Type 35B, which had a straight-eight engine with a single overhead cam, roller rod and main bearings, and was supercharged. It was a gorgeous car, black with cycle fenders, and every detail was painted or plated. "Today the car is owned by a wealthy collector, who uses it regularly in eastern Bugatti Club events," said Bob. But I'll bet he doesn't drive it like Bob did — to the store, to the beach with Gina, and then to a bistro to enjoy an interesting meal and listen to Dixieland jazz.

A book at-hand notes: "…the 35B and 35C enjoyed three outstandingly successful seasons, winning the Grand Prix of France (1929 and 1930); Belgium (1930); Monaco (1929 and 1930) and Spain (1928 and 1929); many secondary races and literally hundreds of minor events." (David Hodges, *Famous Racing Cars*). What, I wondered, could it be like to drive what is essentially a race car in traffic? The four naked tires, the rumble of the exhaust, the wind — perhaps it would not be too different from driving a '32 Ford roadster to a Goodguys event. But Bob cited the "smell of hot castor oil, which was the preferred lubricant for the roller bearing types." Then the supercharger would begin to shriek, the engine winding up to 5,000 rpm and there would be terrific sounds from the bare floor and side sheet metal, exhaust note rising, the wind buffeting the driver's head mercilessly, bugs and pebbles flying past with only goggles to save his eyesight. It could be thus — or so I think.

The fact is that Bob drove his Bugatti a lot. He was a founding member of the American Bugatti Club and, for several years, the editor of its publication, *Pur Sang*. He knew everybody who had an interest in Bugattis. Some of the names may not resonate today, but they were important people then. Bob's good friend, Bunny Phillips, for example, had raced at Indianapolis. Bob recalled: "We, the Bugatti owners and fanciers, used to gather on Saturdays at Overton 'Bunny' Phillips' shop in San Gabriel. Bunny had maintained a Bugatti service department since the 1930s, and he had raced a T35 for years. We would look at Bunny's progress on whatever the current project was, and then go for lunch and beer."

Bob added, "After the American Bugatti Club was officially formed, the club events became more organized, usually a picnic at someone's estate, or an overnight tour that included some country roads, where the GP cars could be 'extended' a bit. The fenderless GP cars were usually harassed by the California Highway Patrol, but then the drivers would explain the cars weighed less than 1,500 pounds, so they were legal. That usually confused the CHP enough to let them go."

Opportunities to drive the Bugatti occurred frequently. For example, Bob said that in the 1960s "there was a popular television program hosted by Ralph Story … and featured subjects of interest in the Los Angeles area. The subject of one of the episodes was a little shop in the San Gabriel Valley that made a living by restoring Bugatti automobiles." Bunny Phillips told other Bugatti owners about the filming. Bob said, "On the arranged day, I drove my Type 35B from Manhattan Beach to my office at Parker Aircraft on Century Boulevard, just across from the entrance to the old Los Angeles Airport. I arranged to take some time off and drive out to Bunny's shop in San Gabriel (about 25 miles). Also there were Bob Dunlap (T40), Bob Day (T51), Lucille Phillips (T46), and of course Bunny with a T57 or two."

A group of photographs show the club members gathered for a day of fun and food in the parking lot of the Briggs Cunningham Museum in Costa Mesa. Cunningham was a wealthy sportsman whose racing résumé reached back to the 1930s. He was a friend of Bob and Gina, and they shared an interest in exotic machines, including Bugattis. The photographs, taken by Hugo Molnar, show four of the Bugattis that Cunningham brought out. There was a Type 35B, fenderless and in racing trim; and a Type 55, full-fendered and ready to tour, which is probably my favorite Bugatti. Two others, extremely rare, are a study in contrast. His Type 41 Royale, one of six made, has been described as the largest car ever built. His Type 52, a diminutive machine, was built by Bugatti for his son. Bob notes that the Type 52 was a half scale replica of the Type 35, with an electric motor. It was later put into limited production and could be rented for children to run along the beach at Cannes and Nice. For a small group, the club contained some well-known people. In addition to Briggs Cunningham, Bob and Gina Hammel and Bunny Phillips, there were John Burgess, an old-time dirt-track racer, artist and curator of the Cunningham Museum, and Bob Estes, a wealthy car dealer whose racing history was extensive. For the record, others in attendance included: Bob Dunlap with a Type 40, Dr. Milton Roth with a Type 13, Joe Rickets with a Type 37A, Dr. Charles Hascall with a Type 57SC coupe and Chuck Stanley with a Type 57 drophead convertible. On the distaff side, there was Mrs. Lucille Phillips, Bunny's wife, with her Type 49. Also present was Fred Treat with a Type 57C. Bob said that Mr. Treat had a large estate in Beverly Hills, and when he eventually sold it, he moved to central Mexico where he bought an entire village! No doubt the other club members were equally interesting, if we could dig into their histories.

As they gathered, I imagine that they did what Goodguys do today: talk, admire the cars, kick a tire and maybe stretch the truth. Then it was time to drive to a decent restaurant to discuss the appropriate wine to go with the steak and lobster.

Racing the Reaper

I grew up with an inordinate fear of death. Against the darkness of death I learned early how to read and write. The first words I wrote, according to my mother, I copied from an advertisement: "I Love Dole Pineapple Juice." I'm not sure whether I'd had pineapple juice, a rare thing in our house in those days, but then I hardly understood the full meaning of the words I read or copied. Before I started school I struggled with pleasure through the comic strips and the movie page, and it must have been there that I read about someone who had had a heart attack. I was terribly aware of my own heart, which I urged to continue, but I had no idea how it worked. I could understand a heart attack only in the terms of an image, and I saw a flash of lightning, which is pretty much what a heart attack is.

And death? Death was a shadow in my bedroom at night, raw liver, rain on mossy stone, a Gothic house on a North Dakota prairie, lightning rods pointing skyward. If I developed an inordinate fear, what would an ordinate fear be, especially for a kid who realizes that death is that inevitable door at the end of a long hallway — a realization that ought to send every one of us to the loony bin by the age of ten.

I greatly feared, but had little knowledge of, death. We played war in foxholes dug in the field, and there we died with ease. Saturday matinees showed Johnny Mack Brown and Sunset Carson shooting the outlaw's gun hand, without drawing blood. There was radio death, the "Inner Sanctum" and the creaking door. In high school, real death was an ocean away, in Korea, but it was on my mind as I rode in the backseat of my father's car, reading an article in *Collier's* about kids dying of some sarcoma. Did I have anything? I probed my body and felt lumps, every one a potential grenade. This went on until I was certain I had something bad. Our family didn't have a physician, but I thought I could see a doctor if I went out for a sport. Everyone had to be examined, I assumed. A separate problem was that I wasn't very good at any sports. I could run, I was running from death, so perhaps I could go out for cross-country and at some point mention to the doctor that I was dying. Yes, my fear of death was inordinate.

To forestall the inevitable, to take my mind off of man's fate, I did what we all do, even today: I sought pleasure. I read comic books, ate birthday cake, had a root beer float at the drugstore, saw a movie, got new shoes and rode my bike endlessly. At night shadows lurked, a high wind moaned, the floor creaked, a dog howled, and far off, at the edge of the world the Galloping Goose's whistle was a lonesome sound. Daylight affirmed life: Please, I prayed, let it go on. It did, day by day, and most days were pleasant.

A real pleasure was to take the bus downtown on Saturdays with a friend and spend the entire day wandering the streets, with visits to pawn shops, coin stores, sporting goods stores, the row of five-and-dime stores and the antique shops. We watched the woman in a big department store tie fishing flies, and then we'd spit out the sixth floor window onto those far below. We looked at the Roman coins and the pair of two-handed medieval swords in the Art Museum, then ate a wiener at the Original Coney Island.

Along the way, we'd spend hours in the used bookstores. We might buy a dozen old copies of *True*, *Argosy*, *Bluebook* and a couple pulps, such as *Astounding* or *Weird Tales*. As my fifteenth birthday approached, my tastes shifted toward cars. It was still possible to buy the first issues of *Hot Rod Magazine* for a dime, but even at that price I could only afford a few copies. Plus a couple used *Cycle*, and a couple *Motorsport*, a magazine I didn't see on the newsstand.

One Saturday I came home with a used copy of a new title, *Best Hot Rods*. I thumbed through it on the bus, stopping to read an article about hot rods, speed and death. A rodder named George Castera, although five years older, lived a life that was similar to what I wanted mine to be. He grew up in Los Angeles, and had a strong interest in cars. In high school he

This belly tank was George Castera's last car. Powered by a flathead V-8, it turned 157 mph, a new record. The man in the photograph is unidentified (Don Pennington Collection).

studied automotive mechanics, and hung out around garages known for the hot rods and race cars they built. On weekends he went to various race tracks and "became acquainted with the drivers and the pit crews." What a life: That was my dream!

The article was sketchy, with few details, but what I read held my attention. "In 1948, at the age of 18, George Castera built a hot rod in which he managed to hit 126 mph on the dry lakes." The article made it all seem so easy. I pictured Castera in sunny So-Cal, working on a rod in his driveway, helped by older rodders who knew what they were doing. That's what I needed, plus some money, which Castera seemed to have. It was like reading a Clint Curtis comic book story, where a high school kid is able to easily build an incredible car.

Then the story took a drastic turn in the space of a paragraph break. "During the winter of 1948 and the spring of 1949 George complained of chest pains." He tired easily too. Unlike my situation, he had a family physician. After a thorough examination, the doctor diagnosed Castera's problem as malignant thymoma — an incurable cancer! My heart raced, then sank, as I read those words, but I was told that Castera "accepted his fate without a whimper." I knew a little about dying, and I knew I could never be that brave.

In the face of death, Castera decided to build a new car and go faster. He built a '27 T roadster with a new flathead V-8. "By the summer of 1949, it was ready for trial runs and his friends helped him tow it to El Mirage where he made 136.14 mph on the first run." During the next few months he rebuilt the engine twice, and eventually the car turned 144.45 mph.

The cancer progressed, Castera got weaker, death came nearer, and then, to fight the darkness, Castera decided he needed to go faster. He built a new car, a Class C Lakester, using a war surplus aircraft fuel tank — a belly tank. Again, the article glossed over the details, but such a car, built from scratch, would require a new frame, front and rear ends, a special steering setup with the driver far forward, and a certain amount of engineering required to locate the engine in the rear. The article said that he built a new flathead V-8, but did not give details. It did mention that even in his weakened state he was able to complete the car, although "he could sit up for only a few hours a day."

The car made it to the June 10th, 1950 SCTA meet; Castera was unable to ride along to see his sleek tank establish a new Class C record of 157.235 mph. His friends phoned the news to Castera's home, and I'd like to think that his car's success, and his success, kept him alive. "A few weeks later," I read on the bus, and again as I walked home, and repeatedly in later years, "in St. Vincent's Hospital in Los Angeles, at the age of 20, he died of cancer."

A postscript notes that the lakester "was raffled off at the SCTA Hot Rod Show" the following November. One hundred percent of the money, $3,000, a considerable sum, went to the Damon Runyon Cancer Fund. The car may have been bought by Ray Brown, because much later in the same magazine, without a reference to George Castera, is a photograph of the Brown and Hooper Class C lakester which is obviously the car Castera built. By 1952 Brown and Hooper had set a Class C record at Bonneville of 163 mph for a two-way average. That's what will have to pass as a happy ending to this story.

SIMPLE

They were called the good old days because things were simple. They were simple because there was almost nothing to know, except how to get a bottle of beer, and how to open it.

Think about it: everything that has happened during the past 50 years was a big void. There were no computers, iPods, remote controls, microwave ovens, Xerox machines, DVDs, pocket calculators, color TVs, cordless phones, home scanners, disposable cameras, digital whatzits, lasers or a hundred other things. It was an innocent time, years before the sexual revolution, rock and roll, X-rated movies, hard porn and the assassinations of Martin Luther King Jr., Bobby Kennedy and JFK. It was a time when these words would have made no sense to the average American: uppers and downers, LSD, jet-set, internet, swinging singles, uni-sex, Gore–Tex, Godzilla, clones, sit-ins, Vietnam, Beatniks, groupies, black holes and Sputnik.

Whatever millions of books were published during the past fifty years did not concern us then, nor a zillion songs and movies. We didn't need to know — couldn't know — about that army of public figures, politicians, singers, actors and cultural celebrities that have risen to prominence during the past half-century. Just wipe your brain clean of all that and you have an idea of how little we needed to know back then.

Moreover, things were reduced to the simplest terms. Everyone accepted the concept of Christmas, and Christmas trees, cards and greetings. Christmas was even celebrated in public schools. Meat was healthy. Criminals were people who stole cars or robbed banks and they deserved to go to prison. We believed in capital punishment. We voted the same party line that our parents voted, and we drove the same make of car that our father drove. We didn't debate these things. There was no grey area. Life was as clear as the sky on a sunny day.

Oh, there were a few problems, such as how to get booze. I have never been a drinker, and now I've lived long enough to know what immoderate drinking can do. But that first sip, how it danced on my taste buds! I opened the refrigerator, opened the quart, took a couple delicious sips and stuck the cap back on. When my father poured a glass the beer was flat. I think I learned something.

About thirty years ago there was a best-selling book called *Future Shock*. Its premise was that the world of the future would approach chaos because of the number of choices a person would face. That future is with us already. Simply buying a cup of coffee can involve fifty choices. There must be a hundred kinds of bread on store shelves, and an equal number of cereals. Call city hall or a utility company and you'll collide with a recorded menu that asks you to make perhaps twenty choices before you get to talk with a real person, if you ever do.

There's a specialty store here in town with perhaps eight hundred types of beer — domestic, foreign and micro-brews. How does one choose? When I was a teenager I was aware of perhaps six, and only two stood out: Blitz-Weinhard and Olympia. I felt a loyalty to Oly, my father's choice. But I couldn't get any! The memory of Oly dancing across my taste buds remained only a memory. It wasn't that I wanted to get drunk, I wanted to have a beer ready if I should meet a girl. I had everything planned, and later I kept a stubby behind the spare tire of my '37 Ford until the bottle was better aged than the beer. I don't know what happened to it but I'm surprised that it didn't explode with the heat of that summer. I think beer came only in bottles: stubbies, tall-necks and quarts. I can't remember beer, or even pop, in a can.

So if you ever got a girl and a beer in the same car at the same time you had to figure out how to open the bottle, because there were no twist-off tops. This was a problem, but car guys are resourceful, and it was said that every car had a built-in bottle opener. In some cars it was the space between the bumper guard and the bumper. In others, the hood support or the front seat adjustment lever, etc. On the 1947 Ford the steering column support forms a U, and it works perfectly as a bottle opener.

So let's say, hypothetically, on this one night, a guy, a girl, and a slightly warm stubby of Oly are parked in a place with a view. All of the stuff that nags at us today, talk shows, endless violence, racial and ethnic strife, illegal immigration, gun control, gender wars ... none of that matters. The full moon that floats overhead is unsullied. The steering column support works as an opener and somehow not a drop spills. Our hypothetical couple each take a sip and look at each other. The guy carefully scratches the Oly label with his thumbnail, and when he gets to the bottom the label swings open like a door. On the backside of an Oly label there are two, three, or occasionally, four dots, and as everyone knows, the number of dots signify ... well, let's just say that it has to do with getting lucky. He tips the stubby slightly, turning the backside of the label to the moonlight. He counts, unbelieving, the light is poor, but yes, five! Five dots! He's never seen that many. He takes a quick sip and shows her. Their heads touch as they stare at the label. He smells Evening in Paris, mint, blondness, slightly warm beer, and knows that nothing else in the whole world matters at this moment.

YARD ART

Many of the old cars that we enjoy today exist because they sat in someone's yard or pasture for decades. Until fairly recently it was okay to store a car, whether a Ford or a Cord, in the backyard or beside the garage for an indeterminate time. It was usually a spouse who got it moved eventually. Now an old car gets moved due to the combined forces of big business and local government, and they're cracking down on everyone.

The answer is to call an old car by another name, or have valid reason for parking a hulk. Years ago, when I lived in Michigan, I remember that the city of Flint bought a police helicopter; the city was nearly broke, but the city fathers justified this expensive purchase because with it they could locate old cars *that could not be seen from the road!* I lived about 40 miles away, and had ten cars in open storage; I had put them behind a huge woodpile, and they could be seen only from overhead. I found out later that the local police talked with all my neighbors, trying to find someone who would complain. Finally, someone did, and one day the cops came by to check out the cars, which were a thousand feet from the main road and well away from any houses. My then-wife said that I wrote about the cars and made movies of them, both true, and the officers left, apparently satisfied.

A friend, "Junkyard" Jim Creighton, had a better idea: he turned some old parts into "yard art." He has a 1934 Plymouth coupe body which he wanted to get off the ground to help preserve it and to be able to move it around his yard. He built a frame using wooden 2 × 4s, put Chevrolet pickup axles under the timbers and placed the body on that assemblage. Then he added what appears to be a Hudson hood and possibly a Terraplane grille. The unpainted hulk looks presentable, and it's a convenient place in which to store additional parts. While there may be a neighbor who would not enjoy looking at this piece of "sculpture" I think most people would prefer it to a pile of parts. Another "sculpture" is a more complete car. It uses a 1928 Model A sport coupe body that Jim bought from a farmer for $175, and other parts that he either found in fields, got from friends or picked up at swap meets for little money. Later he was given a '30-'31 coupe roof which he grafted on. Jim moves the car around, sometimes putting it in the backyard, sometimes parking it in the driveway. He and his wife made a life-size male stuffed figure and put it behind the wheel. As Jim says, "It takes a real dummy to drive this car!" They're now working on a female figure to put in the passenger seat.

Down the road Jim's friend, Tim Klausing, has a good-size yard with a bunch of old cars sitting around. Like Jim, he holds open the option of using parts from the cars for other projects, but until then he considers them "yard art" and enjoys looking at them. Beside a large pond that Tim dug by hand sits what he calls his "rhododendron roadster." It uses a very rusty '27 T cowl and quarter panels, '29-'29 A roadster doors and front fenders and it has a pair of mature rhododendron bushes growing through the deck and engine, areas. No one could object to this novel planter, especially when the bushes are in bloom.

Nearby is what at first glance is a nearly complete Model T touring, circa 1925. It's actually built on a frame made of 2 × 4s, with the sheet metal held together by sheet metal screws and the wheels propped in place. Tim's *piece de resistance* sits in a landscaped corner of the yard, with a tall board fence around it and a pool ahead of it. The "sculpture" is a collection of Model A parts; the 1931 tudor body sits on the ground, with the headlights, radiator shell and '29 front fenders propped into place and secured by metal screws. The left front wheel is *in* the pond, and a continuous supply of fresh water flows over the top of the radiator shell and into the pond.

So if you're being pressed to get rid of that pile of parts beside the garage or that car in the backyard, consider making the old metal into something that others might consider attractive, or at least useful.

SMALL WONDERS

From the late 1970s until a few years ago I have had approximately 250 car features published in magazines. I wrote only about rods and customs that mattered to me, and since I have a good knowledge of pre–1960 cars, I was able to discuss the car, its notable features, modifications, and so on. I usually wrote lengthy articles about the car, the builders and the owner(s), and I was able to give the reader information that he wanted to know.

But sometimes, when looking at a neat car, I'd think about the shortcomings of the written word. If a car had twenty coats of paint, that doesn't describe the work that went into that paint job. I've had cars painted, and I've painted several, so I know the work involved, and yet the process had to be summed up in just a few words. That's the big picture, but what about some detail that I might have glossed over or missed and yet it had importance to the owner. The other day, as the weather turned cold, I thought about a heater I'd had in a 1947 Ford over

50 years ago. In those days a good many cars lacked a heater, and I'd owned a bunch of them. I drove around wearing a sweater and a jacket, savoring any heat that might drift back from the engine. If you saw a car in the classifieds that read R&H (radio and heater), or even heater, you knew it was a selling point.

In October, 1953 I bought a 1947 Ford coupe; although it was about seven years old, and two styling generations in the past, to me it was a new car. My previous car had been a 1937 Ford coupe, with pre-war engineering, such as "cable-draulic" brakes. I wore that car out as summer was ending, and for the next two months my daily driver was a fenderless A-V8 roadster. Yes, it was fun to drive, but as fall turned toward winter, the rains came. Often I had to wipe away a puddle of water on the seat, and when I was moving that left front tire threw a stream of water right where the side-curtain should have been. This went on, day after day, and I kept washing off the mud thrown on both sides of the roadster. Then the mornings grew decidedly colder. It was one thing to be wet, but to be cold and wet ... well, I knew I had to do something.

In October I got a job at Frank Costanzo Automotive, a garage/speed shop. I earned only a buck an hour, but at least I had a steady income. Then I found that '47 Ford coupe and borrowed some money from my dear mother. It took a year to pay her back, and then I began to customize it.

So for the first year I had to be content with washing and waxing the coupe, trying to breathe life into the oxidized paint. I enjoyed the car: it was my first decent car, one that I could use on a date, and feel proud as I pulled into the drive-in.

Most of all, it was warm! The heater was an aftermarket item; it bolted to the inside of the firewall, below the dash and over the hump. It had three doors that could be opened or closed to control the heat: the left door affected the driver, the right door the passenger, and the lower door deflected heat downward. The control knob hooked onto the lip of the dash, and it had calibrations printed in red on the brown plastic. That knob, in addition to adjusting the amount of heat produced, turned the heater on and off. At night it seemed almost magical, because it had a small light bulb inside which glowed when the heater was on. When I think of that knob it seems not brown, as it was during the day, but orange, because of the bulb. Sometimes, driving at night, perhaps on a date, the air chilly, it seemed as if the bulb gave off the heat we were enjoying. The knob was a barometer, a note of comfort, indicating that no matter how cold and rainy the weather might be, there would be heat.

At some point I bought a green cardboard tree-shaped air freshener and hung it from the cowl vent handle under the dash, so it dangled in front of the heater. No chrome accessory was so rewarding as that two-bit air freshener. It gave off an appealing odor, a clean odor; as if the coupe were spotless, and when I turned on the heater, the smell of warm fir filled the car. That mingled with the odor of rubbing compound and wax on the dashboard, and girl smells, shampoo or cologne or perfume and the clean smell of a cashmere sweater and tweed skirt, and the indefinable odor of body heat.

GIRLS AND RODS

In the Fifties, hot rodding was largely a male activity, and unmarried males at that. It's safe to say that most rodders were between 16 and 21 years old, and when a guy got married the roadster was traded for a sedan.

I went to Franklin, a large high school in Portland, Oregon, and recently I was trying to remember the types of cars parked around the school in the early Fifties. There were the teachers' cars, of course, and, a distinct minority, the students' cars. As I viewed in my mind the side streets around the school, I realized that over half the student body would have been under age 16, which meant that they could not have driven a car to school. Of the remainder, aged 16 to 18, roughly half were girls.

In the late Fifties I was going to college full time and working nearly full time in a gas station. One of the guys I worked with was Mike — his last name escapes me — and I think he was a couple years younger, perhaps 18 or 19. He was a tall, good-looking kid, with lots of black wavy hair, and he had a nice customized 1946 Ford tudor.

My sister, Bonnie, had graduated from high school and needed a car. When I looked around for a car for her, my eyes fell on Mike's 1946 Ford tudor, parked at the far pump island.

It was a cool car; although it was his daily transportation, it could have gone into a car show, then or now. The tudor body had been nosed and decked, the headlights were frenched, the taillights were frenched 1949 Ford units that sat low in the fenders, and the grille was from a 1948 Oldsmobile. The entire interior had been done in rolled and pleated blue and white Naugahyde; the headliner was white with blue piping. The original plastic sections of the dash had been replaced with aftermarket chrome pieces, and the garnish moldings were either plated or painted blue, as was the dash. The bumpers were '49 Plymouth, and I think it had electric doors (or at least the handles were removed). The flathead V-8 had aluminum heads, a dual intake manifold, and lots of chrome; it may have had other things, such as a cam and headers, but I'm not sure now. In general, this was a really nice example of a typical mid–Fifties semi-custom, with duals and short chrome lakes pipes, whitewalls and full hubcaps, and it had some unusual touches, such as the four rows of louvers in the hood. The paint was dark blue-enamel, I think — and the paint and interior had been recently done.

Because I was a hot rodder, and because I would've loved to own that car, I thought it would be fine for my sister. Bonnie must've thought so too, because she bought it — her first car! I can't remember how the deal was financed, but I think she paid $400 total, which was about what a nice running semi-custom went for then. Bonnie bought it in the fall of 1958, and drove it every day to her job across town. I think the car had a dropped axle, but it wasn't extremely low and got around town fine. The dual pipes were mellow, and not loud enough for her to get in trouble with the law. She was an excellent driver, and the stick shift was not a problem. She loved being seen in this cool custom and, of course, boys were extremely interested in talking about the car! She and her girlfriends loved to cruise the drive-in restaurants, where everyone looked at them. She kept the car in pristine condition, always washing and waxing it, and although she lacked a garage, the car was never dirty.

The history of most custom cars is that they went downhill, usually at a rate faster than a stocker. Some guy ran into the fender of Bonnie's custom, and it was totally his fault. Then she began having trouble starting the car, primarily because the louvers on the hood allowed rain to drip on the spark plug wires. One night at The Speck Drive-In she smelled raw gasoline, and seconds later flames came up through the louvers after one of the Stromberg 97s had flooded. The fire was quickly extinguished, but some wiring was charred as was the top of the hood.

This was not a gender thing — the same thing happened to cars owned by guys — in fact, it happened to me in my roadster. What went wrong had nothing to do with her abilities, or that she was a girl. The blame should fall on me — if I had lived in the same town, or if I had driven to Portland and worked on the car, it might have proved trouble-free, or at least have been a good driver for years. An easy solution would have been to replace the hood with a stock hood, and to replace that dual manifold with a stock intake manifold; then the car would have been a neat semi-custom that would have been as dependable as the hundreds of other fat-fendered cars of the Forties that filled the streets of Portland in those days.

Bonnie had the car repaired, and the Stromberg carbs were replaced with Chandler-Grove

These girls might have owned this 1935 Ford but more likely it belonged to a boyfriend.

carbs. She continued to drive the car for some time — months, perhaps a year or more — and then something else happened. No one seems to remember what it was, something minor, but for some reason her husband-to-be took an axe to that beautiful Ford and whittled it into pieces. No one seems to remember what happened to the pieces, which, if one had them today, would make a spectacular swap meet booth. But there were no swap meets then, and the pieces apparently went to the dump, Another example of pieces of the past utterly lost!

HANEY'S HOT ROD

During the late Forties and early Fifties, home-built sporty cars began to appear with some frequency. Neither hot rod nor custom, the sporty car really wanted to be a sports car using American parts. The sporty car appealed to the backyard builder because it attracted attention, was fun to drive, had the dependability of a stock car and often cost next to nothing. Also, during those years, new cars were hard to get, since post-war production had not filled the gap caused by the lack of production during World War II.

Those may have been the reasons that Harold Haney built this neat roadster pickup. Or it may have been, as his son, Doug Haney, said, that "he just wanted to get the hell out of the house. My father rented a small garage three blocks from home. It seemed like he was always

Circa 1950: Sitting in unfinished car are Doug Haney, age two, and his sister, Carol. The front half of the car uses a Studebaker hood, headlights and sheet metal.

down at the garage, working on what he called his 'hot rod.' I think it was a way to relax, to get away from things."

The project was started in Farmington, Michigan, during the mid–1940s. Harold Haney had the chassis of a 1937 Ford that he'd totaled when the car was nearly new. He had junked the body and parked the chassis for several years. Between 1938 and 1945 he developed the idea of building a car around that chassis, and after the war he was ready to begin. The only changes to the chassis were the addition of hydraulic brakes and tubular shocks; the flathead V-8 engine was left stock.

Whatever designs Harold had for a body were apparently done in his head; no drawings of the car have been found. It appears that he started with the hood and headlights of a 1938 Studebaker, and possibly the cowl; the hood and cowl have been narrowed, but the windshield has not been chopped. The front end was enclosed with hand-formed sheet metal, to make a sleek nose; later, because the flathead V-8 heated up, he cut openings and filled them with expanded metal to make a grille.

At some point, perhaps because it was more functional, or because it was easier to construct, Harold decided to build the car as a pickup. The doors, quarter panels and pickup box were made of oak and covered with sheet stock. The fenders came from Montgomery Ward, and were intended for use on a trailer.

Unlike many homebuilts, this car was nicely finished. It eventually had a spare tire, radio and heater, windshield wipers, horn and even backup lights. Harold built a top, using conduit for the bows; he formed them on his bender, then brazed them together. It's notable that Harold did all the work on the car except for the top, tonneau and interior, which were sewn by his wife, Martha, at home on an old Singer. He worked at Fisher Body Plant 40, where he was able to buy salvage materials, such as the convertible top fabric used for the top and tonneau.

The metalwork on this car appears super straight, and is a tribute to Harold Haney's craftsmanship. He obviously cared about how the car was built. Evidence of this is the use of electric solenoids to open the doors; this was a rare feature on custom cars at the time.

The car was assembled and running by 1950. When Harold got a job at Fisher Body the family moved from Detroit to Lansing in 1955, and the car was towed. Shortly after, it was painted gunmetal gray enamel. With the black top and tonneau, black vinyl interior and chrome wheels, it was a sweet looking and unusual vehicle.

Doug Haney remembers that it had a lot of power and "handled super." Although it was street legal, road worthy and titled, it was never licensed (the plate shown in the photographs was from another car). Harold never drove it, except for a spin around the block. He must have loved the car that he had spent over ten years building, but for some reason he didn't want to drive it. Perhaps, as Doug suggested, Harold built the car as a diversion, a way to get away from things, to be alone, to relax, and if so it was probably good therapy.

Harold didn't want to drive the car, but his sons did. They had played in the car for years and had dreamed of driving it down unseen roads. When Doug's older brother, Norris, turned 15 he almost expected to be given the car, and saw himself driving it to school. Doug, age 10 in 1958, had similar hopes. But Harold didn't want his sons driving the car either, and so the car that had become a fixture in the family was sold for $500. That was a lot of money in 1958, but not enough to cover the loss that Norris and Doug — and perhaps Harold — felt. Harold did not build another car between 1958 and 1983, when he passed away.

Over the years Doug has often thought about the car. He's built several pro-street machines, and is now building a chopped '49 Merc with a full race engine, and while scouting for parts he's kept an eye open for the once-familiar roadster pickup that his father lovingly assembled. All he knows is that it was sold to a man in Jackson, Michigan, and he last saw it thirty years ago heading toward Grand Rapids.

He's grateful for the dozen photographs taken when he was a tyke that document the building of the car. He notes that several of the photographs were taken in Ferris Park in Lansing, a huge park in the Fifties that is now a state parking lot, and that other photographs were taken by the Nazarene Church at Butler and Genessee, an area that has also changed greatly. Whole neighborhoods are gone, and yet he likes to think that possibly, in a garage, under a tarp in a backyard, or behind a woodpile, the car his father built might exist. He'd love to see it, or, if possible, get it back in the family

OUR '40

Joe and Vera Hicks may not hold the record for one-owner street rods, but they're in the running. They bought a 1940 Ford coupe in February 1941, and they still have it! Think about that — that means they've owned, driven, worked on and loved the same car for forty-seven years! During the time they've owned this car the country has gone through a world war, a couple major wars, innumerable holding actions, economic highs and recessions, the birth of TV, the advent of the Beatles, hippies, Woodstock, mind altering substances, *Mad*, pet rocks, you name it! When they bought this car, their sleepy town of Noblesville, Indiana, was getting used to the magic of radio, and World War II was still almost a year and a million miles away.

In February 1941, when they bought it, it was a standard coupe with 4,000 miles and painted Arabian Green. When Joe entered the service, Vera continued to drive the coupe; upon his discharge, she had the coupe painted black to surprise him, They continued to drive it every day

Vera and Joe Hicks beside the '40 Ford coupe they've owned almost since it was new.

until 1950, when they bought a new '50 Ford, and then it became their second car. It was good, dependable transportation, even during the harshest winters. Vera drove her relatives' children and neighbors' children to school in it, so Joe put a small bus seat in the back. Vera got through the snow drifts in the '40 when the school bus couldn't make it! And, of course, in those days the state didn't use road salt so the coupe's body held up well.

Joe made other, minor changes to the coupe over the years—the little turn signals under the headlights, for example, were added in 1947, and those skirts, which he re-worked from a pair of early Forties Buick skirts—but it wasn't until 1952, over eleven years after he bought the car, that he really got serious about making it into a hot rod. The average hot rodder in those days was 18 years old. Joe was 33, too old, some would say, to be playing with hot rods. But he read an article in *Hot Rod* about chopping and channeling your car at home, and it motivated him to try his hand at reworking the '40 coupe. He had experience with the torch and hand tools. He had worked in his father's blacksmith shop in the late Twenties and again in the late Thirties, when the country was in a Depression; between times he had worked for Delco Remy as an assembler, so he also had knowledge of automotive electrical systems.

In 1952 hot rods were still pretty new to Indiana; lacking observable models, Joe followed the ideas put forth in *Hot Rod*. He got out the torch, cut away the floor and dropped the body over the frame; when the body was secured, he raised the fenders three inches. Then he got a deluxe hood and grille, and sectioned the hood three inches without warping the metal. He frenched the headlights, blacked out the hood center chrome, side chrome and trunk trim, and shortened the drip molding to a point just behind the door. The running boards were trashed when the car was channeled, so Joe made the stone guards for the rear fenders. To update the car, Joe added 1951 Ford bumpers front and rear. He installed a heater from a 1951 Ford, and cut holes in the front fenders to create a fresh air intake; to finish off the holes he made a screen and held it in place with bezels from a Dodge parking light.

When finished, the car created a flurry of excitement in the mid–Indiana area. It was still daily transportation for the Hickses, but it was a damn exciting car too! To give the coupe more beans, Joe built a new engine. He bought a brand new Mercury flathead V-8 from the dealer, and added Edelbrock heads and dual intake manifold.

The Hickses' '40 is good evidence that if a rodder keeps a car he or she is never finished tinkering with it. Joe had flirted with the idea of chopping the top, then decided against it. He decided that he wanted to be able to see out from the coupe more easily. The solution struck him one day: use a back window from a 1950 Ford for the windshield and the back window. And that's what he did. Rather than cut the glass, he cut the coupe, cutting into the roof at the front and cutting into the cowl, beyond the vent, at the bottom. The result is a distinctive, one-of-a-kind coupe!

Joe and Vera continued to drive it that way for the next twenty-three years, doing little to the car except to paint it twice. Then in 1975, Joe got itchy. He bought a 1966 Cadillac and transposed much of that car to the '40 coupe. Joe had built six flathead V-8 engines for the coupe, but he deep-sixed the flathead in favor of the Cadillac V-8. This wasn't an easy task, and required Joe's smithy skills. The sump on the pan of the Ford is in the back, but on the Cadillac it's up front. To miss the crossmember and steering, Joe cut the pan off and reversed it, using a long pickup tube on the oil pump. He had to rework the pan on the starter side, so he added a piece on the other side to retain the original oil capacity.

He also used the 400 transmission, the tilt-telescopic column and wheel, the power steering, power brakes and wiring harness. He also used the Cadillac speedometer, adapting it to the original standard panel. Recalling the years when he worked for Delco Remy, Joe rebuilt the starter, alternator, distributor and electrical systems. A late model Ford radiator with built-in transmission cooler is used. A 1971 Torino differential has been narrowed 2½ inches; the wheels in back are 15-inch Dodge Diplomat police car items, and up front are 14-inch Chrysler wheels.

In addition to being a fun car that always attracts notice and comments, the '40 has been part of the Hickses' social life and family traditions. Their nieces and nephews have learned to drive in the '40. One niece who learned to drive in this car now has a 14-year-old daughter who is also learning in the '40. Joe and Vera drive the car each year in the parade in Noblesville, and they hit many street rod runs. Joe's 70 now and Vera is close behind, but they are young in spirit and perhaps that's due to the long-time love affair they've had with the coupe as well as with each other. In 1984, at the James Dean Run, they won top prize in the dance contest; they still compete, and are among the most energetic on the floor.

They hope to continue dancing and rodding for years, and I think they will.

The Fabulous Fifties: Chopped and Channeled

In the Garage

In the garage, and to a degree outside of it, I was always looking for a role model. I'm not sure people used that term then. I certainly didn't. The search was not done consciously, but I was aware that there were people that I admired for whatever reason and, in the same way when I left a movie, I found myself imitating what I'd seen. Even though in eighteen years my personality, for better or for worse, was mostly formed, I felt I could, chameleon-like, absorb someone else's manner of speech or appearance or gesture or whatever it was that I wanted to emulate.

In the garage, Jim, the boss, irritated me and perhaps some flaw of my character irritated him. Why else would he stand behind me in the lunchroom, hands in the pockets of his shop coat, rocking on his heels, asking me questions as I tried to eat my lunch? What's the capital of Bolivia? Who laid the Atlantic cable? How high is Mt. Everest? This quizzing was intended to make me look stupid, and also pointed out Jim's belief that the only reason for reading was to gather information. In his opinion no one read simply for entertainment.

On the other hand there was Wayne, a tune-up man with dark wavy hair, a mustache and a honey-sweet southern voice. A ladies' man, I thought, although I knew nothing about his personal life. Since his workspace was next to the big front door he often greeted customers and he was good at it. I could have learned from him. Buck, the other tune-up man, was serious about his work and his one expression revealed nothing to me.

I had just graduated high school and this was my first full-time job. In the garage I found myself in a community of men, each quite different. I think the person I most wanted to emulate was Phil, a mechanic, but he was such an extreme character that any attempt I might have made would have been considered parody. He was a true eccentric. A curmudgeon at age thirty. He always wore a leather cap with earflaps and smoked a corncob pipe that gave him a resemblance to General MacArthur. His car was a 1938 LaSalle tudor, a rare model I'm told, and it was always immaculate. On the back seat was a huge Webster's dictionary and the complete poems and plays of Shakespeare in one volume. As proof that he had read the plays Miller liked to quote from them, such as: "Arroint thou rump-fed runyon." I doubt that anyone in the garage knew whether the quotes were accurate but we knew that they drove the boss crazy. Jim said it was bad for the customers to hear such things.

Then there was Wes, also a mechanic, who, when he wasn't rebuilding an engine, was putting dual pipes on cars. That year Cadillac began putting dual pipes on cars at the factory and therefore it seemed that everyone wanted dual pipes on whatever they were driving. Wes and I were somewhat alike and I identified with him in various ways. He was from my area of Portland and we attended the same high school, but he'd been there seven years earlier. Like me he was short and scruffy. He was a scrappy guy and reminded me of Leo Gorcy except Wes had narrower eyes, was usually smiling and moved and spoke quickly. There was a toughness about him even though he was about my size and seemed slight within his coveralls. I admired his mechanical ability and his willingness to confront a problem. He drove a 1941 Ford tudor and it was a mess. Never washed, mud and dirt everywhere and diapers on the backseat and floor.

Although his car was unlike mine, which I labored to keep clean, it held my interest. Outwardly stock except for the stubs of dual pipes the car had, according to Wes, some speed secrets. It was a Ford block bored to 3⅜" with Mercury heads and cam. The real secret was the "big, heavy flywheel, a 1936 I think. It is heavier than hell! Once that sonofabitch gets to turning, she really turns!" From experience I knew a 1936 Ford flywheel was limited to a 9" clutch; I had no idea how much it weighed but I was a kid so I kept quiet. Besides, I had a fondness for a flathead V-8 that appeared stock but ran strong and had been built on a limited budget. Milled heads, dual pipes, dual breaker springs, maybe a Stromberg EE carb and, in my case, a chopped flywheel. I could identify with Wes.

Next there was Scoffie, a long time customer who came in often. He got his nickname from the Miller-Schofield head he'd had on his Model A in high school. He was now around 40, tanned and good looking with bulging arm and chest muscles. I know now that during his life he owned a string of beautiful cars and they were always immaculate. Unlike Wes, who had a wife and lots of kids, Scoffie never married. At that time he owned a 1947 Cadillac convertible, a car I loved. Scoffie's was gorgeous: black with a white top, whitewalls and a red and white, rolled and pleated Naugahyde interior. The Cad flathead V-8 under the hood was painted red with lots of chrome and an Edmunds dual manifold. That was my dream car and I would still love to own one today, 50 years later.

The Cadillac was in the garage for engine work and, as usual, Scoffie was helping out. I wanted to talk with him but he never said much. Not to me anyway. I watched as he finished unbolting the right side head and attempted to remove it. His biceps bulged, chest muscles strained under his black shirt and his face turned red. He tried again and again, the vein at his temple growing larger. That Cadillac head probably weighed 60 pounds and had to be lifted straight up. I realized that while Scoffie had huge muscles, they got in the way on this job. It came to me like the answer to Jim's possible question: What is muscle bound?

Just then, Wes rolled out from under the car on a creeper, wiping his hands on his floppy coveralls. Maybe Scoffie said something or maybe Wes just sized up the situation but he adjusted the fender cover, leaned into the engine compartment and came up with that big head, gleaming red like a rare fish. For a long moment he held it in the air, his arms steady, while Scoffie wiped his hands on a shop rag and looked at it. Wes put the head on his workbench and walked into the lunchroom for a coffee break and to tell, for the first time, a story he would tell often in the coming years.

LUKE THE DRIFTER: HOT RODDERS' TROUBADOUR

I want to be the first to nominate Luke the Drifter as the musician whose songs best capture the spirit and mood of hot rodding in the Fifties, especially the early years of that decade.

I know that's heresy. Years ago someone decided that rock 'n' roll was the music of rodding. Perhaps that decision was based on the hard beat and heavy repetition of music that resembled dual pipes. Perhaps it was based on a single event such as Jerry Lee Lewis banging away on a piano mounted on a flatbed truck in the opening scene of *High School Confidential*. Maybe it's the fact that Elvis drove a genuine hot rod in his second film, *Love Me Tender*. Maybe it all had to do with a PR man's pitch, based on the accelerated growth of both hot rodding and rock 'n roll by 1956 or '57. It is a happy music, even with songs about lost love and car accidents, and it's the music of young people — happy young people. If you include poodle skirts, a Green River, bongo drums and people saying "cool," you have the popular picture of the Fifties.

It's certainly the picture that's accepted now, a half century later. Since few people around

The telephone pole shadow divides this Manichean world: beauty and ugliness, good and bad, life and death, yin and yang.

now were actually teenagers during the Fifties, most accept this version. For them it's based on a later source, a 1970s version of the 1950s, something like *Happy Days*. Because many of today's rodders were young when that show was on TV, it has replaced the actual 1950s that they never knew. Both versions are sanctified, with neat crew cuts and pageboy hairdos, white Dickies and crisp Dan River shirts, flipper hubcaps and angel hair.

The Fifties were a good time, but the early years of that decade had a harder edge. The Korean War began in 1950 and pulled many men who had served in World War II out of the lives and careers they were just getting started. It threatened a generation of young men of draft age, especially those between 18 and 23. Some 55,000 young American men were killed in the Korean War. For others there was the confusion of what to do with one's life at a time when everything seemed uncertain. I joined a hot rod club in July of 1951 after it had formed again. Earlier 20 of its 25 members had been drafted and the club disbanded. A truce was called in Korea shortly before I finished high school, so I missed that war by months. But it was heavily on my mind.

The rods and customs of the early 1950s reflected the tenor of the times. If they were painted they were black, dark blue, purple or dark maroon. They lacked striping, flames and even louvers. Unadorned, they seemed sinister, especially at night. The drivers were young men back from Korea or about to go, working stiffs, pump jockeys, often without promise and with uncertain futures. They were considered outlaws by the press and solid citizens, or were at least living on the edge of society, outsiders whose pipes cut through the night in impromptu and illegal drag races on city streets. What did they listen to if the car had a radio? In 1951 Sinatra was in a serious decline and was replaced by Johnny Ray. There were Perry Como, Connie Francis, Kay

Star, Teresa Brewer and many others; crooners and canaries. Then suddenly there was Hank Williams. He'd been performing in the south for years, to a limited audience, but found instant fame when he sang "Lovesick Blues" at the Grand Ol' Opry. He recorded it and it stayed on the charts for 42 weeks! His popularity continued even after his death a couple of years later on New Year's Day, 1953. "I'll Never Get Out of This World Alive" went to number one on the charts after his death. Car guys would listen to Hank not only because of the line in one of his songs referring to a hot rod Ford, but because he was soon heard everywhere.

Earlier he was forced to record songs under the name Luke the Drifter because his producers thought most of his songs were too dark, too despairing. Those songs include "Pictures From Life's Other side," "My Son Calls Another Man Daddy," "Be Careful of Stones That You Throw," "Men with Broken Hearts," "Just Waitin," "May You Never Be Alone (Like Me)" and "The Angel of Death." Except for some sentimentality they are beautiful songs. They're about loneliness, isolation, lost love, cheating women and death, things that a young hot rodder might have been thinking about.

A favorite of mine in those years was "Lost Highway," written by Leon Payne and made famous by Luke the Drifter. The narrator of the song is in prison for a crime involving a card game, wine and a woman. For many young men that explained how easy it was to enter a life of crime.

I got the lesson. In 1951 I got my A-V8 roadster on the road and I was a model citizen — more or less. A year I later I'd channeled it, put in a dropped axle, a Smith and Jones 272 cam, replaced the '40 Ford dash with a tiny piece of aluminum that held only an ammeter and three switches. When I got it running it looked awful. The paint was burned off the lower edges of the body from when I cut away the floor, no floorboards, dash gone, lower half of the firewall missing — but it ran like crazy. That car never ran so well, and I raced everybody. What did I have to lose? Years later I realized that during that desperate year I was I mourning and protesting the death of my father — the stuff of a Luke the Drifter song. But at the time I was simply a kid in dirty Levi's, an overgrown crew cut, looking as scruffy as my roadster, a marginal person in high school society, an outsider, an outlaw.

OREGON ORIGINAL

I was able to attend the first hot rod show held in Portland, Oregon. Not many can say that; I've asked extensively, and found only a few people who saw that show. Many who might have been there were off fighting in Korea; many who were there are now dead. It was held long ago, on a weekend in mid–March, 1951. I was 15 and nuts about cars, although I knew little about them. I went with my father, who knew everything about cars but almost nothing about modifying them. I had the impression that hardly anyone knew how to build a hot rod, which was a good reason for having the show.

One guy who was there and who certainly knew how to build a hot rod was Wayne Mahaffey. His 1935 Ford phaeton was one of the thirty cars on display, and it was stunning. It was long, low and sleek, the kind of car I drew on my Pee-Chee notebook. In my ignorance I could judge cars only in a visceral way: in the case of Mahaffey's phaeton it was the chopped (4" by Portland Top Shop) and padded white top, gorgeous black paint, and red and white rolled and pleated interior (by Gaylord of Los Angeles). In the same way I could appreciate the solid side panels, Packard skirts and filled spare tire cover that smoothed the car's lines. I could see that the dash had been chromed and the display sign said that it had '41 Buick instruments. I appreciated the whitewall tires and full hubcaps (now-rare Lyons): I no doubt recognized the '40 Ford

Wayne Mahaffey's brother, Don, beside the 1935 Ford phaeton in 1950 (Mahaffey photograph).

taillights set low in the fenders and the 1949 Plymouth rear bumper. The hood was closed, but the sign indicated that power came from a 1946 Cadillac V-8 (flathead) hooked to a Hydramatic transmission.

Mainly, all I could do was admire it, and dream about owning such a car. I've always loved '35–'36 Ford phaetons, and although they were rare there was always several around. After all, they were only 16 years old! I thought if I had a phaeton I'd also have friends, including a girlfriend, and the gang could pile in and we'd drive to the beach or the mountains and I'd be invited to join a social club, etc. The dream went on and on, well beyond the car.

What I did have was an A-V8 roadster, bought a month before that show; by summer we got it on the road. In July my father and I drove to Eugene, 120 miles to the south, to attend the first legal drag races. Somewhere south of Salem, as I fought the wheel on bumpy Highway 99, a two-lane road, I saw a black car in the mirror coming up fast. It was Mahaffey's phaeton, and I can see that image today: the car pulling along side to pass, Mahaffey calmly steering with one hand, his right arm draped on top of the seat; then he stepped on the gas and shot smoothly past me and out of sight. When we arrived at the drag strip Mahaffey had removed the skirts and hubcaps and was ready to compete. This is a heavy car, but fast, and in the early 1950s Wayne drag raced wherever there was a race — Eugene, Aurora, Scappoose, Newport.

I saw the car again that same month when it was in *Hot Rod Magazine* (July, 1951), the first car from Oregon to be featured in the magazine. The photographs were taken by Tom Medley, who grew up in Salem but was then working for Petersen. In the one paragraph of text I learned that Mahaffey paid $425 for the phaeton, which was in a "sad state," but it was now "valued at more than six times the purchase price." I also learned that Mahaffey won the top trophy in the sedan class at the drags in 1950.

Mahaffey sold the phaeton in 1954; then came a long line of hot rods, including a 1923 Ford roadster that set an NHRA record in 1960 with a flathead V-8 that scared the competition. When

I ran into Mahaffey in 1985 I mentioned that I'd heard his old phaeton was in Denver, and the next thing I knew he'd bought it back; it looked good, and largely unchanged, except it had an Olds V-8. Then Mahaffey sold it to a close friend, and upon his passing, Mahaffey got the car back in 2001. A master bodyman and mechanic, Mahaffey went through the car he'd built 50 years before. He rebuilt the '40 Ford brakes and running gear, and he rebuilt a Cadillac V-8, which must have given him a sense of deja vu. The car also got new red and white rolled and pleated interior, new padded top, new black paint, new bright-work and a '49 Plymouth bumper for the front. It looks stunning!

Mahaffey got the car finished in time for the new event season, where it consistently took top honors. It won Best of Show in the Obsolete Fleet Show in Salem, Oregon. In the 2003 Eugene Autorama it cleaned up, winning Best Street Engine, First in Class and the major Award of Excellence. At the 2003 Goodguys Northwest Nationals the car won the Memory Lane award. Mahaffey had shown the car only twice during the 50s, but now enjoys getting it out in public whenever he can.

The First Ticket

Probably everyone remembers his first car, but how many remember that first ticket for a moving violation? It's an event that most people repress. Because I always try to do the right thing and because I have an acute sense of guilt, earned or unearned, I remember my first ticket vividly. I felt I was branded, scarred, my driving record sullied. Although others might find my personal experience as interesting as, say, looking at someone else's baby pictures, I think it's worth discussing in the context of the times.

In January 1952, my friend, Larry Deyoe, told me about a roadster parked at the rear of the yard next to his house, and since it wasn't being driven he thought it'd be for sale. I already had a '29 Model A roadster that I'd owned for nearly a year, and after driving it for a few months I'd taken it apart. I was a junior in high school, with little time and no money, and I did not need to own another car. But this roadster was only a few blocks away and because I was crazy about cars I had to take a look—just a look—at it.

The car was at the far end of the yard, covered with leaves, tires sunk in the mud. When we brushed away the leaves I was disappointed, because I had hoped that it was a '32 Ford roadster, or an A-V-8 with speed equipment, or an old race car. It was, in fact, a 1929 Model A roadster body mounted on a 1937 Willys chassis with a 1942 Jeep engine. It had bobbed Model A fenders, no running boards, a '32 Ford-style grille shell, a hood, a very old top, and it even had a little radio and heater. Although it was a combination of junkyard parts, the parts fit neatly and it was a cute car; it was fairly well-made, and obviously someone's idea of fun transportation. It was a good example of a rod built immediately after World War II, when cars were hard to get and a guy reworked an early model car, following his own vision rather than building a car like the next guy's car. I called it a hot rod, but a better description would be a street rod, a term none of us used back then. It was not built for speed, but for transportation.

The current owner of this roadster was fighting in Korea, his mother said, and, yes, he would sell it. One thing that interests me about this story is that it reminds me that old cars were allowed to rest in pieces, often for many years, without someone pouncing on them as an investment. No one cared. Another thing that interest me was how cheaply on could buy an old car. In this case, the guy wanted $25!

That also reminds me of how little money most of us had. Sure, I could dig up a nickel for an occasional Coke, or two bits for a magazine, or sometimes, $3 for a pair of Levi's, but every-

Al Drake, in 1952, beside the '29 Ford roadster he bought for $25. He stripped it to create a California hot rod. The fields in the background are now filled with houses.

thing beyond a fin was big money. I frequently hitchhiked home from school to save a nickel. I quit buying clothes my sophomore year, and any money I had I spent on my car. In the winter of 1952 I did not have a job, and my father was taking home only $50 a week from his service station. I have no idea where I got the $25 to buy the roadster — perhaps I sold something — but a week or so later my father hauled the car out of the mud with his 1942 Lincoln Zephyr and we got it home.

At school I drew pictures of that car in my Pee-Chee notebook, and dreamed. I imagined it fenderless, channeled, with a race car nose and a full-race Willys engine. I actually imagined that I could build this rod into an Oakland Roadster Show winner! But study hall dreams translated badly. If I'd had good sense I would've left the car intact, got it running and driven it. Instead, I stripped the roadster to make it look like a traditional hot rod. I removed the fenders, grille, hood, windshield, top, heater, radio, even the headlights. I got it running, and, once started, it ran well. I'd get a friend to tow it behind his mom's Plymouth and we'd tow it for miles, the engine catching, quitting and catching again. We had a gallon of paint thinner and I'd pour a shot in the carb and we'd tow it some more. Today when I think of that car I can recall the odor of exhaust tinged with paint thinner, and it's indelible in my senses.

Finally the engine would sputter, catch and run smoothly. Once it was running I didn't want to shut it off. I drove around for hours, cruising the back streets, and occasionally venturing out on a main street, where I could open it up. It didn't have terrific acceleration, but to be going 40 mph in a roadster without a windshield was cooking! The car handled well. That Willys frame was light, stiff and low. The car had elliptical springs front and rear, and tube shocks at all four wheels. It'd take city corners at speed, riding flat, and if the rear tires broke loose it felt like a controlled slide to me. Hey, I had nothing to lose — I didn't think about personal injury — and so I drove it hard and fast.

The traffic ticket Albert Drake got when he was 16.

Another thing that interests me about this story is the memory of how little traffic was on the road in those days. I lived at the edge of a big city, and except for the eight A.M. and five P.M. rush hours the streets were nearly empty. Husbands were at work, wives were at home and kids were in school. Except for me — I was whipping the little roadster around the neighborhood every chance I got. This went on for two or three months. One sunny afternoon I'd been driving around for a couple hours, and I kept telling myself to park the darn roadster in the driveway. Perhaps I feared the cops, although in those days you didn't see them often. Besides, I couldn't imagine that anyone would complain about a kid racing around the neighborhood in a stripped down roadster, taking city corners in a controlled slide!

Some places there were no houses, just empty fields that made the transition to country. The street I lived on was half houses, half open fields; it was paved with oiled gravel to a point just beyond my house, where it became a bumpy road filled with mud puddles so there was little through traffic. I went past my house and around the block. I bounced over the bumpy dirt road, floored the gas in second, and whipped around the corner. Three more corners and I was back home. Just once more around the block, I told myself, and I'll park it.

As I hit the bumpy part again a cop car came slowly around the corner, and my heart sank. I didn't need a siren or flashing light to tell me what to do; I stopped. The cop slowly got out, looked the car over and asked to see my license. I didn't have it with me! I'd had a license for only a few months and had not become used to carrying it with me. I told him I had to get it and ran for home! I'm surprised he let me leave.

When I came back a couple minutes later the cop was already writing. He pointed out that the car lacked essential equipment, such as lights, horn, windshield wipers and the damn windshield! It lacked the required four fenders. No license plates, and no insurance. I was probably shaking. I knew that the fine was $10 for each missing fender. This could add up. But I think cops were different back then. He wrote me a ticket for driving without current plates and told me that he never wanted to see the car on the street again.

The ticket required me to go to traffic court, where I saw a movie about reckless teenage drivers. Rather than follow my dream and make the roadster into a show car — or at least a legal machine — I took the headlights, windshield and Gemmer steering off for my other '29 and traded the Willys-powered roadster to a kid in Oswego for a complete, nearly running 1930 American Austin sedan. That ticket caused me to drive with great care — at least for a few months, until I got my A-V8 back on the road.

Traffic Court

In the Fifties, in Portland, Oregon, there wasn't much crime. My friend, Steve Sauer, a retired Multnomah County Sheriff, told me that a stolen car or a bar fight or a traffic accident was a big deal. In all his years of service, he fired his .38 Colt revolver only once, and it was aimed, not at a person, but the radiator/engine area of a 1948 Dodge!

So what did cops do? Well, they kept busy with parking and pedestrian violations. In 1956 I worked at Lee Cosart, a Dodge-Plymouth dealership, and sometimes I had to park the parts truck across the street when trucks filled the loading dock. It was a side street, perhaps 20 feet wide, with very little traffic. On one occasion as I parked and walked across the street a motorcycle policeman came from nowhere and gave me a ticket for jaywalking. I think a fine was involved, but if I were to attend a session of traffic court the fine could be avoided. I wasn't making much money, so I naturally opted to go to court.

One evening after work I went to the courthouse and sat in an uncomfortable chair with rows of other lawbreakers. The occasion is fuzzy in my mind, but I do remember that I saw a film about safe driving (and safe street crossing, I assume). I'd love to see that film again, just to refresh my memory. It was in black and white, featuring several people, one of whom drove a hot rod, and there was a wreck at the end. It humanized the kind of story one read in the newspaper, and showed that just driving to work was a lottery; you might be the person who doesn't make it home.

Those fragments of memory came back when a friend, Dave McCabe, a member of the Vespa club, mentioned a DVD set he'd checked out from the library. It's called *Hell's Highway: The True Story of Highway Safety Films*. The album blurb notes: "Highway Safety Films recovers a missing chapter of American film history as it examines the fascinating and shocking driver education films of yesteryear. Produced between 1959 and 1979 by a group of volunteers in Mansfield, Ohio, these films promoted safety by presenting color footage of careless driving's dark consequences: blood-stained wreckage, injured bodies, fresh corpses. In the 1970s and 1980s, these films disappeared from the American classroom and assumed an almost mythical status among those who had once seen them."

These films are frank. A blue '55 Chevrolet is wrapped around a telephone pole, and they haul the bloody body away in an ambulance (which was usually a hearse supplied by the local funeral home). The camera pans over twisted metal and the bloodstained interior. There's a good deal of real blood in these films, and the victims are shown in the sad state that's the result of a horrific wreck.

A narrator emphasizes that these films, made between 1959 and 1974, are a new kind of safety film, using color motion picture footage of actual highway accidents. An historian discusses the history of training films as a means to explain nature, illnesses, woodworking, the dangers of VD or a hundred other subjects. He notes that the safe driving films made earlier emphasize a moral lesson, usually through a narrative. He says that the older films "subvert the intention of the film" by making them interesting.

An example of that kind of film is *And Then There Were Four,* he says. There's about a

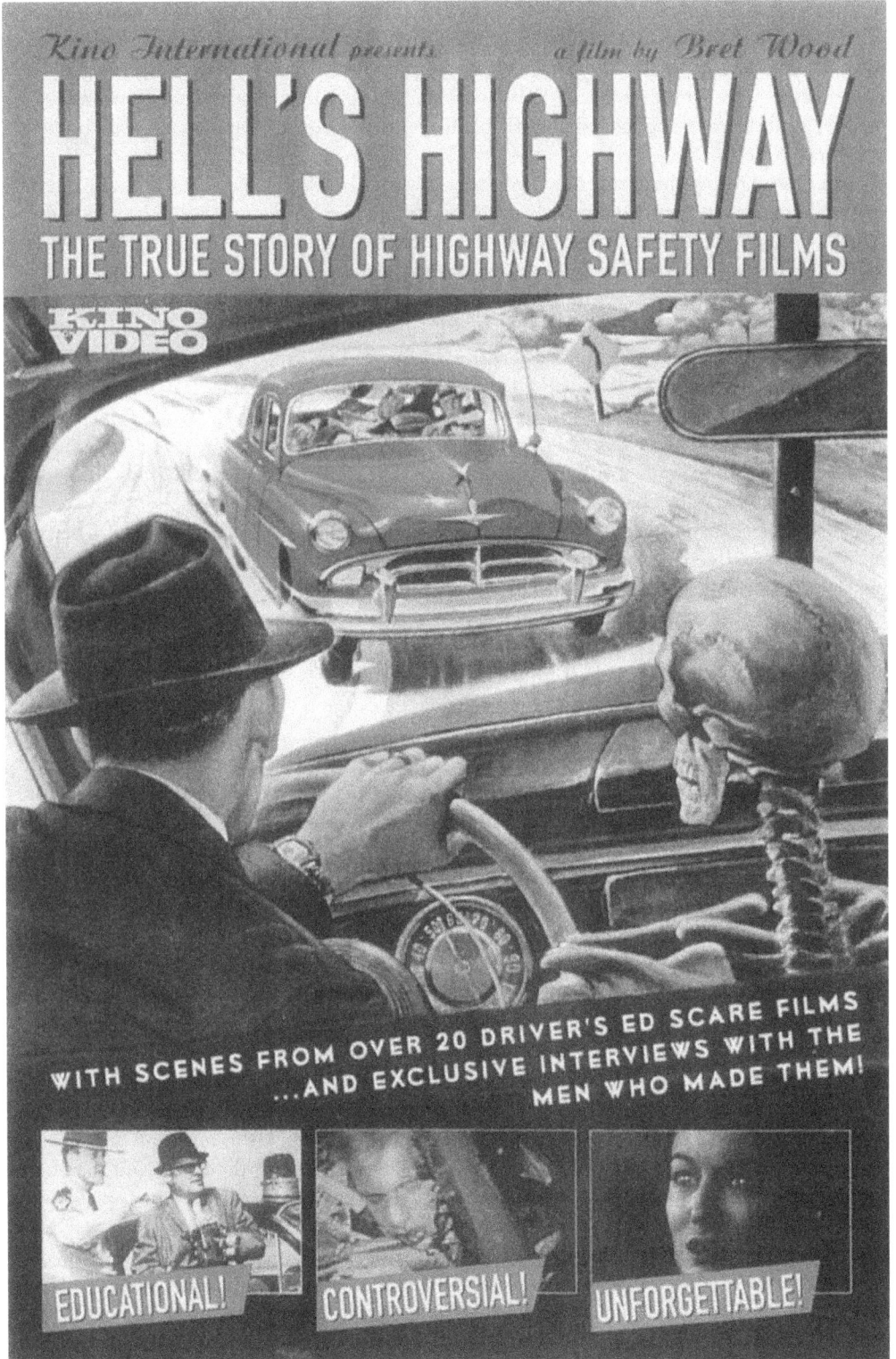

Graphic movie shown as a cautionary tale.

minute of that film shown, but I needed only one image, that one of the old Italian fruit vendor, to realize that it was the same film I'd seen in 1956! It's in black and white, and there is a kid in a fenderless, imperfect '29 A-V8 roadster, ripping away from a stoplight. The images linked me with the night I first saw them, fifty years ago! I'd forgotten that the narrator was Jimmy Stewart, and that one cop looked remarkably like Chuck Connors, who later starred in the TV series *The Rifleman*.

But those things that made the film interesting are also what make it less effective, according to the historian. In the later highway safety films there's no story, no fancy dialogue, no staged wrecks. As an overlay notes, "Most of the actors in these films are bad actors and received top billing only on a tombstone." Nothing is staged; the blood and the bodies are real. A truck falls off of an elevated bridge, killing two. A car is pulled from a river, upside down, all killed. A driver goes off the road in his '56 Pontiac; his upper body falls from the car and when the door hits a stump, closing it, the door crushes his head. The narrator notes the irony: "Damage to the car was slight — it'll cost about $75 to make repairs." A foreign car driver drove under a truck trailer, neatly removing the car's roof and the driver's head; the truck driver became aware of the car after he'd dragged it for seven miles! An especially horrible example is the accident where the police note a baby bottle in the car but no baby; a dozen men lift the car and discover the dying baby beneath it.

These are realistic and powerful films; the camera reveals all and does not flinch. They aim, in large part, at teenage drivers whose driving record was lousy; the recklessness of many teenagers behind the wheel is a form of suicide, and they coined a new word to describe it: "Teenicide." Most of the cars in the films are 1955–1965 models, with 200-plus horsepower; sometimes alcohol and icy roads were part of the fatal scenario. One thing is clear: seatbelts save lives. Most of the cars in these films lacked them, and the victims went through the windshield, were ejected, or were tossed around inside the car, and were often half in and half out, with fatal results.

Today there's seemingly a freewheeling attitude in the media regarding sexuality, nudity and violence. But, in fact, the camera cuts before things get messy. When I was young, insurance offices and other businesses displayed blown-up photographs in their window showing car wrecks and disasters. For example, a large black and white photograph of a Buick convertible against a tree, the driver's door torn off, the driver smashed into the dashboard, and blood everywhere. I'd stare at the scene of horror for minutes, absorbing that awful moment. Did I think about that photograph later, when I was driving? Maybe.

I'm not sure how you teach someone to be a safe driver, but I think explicit photographs and safety films must help. Or perhaps one learns from experience. I can think of a personal example. One morning I got up early to drive to Detroit, where I was a guest speaker at a writing conference. We were in a hurry, and after my wife and kids were in the Travelall I remembered I had to pick up a lady, a person I'd never met, who needed a ride. It was still dark when I turned down a two-lane road near our house and suddenly a bell sounded and a red flashing light indicated that a train was approaching. I saw the train's light far to my right, and, because there were no arms to stop traffic, I decided to go ahead. I got on the tracks and the engine coughed, spit, balked; perhaps it was not yet warmed up; perhaps it behaved in a way I would not have noticed under ordinary driving. It continued running and I was a block away when the train rushed past the crossing, going faster than I had imagined., Perhaps there was no danger, but in memory I have envisioned the most incredible scenarios. In memory I put the Travelall in low gear and push the starter button, slowly grinding my way across the tracks. Or I realize that we need to abandon the vehicle, and I'm fighting to get three kids out of their seatbelts as the headlight approaches rapidly. How little time I would have to make a decision: crank on the starter or save the kids. Over the past thirty years I have thought about that moment a thousand times, and I've had nightmares where I'm trying to move the Travelall forward by rocking my body. And if something had happened it would have been my fault entirely. I've been guilty of bad judgment numerous times, but in this case the lives of four other people were at stake. I learned from that event, and over the past 30 years I have never tried to beat a train. On the other hand, I have jaywalked.

One narrator thinks the Highway Traffic Safety films are passé. He says they're "shocking" but would have little impact on today's youth, especially when compared to the violence of today's video games. A cultural historian considers the films "wonderful time capsules" but thinks that the current footage of crash tests using dummies is a more effective way to teach safe driving. That's the kind of film the group might be making today, if it hadn't folded up in 1974. The story of their rise and fall is complicated and unclear. They branched out to make police training films about shoplifters, bank robbers and "paper hangers," and bought a new bus outfitted with a bedroom, bar and various luxuries. The organization had important people on its board, including Sammy Davis Jr., who wrote a weekly newspaper column espousing safe driving. In 1972, the organization held a TV telethon to raise money—it was opened by President Nixon. Then there was a big wreck within the organization. A key member died, and it was rumored that she had been murdered. Several million dollars were missing, and the organization was $5 million in debt. Then things got stranger. One safety film, *Carriers or Killers?*, was about truck drivers; it opened the door to Jimmy Hoffa, the Teamsters and organized crime. Then a private investigator asserted that the organization got into porno films, and alleged that some were filmed on that fancy bus. One police instruction film was *Camera Surveillance*, and it used a two-way mirror and a hidden camera in the towel dispenser in a public restroom in downtown Mansfield, Ohio. The purpose was to get evidence on "deviates." The investigator mentioned that an uncut version of the film was popular locally because several well-known citizens of Mansfield were shown. The Highway Traffic Safety group became defunct in 1974, amid great scandal and a long way from bloody wrecks.

THE MINISTER'S SONS

Because he died in another state, the death notice in my paper was tiny. David Cotton, MD. Then a couple words indicating that he had been an oncologist and had died of cancer, a sad irony. However, rather than sadness, I felt that shock of recognition. I hadn't known him well enough to feel sadness, but I had known him. I'd gone to high school with him, or at least his final two years, since he had transferred from out-of-state. I hadn't seen him or thought about him for 50 years. I was shocked because he'd looked so healthy two years ago at the 50th class reunion, and he was one of the few who closely resembled his youthful self. There was an assured, even prosperous air about him, and I was reminded that he had done well in life: student body president, college grad, medical school, an internship, a practice. One could suppose other things, such as a posh home, investments, expensive hobbies and travel. He had done well, no doubt about it.

It was only after I read of his death that I began to recall how his life had intersected with mine, albeit slightly. Dave and his brother, Dell, arrived in my neighborhood because their father had been transferred there. He was a minister, and his new position brought him to the Lents Evangelical United Brethren. That was a church I had attended for years, until legal drag racing began to be held on certain Sundays; the sound of open exhausts had a greater hold on me than religion could. Since I no longer went to church, I never knew Pastor Cotton. I saw David at school, but at a distance, since he was involved with school politics, clubs and the social scene. That makes what I do remember about the Cotton brothers all the more remarkable.

During my senior year I dropped by the Cotton house for some reason. The house, owned by the church, was next to it, and in a one car garage the boys were working on a pretty sad 1936 Ford tudor. It had been rolled, the cloth roof in tatters, the top depressed and askew. There was enough body damage to discourage most guys, but the Cotton boys were not afraid to tackle the project, even though they lacked the proper tools. They had removed the broken glass and, using jacks, a chain fall and a sledgehammer, wrestled that top into position. When I returned a couple of weeks later the top looked fairly normal and the doors would close. Maybe prayer had helped. But in those days a guy could buy a pretty cherry '36 Ford tudor for $50 and save himself a lot of work. The Cotton boys must have been pretty desperate.

Later they were working in a larger garage across the street from the church. They had a 1930 Model A coupe that they were transforming into a hot rod, and once again they were doing all the work. They had chopped the top and welded the two halves together, and I was impressed. Not that the work was perfect, it wasn't, in fact, it was rough, but they had not been afraid to tackle the job. They'd also channeled the coupe — a lot — and made new supports for the body. The problem was, they had not lowered the chassis, so when you opened the door the frame rail was even with your pants pockets. When I stopped by they were building motor mounts, trying to position a master cylinder and figure out the steering.

I never saw either car on the road, and can't remember any other car they owned. They obviously worked on a shoestring, doing their own work because they couldn't afford to have others do it, and they didn't have enough money to buy another car. Perhaps the two cars I saw them working on had been donated to Pastor Cotton for the church; if so, they must've been put in the poor box! But I was impressed then, and again now, at the way, in Horatio Alger style, with grit and gumption, they had pulled themselves up by their bootstraps. They had apparently continued in this fashion in later life, and had found success.

Months after that 50th reunion, I was talking with Ann, a friend who actually graduated in the next class, and I mentioned David Cotton. She said she had sat next to him at dinner, and she asked about his brother, Dell, who was in her class. "He told me Dell was working for Uncle Sam. Then he smiled and said that Dell was in a federal prison, that he got ten years for fraud!" I was astounded. Then she added, "Well, remember when their father, the Pastor, was arrested for being a peeping Tom?"

"Really," I said.

"Yes," she said, "it was in the news."

None of that diminishes the respect I had for their self-reliance and initiative. But then I thought, and I remembered that I had sold them an engine, and they had failed to pay me. So, I thought, that trail of larceny began many years before.

But why did I sell that engine anyway? It was an excellent engine that my father and I had built for my roadster only three years earlier. It was a 1949 Ford V-8, bored .040, new pistons, rings, bearings, valves, gears — new everything. It had Johnson adjustable tappets, a chopped flywheel and milled heads. The key pieces were the Edmunds dual manifold, bought new, and a rare, even then, Blackburn-England converted Nash ignition with dual points and condensers. A year later, in 1952, I had Keith Randol, a top-notch race car builder and mechanic who built 90% of the Orange Crate, install a Smith and Jones 272–2 cam. The engine ran like gangbusters.

So why did I sell that engine? Well, I told myself, at the start of 1954 I tore my roadster apart for a rebuild. I quit driving it for two years. I guess I told myself that I didn't need that engine.

But why did I sell it? I could have stuck it under the workbench. I could at least have taken off that Edmunds intake and that Delco Remy distributor and put them under the bed, where they might be today. If I hadn't sold it, I'd probably still have that complete engine.

Think: why did I sell it? I guess I didn't value it enough. It was an excellent engine and ran like stink. But that Edmunds intake was never seen on any magazine feature car; I thought I needed an Edelbrock or an Offy. And the engine was an 8BA; I had seen only one such engine in a roadster in *HRM*—Bill Likes' '32 roadster—and I thought I needed a 59-AB type engine. I liked the symmetry of the water hoses, in the same way I liked a Stromberg carburetor better than a Holley or Chandler-Groves. Petty ideas! Foolish youth!

Why exactly did I sell it? I needed money. Of course I needed money. But whatever I would have gotten for it would not have been enough to build an equally good engine. Face it: it was just one of many stupid things I've done in my life.

I can't remember whether the Cotton boys asked me about buying the engine or if I asked them. At any rate, one day I pulled the engine from my roadster, loaded it into the trunk of my car and drove to their garage. By then they'd built motor mounts and we set the engine in. I do not remember shedding any tears as I drove off. I also do not remember whether or not I had money in hand as I drove off. I stopped by frequently, trying to get a payment. After all, their father was Pastor Cotton, a man of the cloth, God's servant, leader of the flock, and that meant his sons were absolutely honest.

I'm slow to learn, so I assume my visits to collect money, any amount of money, went on for some time. Finally, I figured things out: despite the Cotton boys' protests and oaths of intent, they did not intend to pay me. At all! So one day I went to their garage with some tools, took the engine out myself, wrestled it into the trunk of my car and took it home. Had I learned a lesson? Probably not.

THE ORIGINAL FONZ

The first time I saw the Fonz on TV's *Happy Days*, I thought back to my high school years and a guy I knew named Gary Guthrie. In those days there was a terrible caste system; you were either a jock, a social type, an intellectual or a greaser. The jocks tended to be social types, but otherwise there was little overlapping. You were stuck in a niche, and everyone, students and teachers alike, forever saw you in only the most narrow way.

Most of us who fooled around with cars were greasers; we had baggy pants, shoes run down at the heels and terrible haircuts. Gary, on the other hand was cool. He was a sharp dresser, with a closet full of pastel Stradivari shirts, white cords, pegged suntans and a pair of perfectly clean saddle shoes. His crew cut was always perfect, which meant he probably had it cut every ten days. He was tall, lean, angular, with an athlete's body, although he did not participate in school athletics. He was handsome, and could have joined the best social clubs, a ritual that seemed terribly important at the time; he chose to not join a club. He had a certain toughness, with moods that shifted quickly from joking to serious, and in my mind he could be somewhat menacing. He was certainly unpredictable. And he was truly independent. He was one of the few who hung out with jocks, social types and the greasers. It's hard to go your own way in high school but Gary did.

All that is preface to his car activities, because I think he showed some of those same qualities when he built a nutty '32 Ford three-window coupe. He traded his first car, a 1936 Ford coupe, for the '32, which was bonestock except for a dropped axle. This was in 1951, when Gary was still 15; he drove it occasionally—and illegally—until he got his driver's license in January, 1952. Then he got serious. In an afternoon he removed the fenders and running boards and threw them in the junk pile. But, as he told me years later, "even with the dropped axle the car looked awful. I knew it had to be channeled!"

The '32 became a daily driver and was later traded for the 1940 Merc coupe beside it; Gary Guthrie later sold the Merc for $200.

A couple friends had had their cars channeled at a local shop. The price was about $35, depending upon the amount of gas used. Gary recalled the operation: "This sounded fine to me so I skipped school on a Friday and drove the '32 (to the shop). I watched the fuel line while Gene had at it with the cutting torch. By the end of the day, the body had been cut loose from the floorboards and allowed to settle down over the frame about six-to-eight-inches. Gene then made little short welds wherever the body inner structure would touch the remaining floor boards. This was the epitome of the a phrase 'Quick and Dirty.'"

Gary moved the radiator and grille forward and down until it was level with the cowl, and built a sheet metal hood sans side panels. To solve the problem of the rear tires rubbing on the body, Gary did something I have never seen anyone else do: He simply reversed them by mounting them backwards! He pointed out that this was perhaps safer than the original, because he used $5/8$-inch grade 5 machine bolts for the stock wheel studs.

All this was done in a day or two, and on Monday we were surprised to see the '32 cruise down Woodward in front of Franklin High; it was now half as tall as it had been on Friday. Gary remembered that "this '32 was now the coolest looking thing on four wheels. No mention that there was only about two feet between the headliner and the top of the seat, all the blow-by from the tired engine came directly into the interior and the mechanical brakes scarcely worked. The exhilaration of driving this fine machine cancelled all those negatives."

Gary later sold this '32 to a friend for $100, but he knew that he would build another '32 someday. After a couple sharp '40 Ford coupes and a cherry '40 LaSalle coupe, he decided to build another rod. In 1953, after he had graduated from high school, he found an original 1932 five-window coupe and bought it for $260. "It was drivable but the engine was about to go. My approach to this '32 was totally different. We took it directly to the Blue Bell garage and carefully unbolted and hoisted the body off ... so I could begin reworking the frame, suspension, brakes and cross members."

Gary knew he wanted this coupe to be low, because low was cool (he says he still feels that way!). He often saw a channeled but not chopped '32 five-window around town, and "every time I saw it drive by I liked it more. Something about the larger top and low small body really did it for me."

Gary took the two frame rails to a body shop and had a step put in the rear. When he got them back to the Blue Bell garage he assembled the frame. "I used the original rear cross member, a pickup truck center cross member and the suicide style front. We carefully set the frame up in a jigged fashion and with the help of a friend, the major frame components were electric welded together in one evening. We then proceeded to mount the dropped axle, springs, reversed wheels, engine, rear end, hydraulic brakes, steering, gas tank, etc.

"At this point it was drivable (no body) so (George) Sabin and I sat on a couple of milk crates and took off for Mount Tabor. What a rip! We somehow got through the excursion without trouble with the law. We were lucky since the vehicle had no fenders, license plates, just two frame rails, an engine, four tires and driven by two wild teenagers."

Unlike the work done on the '32 three-window, the flooring on the five-window was carefully removed and the body dropped over the frame. When the bodyman lost interest in the car Gary had to finish the work; he now knows that this was a blessing, since it gave him reason to learn how to weld and work metal. By mid-summer he had the car on the road, and drove it until a friend offered to trade a '40 Merc coupe for the '32, straight across, and Gary reluctantly agreed. He remembered: "This '32 had the possibilities of becoming a first class show rod because structurally it had no flaky or sloppy building techniques. The trouble is, once you start driving the project and it is your only transportation it's difficult to stop, tear it down and finish it."

These days Gary does not own an old car, but he does own a 1948 Piper Vagabond plane and a 1968 Breiglib sailplane. The Piper came with a 65 hp engine, but Gary has put a 100 hp engine in the plane. This does not surprise me: He is still going his own way, doing neat things that are truly different.

BONNEVILLE SPEED WEEK, 1955

If a negative can be something, what is most vivid about my first trip to Bonneville is what I do not remember. I cannot remember where we slept during that entire week, or where we ate or cleaned up. We had to eat and sleep, but is it possible that we didn't shave or shower for days? I know we had to have drinking water in that hundred-degree heat, but where did we get it? And what did we carry it in? There were no plastic gallon milk jugs in those days, and I don't remember any metal Jerry cans. And did we have a change or two of clothes?

The other guys must have faced the same problems. I don't remember more than one motel in Wendover. I don't remember anything like today's RV rigs, trailers or campers on pickups. There were around fifty cars competing, which would mean around two hundred guys crewing the cars. Later I learned that some guys slept in an abandoned building on the old airstrip, and I know guys who slept in an old military truck cargo unit, big enough to hold ten people. But where did the other 150 guys sleep?

Wendover was a small group of buildings. It must have had a store, a place where we probably bought bread, baloney, milk and pop; I suppose we lived on sandwiches, but I can't remember a single meal. However, I also can't remember being hungry, thirsty, sleepy or uncomfortable: chalk that up to the resiliency of youth. I was in such a state of perpetual excitement that I would have slept with scorpions and drank from the drainage ditch, if necessary.

The 1955 Bonneville souvenir program.

Much of what I can remember are images. Loading tools and a rebuilt flathead in the trunk of my coupe, as I quit the job I'd had for two years in order to go to the salt. I don't remember talking it over with fellow club member, Frank Hahn, but he owned a new Buick and that's probably why we went. A two-lane road across Idaho, through a long hot day, with Frank checking tire temperature with his hand every fifty miles. A two-lane road in Nevada wiped out by a gully washer. The excitement of seeing the first fast car, Joe Mabee's 200 mph sport coupe, cruising Wendover. The blinding brightness of the sun (Frank had sunglasses, did I?). The coolness before the dawn. The terrific heat by midday (110 degrees I wrote on a postcard to my mother). My pith helmet, army surplus, which I'd painted white and awkwardly lettered several years earlier; it was useful. The overwhelming odor of Ski 'N Sea, which I thought was a new product; was it also a cover for being unable to shower? The exciting mixture of exhaust sounds from the pits and far out on the course. Seeing machines I'd read about in magazines: the Kenz-Leslie Special, Fred Larsen's modified roadster, Art Chrisman's competition coupe, the Ruddy-Weinstein roadster with bodywork by Chuck Porter and Don Waite's modified roadster. Seeing familiar names in the program, people who were no doubt beside me at some point: Niekamp, Fox, Hashim, Sanchez, Voigt, Harold Johansen, Betz, Tom Cobbs, Virgil Gardner and the LeBlanc brothers.

I had a BSA Gold Star, and was nuts about cycles. A bunch of them were running, and again I saw names I knew from magazines: Bud Hare, Joe Simpson, Bus Schaller, Marty Dickerson on the first Vincent I'd ever seen, and the Brute, built by Chet Herbert. The Texas Cigar was running with its streamlined body and, I think, two Triumph motors. Pat Connoly, the noted cam grinder from Portland, was running a Triumph. A guy from the Midwest was running a lengthened chassis with two Harley Davidson motors; it was aptly called The Monster.

Top: The official window decal for the speed trials. *Bottom:* Frank Hahn, who attended with the author, beside the Kenz & Leslie pushcar, a '32 roadster.

Top: Bert Leithold's 29-A roadster had a lengthened frame, ran 270 GMC, and turned 127 mph. The car is a street roadster today. *Bottom:* Art Chrisman's radical Model A coupe turned 195 mph. The nose was made from two '40 Ford hoods, one upside down. The car still exists.

The author beside the old sign at the entrance to the Bonneville Salt Flats.

We ran into a fellow Road Angel, Jim Davis, who made it to Bonneville every year, and we found much to marvel at. Until 1955 I had seen only one car with real flames, a 1941 Merc sedan from California. Cars I was familiar with had flames painted in a single contrasting color, like scallops. At Bonneville in 1955 there was a new Cadillac, owned by the Yeakel brothers, and it had gorgeous multi-colored flames with lots of purple, lavender and orchid. They had a new Ford pickup with matching flames; it was the tow truck for the Cortopassi brothers' Glass Slipper, which was purple with lavender striping. It ran 181 mph on the salt.

There was Dana Fuller's GMC diesel streamliner; the first time I saw it I thought it was on fire. It was a piece of work, but it bent 20 exhaust valves on a run; I never saw it in a magazine. However, I took three photographs of the car. I also took three photographs of the Kenz-Leslie Skyland Ford streamliner, and two photographs of their '32 Ford roadster push car. I took one photograph of a new Porsche Speedster coupe, and three of Bill Scace's Mercedes 300 SL gullwing coupe; I never expected to see such cars again. I could have taken a hundred photographs, but given my budget, I only took three dozen that entire week. One, taken through the windshield in the morning, with a single car on the road, shows the arch across the street with the word Ogden; it might as well have spelled Paris or Shangri-La.

SUMMER 1955: A SUNDAY

Of a particular Sunday during the summer of 1955, I remember almost nothing. If that sentence has the tone of confession, I do confess that I do not remember everything that happened on a given day over 50 years ago. Unlike some, who may or may not have experienced those distant days, I have never claimed to remember everything.

Gerry Burger wrote at least two really funny columns for the *Gazette*. One was based on the idea that some rodders have an unreasonable yearning to be old because they claim to have been rodders during the Fabulous Fifties. Burger said he looked at those smooth cheeks and thought, no way, not possible. To have lived in the Fifties and be working with rods, a guy would have to be somewhere around 65 or 70 — and who would wish to be that old? The impulse is to roll back the years, to become younger, to merge into that youth market that dictates fashion, film and food.

Some cultures equate old age with wisdom; in America if you're old your doctor, the store manager, and the cop consider you a nuisance. The only virtue to having achieved a certain age is that you have lived the history others are wondering about. They ask what the 1950s were like. That's a question I consistently ask myself, and when I think I've arrived at an answer I ask it again, my personal version of the myth of Sisyphus.

I try to see the big picture, but see only small parts. Of this particular Sunday during the summer of 1955 I see only a moment. It's like a silent movie where the screen is black and then the lens opens to create a circle of light that illuminates an actor's face, isolated from any context. In this illuminated circle I see a face, that of a teenage girl, my sister, Bonnie, and as the circle widens I see that she is about to exit the passenger side of the car. The circle slowly opens as the camera pulls away; then I am both camera and subject, able to view the scene objectively, and I see myself exiting from the driver's side of the same car.

Why remember this? What is important about this moment? Well, most notably, that we're alive, that we exist in this time, in this place. It's 1955, the summer, a Sunday. We're young — younger than I can sometimes remember. If questioned by the authorities I could prove that I was once that young, although I would have difficulty telling them what my sister and I had been doing on that particular day. I think we went to Blue Lake Park, and went swimming. I can't remember whether we went with others, or met them there, or whether we rented a canoe. I assume that we did not drink beer because of our ages. Possibly we did not even have a Coke, so I assume we are terribly thirsty.

As the camera pulls back I see the car we are exiting: my 1947 Ford coupe, newly painted, nearly perfect. Not chopped, channeled or sectioned, it was simply lowered, nosed, decked, top grille bar removed, pipes, wide whites, full-disc hubcaps, all period touches. If I can shift this mental movie from black and white into color, perhaps that new CinemaScope — or even Todd-AO — color, we'd see that the coupe is Baltic Blue, a 1955 Buick color, and the dash and garnish moldings are Bahama blue, a 1955 Cadillac color.

Those gorgeous colors, that give lie to the grayness of the Eisenhower years, are repeated in our clothes. I wear a brightly patterned shirt and matching shorts, a cabaña outfit, kind of silly now, but popular at the time. Bonnie is also wearing a brightly patterned blouse over her one-piece bathing suit. Bonnie looks somewhat like Jean Simmons, although her hair is longer and more blonde — maybe like Julie Harris. We are cast in the gold of the setting sun on this summer evening, on a Sunday, 1955, which gives us an unreal appearance. We are healthy and tanned, more so in this light, and we might be apparitions, figments of an imagination, fragments of memory, but having been brought to the present we have a reality, and we are hungry.

Al Drake's '47 Ford, a mild custom, in the summer of 1955.

Because it is 1955, we park and walk to the window at Dickeys. There are lots of drive-ins, but in the past year or so walk-up burger joints have become popular. The building at Dickeys is modern, with lots of red, white and black tile, plus aluminum accents; the entire front is glass, and the place looks super clean. The food is good, and the price is right: 19 cent hamburgers, 11 cent French fries, 15 cent milkshakes. We order and within minutes the girl hands us a sack and two tall drink containers.

The odor of hot food fills the car. We eat with gusto. We are lean and tanned and hungry. If the battery was up I no doubt turned on the radio; in that pre-rock 'n' roll time we might have listened to Tony Bennett sing "Stranger in Paradise" or "Because of You," or maybe something forgettable, like "Cabbages and Kings." The sun glares off the chrome dash pieces, the horn ring, off the windshield of a car on 82nd. Because it is 1955, a Sunday evening, there is almost no traffic. Against the glare some things appear sharp-edged, others fuzzy; I closed my eyes tightly, saw a galaxy of colored lights against the lids, then opened my eyes, hoping the view, and my thinking, were clearer. It's clear I have to go to work the next day. But something has skipped, like a needle on a record. The sunlight is blinding, the milkshakes cold. I can't remember what songs were on the radio. If I had known a half a century later that someone would ask me about the 1950s I would have taken notes.

Here's the meaning this moment has for me: because I do remember it, however imperfectly, that suggests it happened seldom, maybe only once. I wish it had happened often, this kind of getting together, Bonnie and I, being close in the way siblings should be. But I'm glad it happened this time, this Sunday during the summer of 1955, and between the dazzling sunset and the hamburgers and Teresa Brewer on the radio, perhaps Bonnie and I talked; I hope we did.

A reader, years younger, might say that he already knew that there were kids, cars and hamburgers in the 1950s; so what? I'm reminded of a time, 40 years ago, when I heard Gary Snyder read an early poem from his book *Riprap*; it was only ten lines long, and mostly description. A person in the audience questioned whether that was a poem. Snyder simply said: "You need to have had the experience."

1956: The First Portland Roadster Show

I'm possibly the only guy still alive who had a car on display at the first Portland Roadster Show.

That was in November, 1956, half a century past. I've reviewed in my mind the cars in the show, the owners, and the images drift past, sepia toned, like dried leaves blowing along with the pages of a calendar — a film device to show the passing of time. Some of the faces are blank; some lack names. I'm not going to pretend that I remember everything from that distant time. I have forgotten far more than I remember about that show.

However, I do remember a kind of excitement I felt when I first heard the show's name. There had been hot rod shows in Portland for the previous five years with words like speed and rods in the title, but the use of the word "roadster" suggested much. I used that word to describe my own A-V8, and I considered it in general a more appropriate term than hot rod, which still had negative connotations. Portland Roadster Show: the name evoked in my mind a race car nose, bobbed deck, rolled-under pan, and of course it evoked connections with that show in Oakland.

It was a fitting name, and the show came at the right time; since 1950 rodding had accelerated. The first hot rod show in Portland was held in 1951. The first legal drag races in the Portland area began in the summer of 1952. The Multnomah Hot Rod Council was formed in 1954–55; it was the governing agency for the many car clubs that were multiplying like rabbits. With a strong membership and strong leadership under Dee Wescott, the MHRC got lofty ideas; it wanted to buy land in Woodburn, a few miles south of Portland, and develop a drag strip. To raise money, it decided to hold a car show.

It was a small show by today's standards. The Portland Armory, the site of the show, could accommodate only forty cars and a few displays. Given the space limitations, and the large number of cars available, I'm surprised that my roadster got in the show. I'm also surprised that it was in show condition or even running, because I'd moved away, albeit slightly, from hot rodding. By 1956 my interests had shifted to customs, motorcycles and girls. Or, more accurately, to girls, motorcycles and customs. I'd grown tired of using my roadster as a daily driver, and I'd come to appreciate the comforts of heat and music. Therefore, I sold the engine from the roadster (stupid!), tore the car apart and it remained that way for two years. For most of 1956 I worked at a new car dealership and, by the time of the show, at an automotive warehouse. That year I built a 1951 Chevrolet mild custom, and I began taking classes at Portland State College, so I was busy. And yet, I found time, over a period of months, to rebuild my roadster.

I wasn't the only one obsessed with machines. It was car crazy time. Motorcycles were big too. I knew lots of guys with cycles, and most weekends I'd go riding, cutting trails on the hills outside of town. Drag racing had become a huge sport; in 1955 the NHRA Drag Safari came to the Scappoose drag strip near Portland, and *Hot Rod Magazine* covered the event. Custom cars were big; 1956 was the apex of custom cars. Check out the publications; in addition to the features in mixed-use mags, custom cars had four separate titles. It seemed like every guy had primer spots on his car, whether it was a 1936 Ford coupe or a 1955 Merc. I knew one guy who bought a new 1955 Chevy hardtop, had it nosed and decked, and drove the car in grey primer. A new car! In primer! He also installed a Packard floor shift transmission for racing. There was plenty of that going on, and he found the competition on 82nd Avenue at night and the unfinished Banfield freeway. In addition to early model coupes and roadsters with hopped up engines, there were the late models: 1950–53 Oldsmobiles with McCullough superchargers and dual pipes; customized Corvettes; new Chevys with Power Pack options; and an occasional Dodge D-500, an early muscle car.

With so many neat machines available, I'm surprised that my roadster made the show. I'm also surprised because often I didn't hear about things, or was slow in applying. With room for only forty cars, I assume the spaces filled quickly. I can't remember how I made application. As I think about it, perhaps my car got in the show because I had recently met Bill Peterson, an older rodder who was involved with the MHRC, and who was the chairman of that first show. Peterson belonged to the Road Knights, and I was friends with another member, Bob Hooper, who had previously belonged to my club, the Road Angels. The Road Knights rented a clubhouse, and I used to drop in some evenings and shoot the breeze.

The No. 453 1929 Ford Roadster owned by the author of the Road Angels of Portland. The paint is Sierra gold, and body is channeled with handmade rear fenders and a chopped windshield. A 276 cubic inch 1948 Merc engine powers the car. The upholstery is black with white piping.

Or perhaps I made application on my own. I'd rebuilt my roadster three times in five years, and by late 1956 it was, in my opinion, a show car. I'd rebuilt the running gear, chromed parts of the front suspension and various engine accessories, and built a neat dash. The engine, originally built prior to 1949, ran a ⅛" stroked crank, big cam, headers, lightened flywheel, heads and manifold; I went through it a year earlier, when I worked in a garage, and it was sanitary. A local bodyman made the body nearly perfect, and he painted it a new color, Sierra Gold, a 1956 Chevrolet color, which I thought was so beautiful. I had a matching set of big and little white wall tires, and from someone I borrowed a set of Dodge Lancer hubcaps. Shortly before the show I had the interior upholstered in black Naugahyde with white beading. That car looked good! In those simpler times most of us made a simple distinction: if a car had paint and upholstery it was a show car, because most rods didn't have either! My roadster went way beyond those standards, and I entered the show with pride and confidence.

The show was held on the last weekend in November; as I headed for the Armory the sun was out and the weather pleasant. I could have driven the roadster to the show, but for some reason I bolted on my homemade tow bar and hooked the other end to my '51 Chevy; I wish I'd taken a photograph of that moment. My friend, Al Rogers, rode with me. We have been friends for 55 years, and last week when I asked him what he remembered about the first Portland Roadster Show he said "nothing." Nada. "I don't remember anything about the shows I had my car in!" he added. Al spent thirteen years building a beautiful roadster called "The Seven Year Itch," which he showed extensively in 1964–65; it got half the cover of an issue of *Hot Rod Magazine* in 1965.

So between the two of us we remembered nothing about the trip to the Armory. Al doesn't even remember the blob of phlegm a bum on Burnside hacked on the rear fender; I remember it because I had to clean it off. My roadster was on display near the big overhead door on the west side, which I assume means that it was one of the last to enter the Armory, or that the cars were maneuvered to their locations. My roadster was beside at least two neat rods in a roped-off area. One was Bill Peterson's red, full-fendered '32 Ford roadster, which was twice featured in *Hot Rod*; it's still in the Portland area, I'm told. On the other side was a cute '32 Ford pickup owned by Bruce Baer, but originally built by Roger Simonatti, a guy who has built over 100 cars, and is still building them! If there were other cars in that circle I can't remember them, but I do remember that across the aisle from my roadster was a black 1955 Austin-Healey, customized with two side pieces from a 1950 Studebaker grille and chrome lake pipes that ran beside the body. Next to that was a black 1951 Jaguar XK 120 roadster with chrome wire wheels, chrome brake drums and a padded top built by Chuck Blanchard.

Another car in that show that I remember well is Johnny Howard's convert, called the "Starlight Custom" because of the 20 small blue bulbs worked into the headliner. Billed as a 1950 model, it was actually a 1949 Merc with 1951 Merc rear fenders. This was a full-on custom built in Portland by the Beard Brothers, and in 1953 I was able to skip school to accompany the car to the Oakland Roadster Show for a full week. Another radical custom was Roger Cunningham's '50 Ford convertible, which was about as low as it could get. It was painted purple, and the interior featured burgundy and pink rolls and pleats. Beside it was Don Telen's 1940 Merc coupe, which was chopped and dropped to the limit. The paint was "Frosty Grape," and the interior was dusty rose and white rolls and pleats. The owners were friends, both members of the Kustoms club, and they often cruised together on downtown Broadway, where they created a sensation.

A few things of note: there was no angel hair used, that came later. In fact there were no elaborate displays around the cars. Other than a 1956 Ford pickup and the 1955 A-H, there were no "late model" cars. The emphasis was on the early rods and customs. Telen's '40 Merc coupe was the only chopped hardtop in the show, and almost the only one in town. It was not easy to chop a top. 1940 Fords were popular and there were half a dozen or so in the show, all coupes, and half were still running hopped-up flatheads. Perhaps the most striking was Earl Robison's black '40 standard coupe with a black and white checkerboard interior design sewn by his wife. There was also a beauty contest, where young women competed in bathing suits for the title of "Miss Roadster Show"; it was a feature of following shows, until feminist forces deemed the contest "sexist."

But 1956 was such a happy, innocent time, I doubt that most of the guys at the show could have defined the term sexist. We were happy thinking of Cadillac hubcaps and dual pipes. Things were so simple that although a reported 5,000 people attended the show, everyone found a place to park on the street! I guess the show made money, because the MHRC soon bought land in Woodburn and created a drag strip, which, happily, is still very active.

The Portland Roadster Show has celebrated its fiftieth anniversary. Pretty amazing! I suspect that everyone anticipated the 1957 show, but I'll bet no one thought it would continue for fifty years. I know I didn't, but I didn't think in those terms, back when two weeks was a long time and a year was forever.

CRUISING ON A VESPA AT MIDCENTURY

After nearly 50 years, I could be wrong, but I have long believed that I owned the first Vespa scooter delivered in Portland, Oregon.

Top: Here's our man touring France in 1962 on a Lambretta.... *Bottom:* ... and astride his 1951 BSA Gold Star.

In 1956–57 I worked in an automotive warehouse at N.W. l0th and Flanders St. Sometime during that year, a Vespa dealership opened at l0th and West Burnside, on a pie-shaped piece of land across from the building which then housed Wentworth and Irwin, a Nash dealership, and which now houses Powell's City of Books (the world's largest bookstore according to *The Guinness Book of Records*). I drove past the Vespa dealership twice a day, and I could see the two or three scooters on display. What got me to stop was the Vespa with a sidecar that appeared one day; it was terribly cute, and I was impressed by the simplicity of the torsion bar suspension. I knew right then I wanted one.

I grew up at a time when scooters were practical transportation, because new cars were unavailable during World War II and hard to get for several years after the war. A sporting goods store near my house had a row of new Servi-Cycles for sale, and occasionally I'd see a Whizzer motorbike, or a Doodlebug or a Hiawatha or Cushman scooter. I'd find a motorized scooter in the classified ads and I'd try to convince my father that I could use it on my paper route. I never got a scooter, but I spent a lot of time trying to figure out how I could adapt a small motor to my bicycle. When I turned 16 I built a hot rod, and after graduating from high school I had motorcycles, including a beautiful BSA Gold Star, which was sanitary and quick.

By 1957 I was moving away from cycles and hot rods. In the fall I began classes at Portland State College full-time, and I was thinking lofty thoughts and hanging out with a better class of people, so I abandoned my old ways. I bought a car coat, Ivy League pants with a little belt in the back, penny loafers, paisley shirts and V-neck sweaters. As I changed, so did the world. In Portland it became possible to buy beer by the pitcher and to walk around in the tavern with a glass of beer and to throw peanut shells on the floor, just like people did in the joints in Frisco. A coffeehouse opened near PSC, where Beatniks drank espresso, played chess and read *On the Road*.

In this kind of atmosphere, it seemed a good idea to buy a Vespa scooter. Actually, I can't remember exactly why I bought one, but I know I was thinking of the larger world. I wanted to go to Europe. I wanted to enjoy things I'd read about in *Esquire* and *Playboy*, such as seeing a bullfight, eating gazpacho and paella, cruising the Riviera on two wheels and drinking the *vin du pays* of many countries. I wanted to wear a Harris tweed jacket with leather patches on the elbows, suck on a pipe and carry a slim black umbrella. On a more mundane level, the city was installing parking meters around the college and it was getting increasingly difficult to find a parking space for a car. Also, there was a ceramics professor at PSC who rode a Vespa he'd bought in Italy, and he made the scooter sound like fun transportation.

So, one day in the spring of 1958 I went to the dealership and bought a 1957 Vespa 150 for $250. It had been brought to Portland by the dealership's mechanic, used as a demonstrator, and was now fitted with a 1958 engine and titled as a 1958 model. I can't recall the mechanic's name, but I remember that he had a sister, an attractive young woman with reddish-blonde hair, who took classes at PSC.

The scooter was in beautiful condition, and had a luggage rack, the only accessory. It was quick! I was told that the mechanic had milled down the head to raise the compression and had gutted the muffler to reduce back pressure. I never had the scooter apart, so can't testify that those modifications had been done. but I do know that the scooter, although quiet, would run past 55 MPH on the speedometer, 5.5 MPH faster than the top speed stated in the owner's manual. I loved riding that Vespa! After the various problems I'd had with chains and sprockets on motorcycles, I admired the Vespa's engine/transmission/final drive construction, and the fact that the engine had only three moving parts! It seemed that the designers had thought of everything. The lights ran off the magneto, making a battery unnecessary. Below the seat was the fuel lever; when I ran out of gas, as I often did, I'd flip it over to the reserve level, which would always get me home, and later to a station.

On the left side of the body was a compartment that held the factory tool kit and tire pump, two-stroke oil and a measuring can, a couple rags, and other miscellaneous stuff—with room left over. Behind the seat was a pillion for an occasional passenger, and behind that was the optional luggage rack. which would carry a decent load.

I could've got a spare tire, which bolted in place under the rack, but changing a tire was no problem. One Saturday morning, in a hurry to get to my job in a gas station, I found that the rear tire was flat. I laid the scooter on its side, and using a wrench that came with the scooter I removed the four bolts that held the wheel to the hub. Using the socket on the other end, I removed the bolts that held the two-piece wheel together, cold-patched the tube, reassembled the wheel, pumped up the tire with the factory hand pump and was on my way in 10 minutes.

The scooter was terribly inexpensive. Gas cost between 16 and 20 cents a gallon, and two-stroke oil wasn't much. The mileage was around 150 miles on a full tank. A license plate was either $2.50 or $3.00 a year, and I never did have any insurance. I replaced the spark plug with some frequency. I rode that Vespa for five years, and the only expense, besides spark plugs, was a control cable and a new inner tube, the result of taking on a passenger without increasing the tire pressure, as per the manual. I never did any maintenance, other than washing the scooter — maybe I waxed it too. But the total cost of riding that Vespa for five years was around $25!

I had lots of fun with that scooter. I met girls who just had to have a ride. I'd park it anywhere — between cars, on the grass, on the sidewalk. I'd park it in front of a funky-fashionable tavern like the Pink Bucket and enter wearing my car coat, Ivy League slacks and penny loafers, looking, I thought, very smooth.

I cruised from place to place all night, and when I came home, often very late, that scooter was so quiet my mother never woke up.

And yet, sometimes I look back, especially late at night, and wonder whether I should have owned that scooter. Sometimes, these nights, I stare into the darkness and celebrate the notion that I'm still alive. The problem was that I expected that Vespa to be two machines: a quiet, classy scooter that would get me around town in style, and a fast grand prix machine. I had ridden motorcycles for several years, and some of the bikers would get gas at the station where I worked. They'd always give me some guff, indicating that they considered the Vespa a toy. That was a reason for riding the scooter hard. I'd ride between rows of cars at a stop light, as I'd done on motorcycles, and when the light changed to green I'd grab a handful of throttle and run it through the gears, speed shifting. It seemed impossible to over-rev the engine, and so I kept it wound up.

It rains a lot in Portland, and while the leg shield kept my lower body dry, my upper body was quickly soaked. One morning, after a short ride, I was really wet, so I stopped at an army surplus store and bought a cloth coat with a snap-in alpaca liner. Rain could not penetrate that liner, and the coat, with the hood raised, gave me a sense of protection. Of course, I never wore a crash helmet. It scares me now when I think of leaving PSC, going up Broadway, then downhill, through a couple right turns, merging with traffic and then entering a left hand curve and heading over the Ross Island Bridge, going as fast as I could. On a motorcycle I could just lay it over, but the smaller wheels on the scooter required a different kind of control, similar to certain kinds of skiing.

By dumb luck, and a smidgen of skill, I had only one accident in five years. My wife and I rode from Eugene to Ashland, to attend the Shakespearean Festival, using what is now 1-5, and although we had about 50 pounds of camping gear on the rack, we kept up with traffic. Most of the time there was a logging truck or a bus close behind. At Azalea the road widens to a third lane, which is a slow lane for trucks, and they had deposited a sheen of oil. When we hit that oil, the rear tire spun like mad, the engine turned an impossible 20,000 RPM and we went down; my wife fell off, but I hung on to the bars as the Vespa slid and slid, seemingly forever. On our return, at my wife's insistence, we took Highway 99, a slower route.

In 1962 we headed for Europe, and I sold the Vespa to a German student in Eugene, Oregon for $195, a little less than I'd paid for it. We got to Europe, and in Roosendaal, Holland, I bought a used Lambretta scooter. I was told it was a 150cc but it turned out to be a 125cc model, which put us at a disadvantage in places like the Pyrenees. The two scooters were quite different, and because the Lambretta had shocks on both sides of the wheels and the engine in the center, I think it was the better scooter on a long journey, while the Vespa was better in town.

I've told myself many times that I'd like to have another Vespa, but only when the price of gas forces others to ride something with two wheels. Part of what saved me from disaster was that traffic was greatly reduced in those days. It's hard to explain, but look at photographs taken during the 1950s in a city like Portland, and unless the photographs were taken at rush hour, the streets are almost empty. That was also what made riding a scooter so much fun.

Scooters on Campus

From 1959 to 1962, when I was a student at the University of Oregon, there were hardly any scooters or cycles on campus. I had been riding a Vespa in Portland since 1957, and I took mine with me to the UO, where it was ideal transportation because my world had diminished to an area of about two square miles. It was a quick trip across campus, through the Pioneer Cemetery or into downtown Eugene. If I were in no hurry I'd ride through the alleys that intersected almost every block, looking in people's back yards.

So if the Vespa was ideal transportation, why weren't there more? Actually, there weren't many bicycles either. I suspect that most college students considered scooters and bicycles as juvenile transportation. That's my impression, years later. The only other guy I knew at UO who had a Vespa was Ed Nadeau, who I'd met at PSC, Ed also had a fairly new MGA roadster. He probably shouldn't have been driving or riding anything, because he got pretty drunk several times a week. He had plenty of family money, and during the summer of 1959 he rode his Vespa all the way to Mexico, an incredible journey. He wanted me to go with him, but, alas, I had to work.

In the fall I rented a room, the old dining room actually, one huge room in a Victorian house that had been converted into apartments for students during World War II. It was like a Charles Addams drawing, and therefore it attracted Beatniks, loners, outsiders, non-students and some really smart and creative students. My room cost $15 a month. After a few months I became manager, which meant I got the entire third floor in exchange for collecting rents and keeping people from destroying the place. Like Vespa riders, the renters were a distinct minority, and on occasion it was us versus the fraternity and sorority people.

One renter was Kernan Tumer, who went on to have a distinguished career with the Associated Press. He had a 1940s Cushman motor scooter. Today it would be lovingly restored, but in 1960 it was a clunky, noisy scooter with an old blue paint job that'd been put on with a brush. The difference between that Cushman and my Vespa was like night and day. One example, the Vespa shifted by rolling the handlebar grip, while on the Cushman you had to let go of the handlebar, reach down low the right side and slide a lever forward.

Another renter was Brad Reed, an outdoorsman, who loved to boat, fish and climb mountains. He went on to become one of the first serious ski bums in Aspen. He showed up at the house one day with a brand new BSA Spitfire, a full-size cycle with a 250 cc single cylinder motor, I think: it was supposed to be an economy bike, because it had things like a partial seat, with no room for a passenger. But it was a neat bike, with a blue tank and the BSA emblem. I think Brad's bike was the only example I've ever seen.

Then a couple, Garth and Virginia, rented a room. I can't remember the details, whether one showed up before the other or if they came together. I clearly remember that in 1960 it was unusual, even shocking, for an unmarried couple to live together, I don't think there was a rule against it; it just didn't happen. They were the only couple to live together in unmarried bliss during the years I managed the joint. My own wife didn't move in with me until after we were married!

I believe Virginia got a Vespa before Garth did, or maybe they brought their Vespas when they moved in. Garth had a Vespa 150, similar to mine. Virginia, who worked for a delivery service, rode a Vespa Grand Sport, the only one I saw during those years. It had a 200 cc motor, bigger tires and was taller than my Vespa. I don't think they took classes, but they had jobs and rode their Vespas rain or shine. Then one day on their lunch hour they rode their Vespas to city hall and got married. I hope it lasted.

RECORDS

A few years ago I went to Tower Records to get something, and I was amazed to find that, despite the name, they had no records! They don't exist. Cassettes seem rare. CDs are now the ultimate way to listen to music I was told. A couple of days later my son showed me a device called an iPod: it's the thickness of a pancake and stores thousands of songs! I turned my back for a decade or two and something familiar like records, something that seemed eternal, is outmoded! Obsolete! I've become a 78 record played with a one-shot needle — scratchy and skipping grooves. It's a perfect metaphor for how time passes and the world changes.

I grew up with records, and I remember when an LP was a big deal, although I bought only half a dozen in my entire life. For younger readers, which these days, includes most people, I should explain that LP means "long playing." For the guy in the back row, hand raised, who wants to know what a record is, I'll simply say that it's a disc with a hole in the middle and continuous grooves on both sides which, when touched by a needle, produces sound. How archaic is that? To mention a record is to flash back to the beginning of time almost. The first records were played at 78 revolutions per minute; there was one song on each side that lasted about two minutes. Then there were 45s, smaller records with a big hole in the center; they turned more slowly, so the same amount of music could be contained in less space. In the 1950s the LP was introduced. It turned at $33\frac{1}{3}$ rpm, and because it was a larger diameter record that turned slower, it had more songs, perhaps ten on each side. It meant that you could place a record on the player and not have to fool with it for half an hour. This led to improvements in players and speakers, and by the late 1950s, High Fidelity was introduced. For music aficionados, whether jazz, popular or classical, a good LP on a good Hi-Fi system was the ultimate in listening pleasure.

That's not really intended as a survey of the history of records, but as an example of how something evolved, loomed large, then vanished. That's true of most of the past. The buffalo herds, the passenger pigeon, the Dodo bird, leaded gas, all gone. We think we remember them but we remember the memory. It's like a song heard long ago, with sections that we can still hum, or melted snow, gone without a trace. LPs show up today at yard sales, like bleached bones on the prairie. When LPs were new and amazing, they were also pricey, around five bucks, and I bought only a few. For my sister at Christmas I bought Belafonte's first album, also Elvis's first. For myself, I bought one by Kid Ory and another with Louis Armstrong singing Fats Waller.

In New York City I visited a Sam Goody store and bought the two-record album, "Lead Belly's Last Session." I also bought an LP featuring two great drummers, Buddy Rich and Gene Krupa.

I do remember the day I bought that one. The day before it began snowing and by eight o'clock that night 3 or 4 inches had accumulated. Snow is rare in my town, and usually melts quickly. The temperature that night was in the thirties; heavy, dark clouds, hanging low in the sky, promised more of the big flakes. It was a magical night, which is probably why Jack Burns came by my house. Jack and his twin brother, Jerry, were my friends and we had lots of fun. They had a knack for meeting girls and finding cherry cars, which actually were the same for them. Find a neat car, meet a cute girl. They'd had a 1930 Oldsmobile roadster, a 1934 Nash Lafayette sedan, a 1946 Ford four door, among others, all low mileage, all in primo condition. It was easy to find cars from the '30s and '40s, but hard to find a really nice one. The Burns brothers would make a discovery, divide the cost, and then run the tires off of the car. They didn't wreck cars, they just wore them out quickly.

On that night Jack was driving a 1948 Plymouth four door, medium blue, with a perfect body, interior, chrome trim and a faux wood dash. All of that seems remarkable today, 50 years later, but at the time that bone-stock Plymouth didn't interest me, except that it had a radio and heater, and both were on. To describe that night is as difficult as describing the tonal qualities of a Hi-Fi system. You couldn't duplicate the situation. Oh, you could get an original 1948 Plymouth and take it out in the snow, but the experience would be different. A major difference is lighting. Then there were few street lights, often none, and only an occasional porch light. On this night the houses were dark, and the illumination came from the snow that gathered on the trees, yards and rooftops. Added to the odd landscape was the silence; snow on the hood quieted the engine, and snow muffled the tires. The silence emphasized the radio; I wasn't really listening until the band paused and a solitary drummer began some hot licks. I listened intently, trying to identify the snare, the trap, the bass drums, the cymbals; a pause, then the drum solo continued, a rapid, intense gathering of sound. We stopped talking and listened as the drummer went on for several minutes. I dug the drumming, but waited for the band to join in, which was like waiting for the other shoe to drop.

Because the record was an LP, the drumming, in various tempos, stretched on like the white fields around us. Then a second drummer merged with the first, repeating variations. This cat did a long set also. Jerry turned a corner, and, perhaps because of the excited drumming, goosed it and the Plymouth skidded slightly. Jerry laughed and easily straightened the car out, but that skid triggered something because at the next intersection he purposely swung the car sideways and quickly straightened it out. He said something, then turned the steering wheel left, then right, and the car's rear end responded.

I had the feeling that we could drive like this for hours, the endless snow, the endless drumming. There was no traffic, no tire tracks ahead, no kids playing in the snow. There were stretches where there were no houses, just empty lots, softened into beauty by the white stuff. This was a neighborhood, not the country, yet snowy fields spread around like a scene from "Dr. Zhivago." A big difference then was the absence of curbs and sidewalks. When Jerry cranked the wheel hard and stepped on the gas, the car angled, the hood headed left, the trunk right, wheels spinning; it described a circle, big enough to use the space at the tips of all four corners. He straightened the car out and went up the street until he found another intersection that pleased him and he cranked the wheel, stayed on the gas, cutting a brodie, the car skidding effortlessly in a big circle.

But he didn't let up this time, and the car skidded around and around — like a giant record, I'm tempted to say — while on the radio the duel between the two drummers grew to a crescendo. I knew I would buy that record the next day.

BUD'S BEANEE-WEENEE

I recently heard about a woman in Iowa who was asked to write an informal column on farm life for a small newspaper, and she balked, saying that she had never written anything. The editor suggested that she include a recipe in each column, with the idea that readers would at least be interested in that, if nothing else. It turned out to be a good idea (a recipe for success) because she began the column in 1949 and she's still at it, over a half-century later!

Because I wanted this particular piece to be a success, I thought maybe I should include a recipe. Perhaps something that involves fresh garlic, cilantro and olive oil, as a beginning. Or something simple: a steamed artichoke, olive oil and lemon. In the many years that I've lived alone, I've learned, out of necessity, to become skillful in the kitchen. There was a time, many, many years ago, before I was married, when I cooked primarily hamburger patties and rice, day after day, and never washed the frying pan! Those are two of the four basic food groups, and they'll keep you alive; some guys may even consider that a recipe!

When I tried to think of something else I love to cook, I thought of a specific day 51 years ago, when I was trying to get my old roadster to Tacoma, Washington for the 1957 T.T.A. Hot Rod Show. Back then, things were not only simpler, the days were longer. On that particular Friday I worked eight hours at Cronin Auto Parts, picked up most of the front end of my roadster at the chrome plating shop on my lunch hour, drove home, that evening assembled the front end and headed north to Tacoma. That's more than I get done in a week these days!

At some point I had to eat supper, and since my mother and sister were off somewhere I had to forage for myself. I could've gone out to eat, but since there were no McDonalds or Taco Bells (ugh!), I would have to go to a cafe and that would take time. Besides, I did not eat out often in those days—I didn't eat out often until the 1980s, when my wife left. I don't know how restaurants survived back then; most people considered going out to eat a big deal, something you did on Sunday afternoon when you went to the movies

Because I was in a hurry, I could have opened a can of soup or fixed a peanut butter sandwich. But when I saw the can of Van Camps Pork and Beans I knew what I wanted: Beanee-Weenees, the food I'd grown up on. Before World War II my father had a WPA job driving a bulldozer (or "skinning cat," as he called it) on the two-lane highway being built through the Tillamook Burn to the coast. He'd be gone all week, leaving my mother and me alone at home. But before he left he'd go to the grocery store and buy a case of Campbell soup, usually Pepper Pot, which I don't think you can buy anymore, and a case of Beanee-Weenees. The latter consisted simply of beans with slices of wieners, but it was delicious, perhaps because wieners in those days had more integrity.

So after I got the front end of the roadster assembled, I went inside to fix a quick but hearty, and tasty, dinner. I opened the can of pork and beans and dumped it into a saucepan. Then I cut up a couple wieners and added that to the beans, turning the gas to the same blue flame one wants on an acetylene torch. Then I cut up a medium-size onion and put the pieces in with the beans and wieners. I added a couple spoons of plain yellow mustard, and several squirts of Worcestershire sauce (optional). I brought the contents to a boil, stirring constantly, and then let it simmer for 15 minutes while I hooked the tow-bar to my 1951 Chevy mild custom workhorse. I buttered a piece of white bread, poured a glass of milk and ate the Beanee-Weenees from the pan, thinking about the weekend and the excitement of the show. It was dusk when I headed the Chevy north, the roadster in tow, heading up Highway 99 (no freeway in those days), with Harry Belafonte on the radio, singing a new song, "Jamaican Farewell," which echoed through my head all the way to Tacoma.

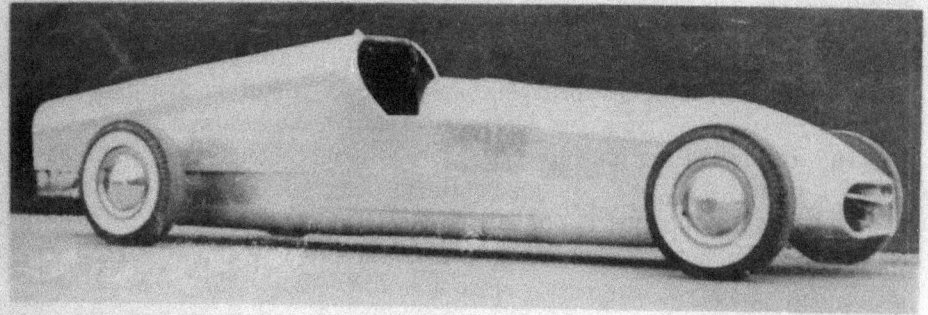

The program for the 1957 Tacoma car show.

Class Angle

I owe John Bartels a lot. He got me a job as a houseboy, which meant that I could attend the university, which meant that I was in the right place at the right time to meet the right woman, who became my wife, which meant that we were able to create a family that now extends to grandchildren. If John had not got me out of town, everything that followed in my life would have been different. What's strange about the situation is that it happened at all, because John and I were so different.

John came from a wealthy family, while mine had nothing. He lived in the affluent West Hills, while I lived on the flatlands. John was bright, well-read, educated, had ideas and was articulate. I, on the other hand, had lots to learn. I think his interest in me was because he saw me as a prime example of the Working Class. It was true that I had had a number of jobs, but the work was done out of necessity, for money, and I could not think of one job that I wanted to brag about. John who, as far as I could tell, had never had to work, wanted to identify with the worker. I'd never thought of things that way, although I often thought I should get paid more.

I met John through friends at city college. He was actually a student at the state university, but his grade point average was below the standard, and he was at the city college for a term, just to get a 2.0 so he could get back into the university. I met several guys like that, all from affluent families, all bright, but they'd partied or goofed off and got bad grades. They were different from guys I'd worked with in garages and warehouses, and I found them interesting. They dressed well, went to parties, drank a great deal, had cute girlfriends and they didn't have to worry. Their parents paid their college expenses and gave them money to live on; I soon realized that if you didn't need to worry about money, then you developed a totally different attitude toward everything.

I was taking a full load at school and working 32 hours a week in a service station, so I was okay. In fact, I was pretty happy, because going to school was more meaningful and interesting than working. But I was living at home, and when John said he could get me a job in the kitchen of a sorority house I saw a chance to get out of town. I had a little money saved, the houseboy job offered three meals a day and I figured I could last two terms. Later I discovered other benefits: I met a variety of interesting people, took classes not offered at the city college, studied more and found that the college experience was more intense because I never got away from it.

I also discovered the difference between casually knowing someone and living with that person. John and I had a nice apartment walking distance from the campus. I'm surprised that we didn't have a cold water flat with roaches and rats. John was disdainful of nice things because they were the trappings of the bourgeois, which, I soon learned, was the worst thing that one could be. He disliked nice clothes too, and preferred worn Levi's, old loafers, a sweatshirt and an army surplus jacket. He drove a 1946 Dodge sedan with Fluid Drive. It was tan, faded to the color of an old bone. It was his idea of the type of car a worker might drive, and with it he was making a statement. It showed everyone that there were more important things than a fancy car. I thought that this was a form of reverse snobbism.

I hadn't been there long before I met a girl named Marni, one of those free spirits that you have to leave home to find. She was trained as a ballet dancer but things hadn't worked out so she took classes and modeled at the art school. We went out a couple of times and I took her home to meet John. Then the three of us began going to the free films on campus or to The Side, a funky college hangout, where we drank hot cider and hand rolled cigarettes. Then we'd jump in John's old Dodge and go past the dry zone for a beer.

I thought everything was fine — my classes, my job, my social life — but as time went by, John began acting oddly, as if he wanted to avoid me. This was hard to do, since we lived and worked together. It took me a while to figure things out, but apparently John had become serious about Marni; we never talked about the various relationships, so I still didn't know whether John felt some guilt or jealousy or resentment. But I was clearly in the way. I had known jealousy but in this case I'd met someone else who knocked me off my feet, and eventually the four of us became friends.

But first, John felt he had to impress Marni, or so it seemed to me. Like John, she came from a family with money and class and good breeding — things he said he'd renounced — but apparently he didn't want to explain himself to her parents. It would take too long to let them and the world know of his ideas about dialectical materialism and the class struggle. He vanished for two days, and when he returned he was driving a new car, apparently a gift from his father. I was surprised, because John had said that material things were built with the blood of the worker. I was also surprised at the car he'd selected: a four year old 1955 Ford Crown Victoria, painted pink and white, with a pink and white interior and very white, very wide, whitewalls. It was the exact opposite of his old Dodge. It looked like an Easter basket, or a car a pimp might drive in a sexploitation film. As a car person, I found it garish. And even I, who knew so little about the theories of class warfare, thought that the car made an odd political statement. John seemed to be saying, if this is the vehicle that will inspire the workers' revolt, then drive on to the barricades!

THE GENUINE ARTIFICIAL ZEBRA SKIN INTERIOR

Pundits looking back at the 1950s describe it as a time of conformity and paranoia. They say that people in the 1950s lived in fear of world communism, A-bombs, H-bombs, Strontium 90 in the milk supply or invasion by Martians. The specter of McCarthyism hung over the land. People feared the blacklist and the loyalty oath. Women worried about being imperfect housewives. Or so we are told by social critics and writers who imposed those characteristics on a decade that took place well before most of them were born. As in a chemistry experiment, there may have been trace elements of those features during that time, but they did not loom large.

I lived through the 1950s, and I recall, it was a fun time. Oh sure, it would have been nice to have had more money. The conflicts were basic: one wanted steak but settled for hamburger, one wanted a Cadillac but settled for a Chevrolet — and generally a used model. Being jilted by a woman, getting fired from a job, not getting a vacation, those were typical problems. Basically, instead of nuclear war or blacklisting, our conflicts revolved around venial sins, or just plain everyday irritations.

Take guys, for example. In general, they got along well, and sought each other's company. Look at all those car clubs; just guys, no women. But sometimes guys could create conflict on their own, simply because they were, well, guys. The result of a trivial conflict might be a fistfight, or it might be something like two bantam roosters, crowing, clawing the dirt, ruffling feathers.

Take, for example, the evening three young guys went to a drive-in theater. It was a perfect example of male bonding. They lived in the same neighborhood, had known each other for years, and ran around together. They liked cars and chasing girls — about the only things for young guys back then. Three guys, on a beautiful evening, and they didn't even argue about which movie they wanted to see.

Larry owned the car, a 1939 Mercury four-door sedan, black, lowered in back, with dual pipes. It was a nice car, and of course the rest of the gang was envious. Larry had dropped out of high school almost as soon as he had arrived, and had gone to work in a furniture factory, which was why he was able to afford such a nice car. I toyed with the idea of dropping out, getting a job, getting a decent car. It was a monumental decision, but an easy one; a guy just never went back to school. Several of my friends dropped out, and no one came looking for them. For whatever reasons, I hung on.

I got a call from Larry after dinner; he and Buzz were going to the 82nd Street Drive-In Theater and he wondered if I wanted to go. Although it was a weeknight and I had school the next day I said okay. I loved movies. What's playing? I asked. Larry didn't know; he just wanted to get out of the house.

What he really wanted to do was show off the car's new interior. The curve of the roof on a 1939 Mercury sedan and the size of the windows make it difficult to see into the car. Larry came around the corner and pulled up; it wasn't until I opened the door that the full impact of that wild black and white upholstery hit me, and my heart skipped a beat. The seats, the door panels, the headliner, even the dashboard were covered in a contrasting irregular pattern.

"Wow!" I said, dazzled by that interior.

"Like it?" Larry asked. "It's genuine artificial zebra skin."

Although the furniture factory where he worked made only frames, a guy who worked there did various kinds of upholstery on the side. Zebra or leopard skin material was somewhat popular then, and one could buy seat covers or lengths of the material from ads in magazines.

"Yeah," I said, still overwhelmed. Because it was new material, the white was very white and the black very black. "Do you like it?"

"It's different," Larry said, but he set his jaw in a way that made me wonder whether he did like it.

We drove the couple of blocks to Buzz's house, and Larry honked twice. After a few minutes Buzz came out onto the porch, shouted something at his father, and slammed the door. As he approached the car his countenance shifted from an angry scowl to a grin. He opened the door and stood there, surveying the car's interior. "Sumsabitch," he said.

"It's genuine artificial zebra skin," Larry said. "I had Fred at the shop do it after work. Like it?"

Buzz grinned, climbed in the front seat and began probing his nose with his little finger, seemingly lost in thought, as if trying to decide whether he did like this wild interior.

Larry drove to the 82nd Street Drive-In Theater, where the first movie, *Gentle Persuasion*, would start as soon as it got dark. While we waited we talked about girls we knew or wanted to know, and cars. I wanted to get mine running. Larry wanted something better. Older, we would have had a couple of beers as we waited, but we didn't even have a soda pop. But it was pleasant to sit in the Merc's confines, away from parents, sharing ideas and opinions, feeling a growing sense of maturity. Even after twilight, even after the cars' spotlights stopped playing chase on the screen, even after the movie started, the talk continued.

Then something strange happened. Light from the movie reflected back, emphasizing the pattern of the zebra skin. As the scenes on the screen shifted, so did the light and dark patterns within. It was like walking through a forest at dawn, trees outlined against the sky. Perhaps because the material was so new the contrast between black and white was so emphatic, even distracting; it was like standing beside a guy wearing a loud shirt. It became harder to look at the film as the pattern on the dashboard carried the eye there. My eyelids began to flutter. This could have been a communist brain washing technique. As the pattern hit my eye, buzzed in my brain, I felt a growing sense of irritation.

Apparently Larry and Buzz felt it too, because a tension grew between them. While my gaze had jumped from the screen to the dashboard and back, and as my brain began to hum, something had been said. Something about a girl, or about the zebra skin interior or whatever, but as I blinked and looked sideways at Larry I saw that his jaw was set. Buzz was miffed too.

There was irony in the air, although I never used a word like that then and probably didn't know what it meant. The irony was that two of the three guys in the car were angry, while the movie *Gentle Persuasion*, was about a Quaker family in the old west who sought peace and ignored the jibes and taunts thrown at them because of their religious beliefs. The film was based on a book written by Jessamyn West, a cousin of ex-President Richard Nixon, and like him, a Quaker. Gary Cooper played the part of the tolerant, long-suffering father, who finally has enough and fights back. Come to think about it, that idea characterized our political thought during the 1950s and later, so perhaps something so simple as an entertainment film and zebra skin upholstery were springboards to something bigger, such as communist conspiracies, blacklists, nuclear weapons, the Cold War, segregation, fluoride added to the water and a plethora of other things.

I became aware of Buzz, on my right, picking his nose and saying, "Damn, it's a jungle in here." Maybe he asked how many zebras it took to get the hides used in the car. I blinked, closed my eyes and looked up; the headliner swirled back and forth before me; when I closed my eyes again I could still see the wild pattern. I was barely aware that Larry had started the engine, but I felt the gearshift move between my legs when he put it in low; as I turned I saw his jaw was set, his head tilted. The car shot forward and the speaker cord snapped. Gravel shot from under the rear wheels as the Merc zoomed down the aisle between cars filled with families watching the drama on the screen as this mini-drama unfolded. The exit was a gate in the fence, with a side road that led to 92nd. In the mirror I saw that we had created a huge cloud of dust that hid the screen and covered windshields.

Still in low, Larry cranked the wheel left, tires squealing as we hit the pavement and the car rolled hard to the right, almost tipping over. The Mercury was lowered in the rear with long shackles, which allowed the car to lean way over. As the car almost tipped over, Larry cranked the wheel, shifted into second, reached over and lifted the movie speaker from the door edge and threw it into the darkness. When the car leaned I was thrown into Buzz, who was thrown against the door. Larry increased the car's speed until we were flying. "Jeez, Larry," Buzz said, gripping the lower edge of the dashboard, "slow down!" Larry, jaw set, kept his foot planted. That heavy Merc was fast; at this rate we'd be doing 100 when we got to the flashing light at Foster!

Past the inter-urban tracks the houses began, and with them house lights and streetlights. As we came out of the darkness I again became aware of the zebra pattern dancing before my eyes. Flashes entered my brain. Car lights came from some direction, illuminating the headliner. The black was a negative, melding in the background, while the white shot out with alarming whiteness. As Larry drove faster the cadence of black, white, black, white increased. My head reeled, eyes burned, I lost my sense of perspective. The vision was like a strobe light on the dashboard.

That's when Buzz said again, "Jeez, Larry, slow down!" Suddenly I realized that Larry had fallen victim to the spell of the zebra skin visual cacophony. Perhaps his mind was on automatic pilot, and he'd keep speeding toward disaster. But shortly before Woodstock Larry let up on the gas and braked hard; the brakes on the Merc must have been better than most because the car slowed considerably, but we were still doing at least 35 when we breezed through the stop sign at Woodstock. Larry shifted into second, using compression to slow the car. Black, white, red, black, the insane color combination assaulted my eyes and brain.

As we entered the intersection at speed, Buzz hit the door handle, threw the door open and jumped out. His feet hit the pavement and momentum thrust him forward; he seemed to be moving faster than the car, his legs a blur, his feet taking gigantic steps, and for a second he actually passed the car, then dropped back. He was still upright as we went past and a block later slowed down. My brain wouldn't slow down however; it was running full speed, synapses open, a monochromatic visual of the Chinese water torture which a bigger kid had once given me, sitting on my chest, tapping a knuckle against my forehead until it seemed he had worn a hole in my skull. Russians, Red Chinese, angry teachers, I was ready to spill my guts.

Odd Balls

People in the Fifties were as smart or as foolish as they are today. In terms of building cars, I think they were more innovative, using whatever they could find or afford, and therefore, they took more chances. Sometimes things worked out; but sometimes the result was a goofy car indeed.

Back then I had a couple close pals, Jack and Jerry, who were twins and lots of fun. Most of their waking hours were spent meeting girls. They also had the ability to find cherry cars, which were a means of meeting girls and, of course, taking them somewhere. I remember an Oldsmobile roadster, about a 1930 model, with varnished wooden spoke wheels and a small golf bag door in the quarter-panel. Then there was a super-nice 1946 Ford four door, only seven years old, Folkstone Gray with an abundance of red trim. By 1955 they owned a tomato red 1950 Mercury convertible with dual pipes; we had lots of fun in that car as we turned 21. What links these cars in my mind was that they were all beautiful machines when purchased, and soon began to go downhill.

In high school they bought a 1934 Lafayette tudor sedan: beautiful body, perfect interior, excellent engine and running gear. I suspect it must have been garaged all during World War II. It was a swell car, and good transportation for a couple of high school kids. It resembled a 1934 Ford, but it was a Lafayette, and that was the problem. They took a lot of ribbing from their peers, including those who did not even own a car!

Jack and Jerry decided to correct the problem. They removed those perfect front fenders and running boards, and built brackets to mount the stock headlights to the frame. It looked better, they thought, but it was still pretty tall. Then one Saturday they unbolted the U-bolts on the semi-elliptic front springs, removed the axle and replaced it on top of the springs, which lowered the front end at least 4 inches. With just those simple changes, and without spending any money, they turned that primo original Lafayette into a hot rod.

They turned the intake and exhaust manifolds over to a friend who took a welding class at a technical high school. He split the exhaust manifold in two, welded a plate on each open end, then welded an outlet with a flange on each section. On the intake manifold he blocked off the stock carburetor mount, then cut into the manifold ahead and behind it. Then he welded on the uprights with a plate that matched the base of the original carburetor.

That Lafayette straight six flathead now had two carbs and two exhaust pipes. To display these changes, Jack and Jerry removed the hood, so the sedan was essentially stripped in front. It was still a Lafayette, but now it rapped through the gears, and it actually seemed to go faster. However, the pipes had exhaust leaks, so the exhaust combined wheezes and flutters with the rap. The reworked intake manifold had vacuum leaks, so the engine ran oddly, especially at low speeds. It seemed to perform best under full acceleration, which was okay with Jack and Jerry. When the guy next to them at a stoplight saw that odd-ball Lafayette with dual carbs, he just naturally wanted to race!

My memory fails me as I try to remember whether that Lafayette ever won a race. I can't believe that fairly heavy sedan with a reworked six could beat even a stock Ford V-8, but Jack and Jerry tried. I was not present for the car's last race, but as I recall the boys were racing some guy in a roadster when they lost control—that front end was kind of goofy after they moved the axle over the springs—and sideswiped a telephone pole. Only the Lafayette was hurt, and Jack and Jerry stepped up to a 1938 Ford tudor, a primo car that had gone all the way downhill by the time I bought it from them.

INCIDENT

Perhaps that's the wrong title, since an incident is a small event, even trivial. Perhaps this piece should be called, "The Day I Could Have Died." That's the way I view it today, although when it happened it was an incident, just one of the crazy things that happened every day when I was growing up. And not just to me — stuff happened to most of my car buddies, whether it was a busted transmission or a speeding ticket or a pregnant girl friend or worse. We were all crazy.

There is a place in Portland where three major streets intersect in a confusion of traffic lights. The city has declared it the worst intersection, and it was not much better 50 years ago, when the traffic was reasonable. Recently I was standing in a parking lot, once the site of a notable drive-in restaurant, looking at that intersection and I had a revelation about something that had happened there, something that seems important but that I had totally forgot.

From 1953 to 1955 I worked in a garage located about half a mile from where I was standing. I remembered that one day, shortly before closing, I had to make a parts run to pick up something small, such as a set of points or a carburetor repair kit. I figured, why take the truck, I'll just run down on my cycle. I had a gorgeous 1951 BSA Gold Star, and I was always looking for a reason to ride it.

Next to the garage was a service station where I sometimes worked, and the kid who was working there that day had recently come up from California on a Triumph Thunderbird. I can't remember the details, but for some reason I rode his bike to the store. Did he urge me? Did I ask? That's odd, since I had grown wary of jumping on strange bikes; every one was different. I learned that lesson when I tried out a Matchless twin that a neighborhood kid was trying to sell. It was an original cycle with all road equipment and appeared to be in nice shape. I cruised on the side streets until I came to a T intersection, and I found that the bike had no brakes! Nothing! There wasn't time to kick it down a couple gears! In those days in my neighborhood there were no curbs or sidewalks, which was a good thing because I shot right over where they would have been, through a yard, across a driveway through another yard and back out on the street! I slowly rode it to the owner's house and parked it.

Maybe I had not learned a lesson, because I got on that Thunderbird and everything was different. The handlebars were a foot wider than I was used to, and that 40-inch twin had a different kind of power than my 30.50 single. The biggest difference was the foot shift; my BSA was up for low, then down three times, and the Triumph was the exact opposite. I moved into traffic which, since it was nearly five o'clock, was beginning to pick up, got through that bad intersection and got to the Stevens Company where I picked up the part and headed back.

I went a short block to Burnside and, still in low, turned right, staying in the outside lane. That Thunderbird had lots of torque and long gears, and I shifted up, into second, and moved up the hill. I wanted to turn left on Sandy, which meant I had to get in a left turn lane pronto. I decided I could rip ahead of traffic and make a fairly illegal left turn, so I cranked on the throttle and that big Triumph responded.

Everything might've been okay, but in the heat of the moment I did a dumb thing. I was moving quickly, and from habit I shifted downward, which put that Triumph back in first gear! Of course at that same moment I grabbed a handful of throttle. That bike leaped forward, engine screaming, the front wheel lifted a considerable distance and I thought I was going over backwards. I felt a sense of stupidity and helplessness which I've since experienced in various situations, but in this one I could have been killed. I figured either the bike would go over backwards or the engine would blow or I'd run into that turkey ahead of me. I think I was airborne clear through the intersection and I had plenty of time — probably two seconds — to consider how hard that pavement was. Perhaps I visualized a bloody spot on the asphalt. In those days no one wore a crash helmet.

I came down, turned left, rode carefully back to the station and returned the bike. Neither it nor I got hurt, which is why this was an incident rather than a tragedy. It's a story with a happy ending. But, looking back, I realize how young, how invincible, invulnerable, how daring we were, and how little good sense we had. Okay, I'll just speak for myself: when I consider things I did as a teenager I question my judgment and lack of maturity. I think that until I was 21 I should not have had a sharp knife, a firearm, any amount of money over $20 or a girlfriend. Especially, I should not have had a motorcycle. But I'm glad I did.

THE MILD CUSTOM

The custom car was a phenomenon of the Fifties. Customs were extremely rare before 1950, and they suddenly disappeared with the advent of the muscle cars of the 1960s. Their popularity grew with the styling trends of the 1950s — the early Chevys, Fords and Mercs of that decade begged to be customized, to have a Merc cavity filled with a floating bar grille, to have the curved GM fenders opened to an air scoop. Their fenders invited all kinds of neat taillight swaps. And if those cars were the favorites, there were all the other makes and models that contributed taillights, grille pieces and scoop teeth.

I had several mild customs during the Fifties— most notably one that was really nice and one that was a dog (hey, not everything that happened in those days was great!) — and thinking about them I'm suddenly struck by two things. One: there were hundreds of mild to wild customs around, but none of us had any money — how'd we do it? Two: between 1950 and 1962 there were roughly a dozen magazines devoted to customs!

These days you need a pocket of the green stuff before a metal artist will begin to beat on a panel, and there isn't one magazine devoted to customs. But that has not stopped the renaissance that is happening among the customizers. Custom cars are booming — on both coasts, but especially in the Midwest. Some of the guys are old cats who had a custom or dreamed of having a custom — back in the Fifties. Some are ex-go fast boys who got tired of going fast and decided to do some slow cruising. Some are young guys who found insurance too steep on a Corvette, or found the family too big for a roadster — or who simply liked the idea of taking an ordinary old car and making it look different. And better, in my opinion. You can restore a '40 Merc, but you have to drop it front and rear to make it look good!

Albert Drake's '47 Ford coupe was nosed and decked, had the top bar off the grill, and dual spotlights.

The main body for the custom guys is the Kustom Kemps of America (KKOA). Recently it held a national meet in Holland, Michigan, and all kinds of neat stuff turned up. The cars ranged from mild to wild, from the popular makes to the obscure, from traditional to weird. There were more chopped '49-'51 Mercs than anyone could have dreamed might exist, and the quality of the cars overall was far higher than what I remember from the good old days. Although the temperature and the humidity were over 100°, these guys were really kool!

X-51

You can't go home again, said Thomas Wolfe, but that doesn't keep us from trying. We return to familiar ground to see the old shake shop, the tavern where we drank the first beer, the gas station where we hung out Saturday evenings, the local theater, the house in which we grew up — even a road, a tree, a bit of sidewalk, something from the past to which we can return and thus confirm that the past is not an illusion.

Which is why I found myself walking across the parking lot at the Memorial Coliseum, on my way, along with thousands of other people, to see a car show called The World of Wheels. The advertising had promised that this year's show would feature hot rods and customized cars from the past.

I wanted to see those old cars, the leaded, lowered, scalloped and chromed cars I had grown up with. They had represented mechanical perfection, ideal examples of automotive artistry, which, like the tableau on Keat's urn, the rest of us were forced to pursue. With the persistence of memory, they had become more beautiful, more dazzling, more important, not only for themselves, but for the time, the world, the way of life they represented.

It's almost impossible to explain to others why one would think that such a quest for the past, or how the past could possibly come alive at a car show, so I went alone. A simple explanation can be chalked up to nostalgia; a dopey affection for times gone; it's not unlike listening to The Golden Age of Radio or viewing old films or collecting Little Orphan Annie Ovaltine Mugs.

To explain an obsession is more difficult.

Fifty-five years ago, half the cars in Portland were modified — nosed and decked, body seams filled, fender skirts, dual pipes, lowered to within inches of the ground — or so it seemed to me, growing up here, a wild-eyed kid always on the alert for an interesting set of wheels. On a Saturday night, if you stood outside the old Penny Arcade, you'd see a traffic jam of the finest cars found anywhere; they rolled up Broadway, dual exhausts rumbling, turned at the Arcade, then down Sixth to Burnside and up Broadway again. They cruised the drive-ins-from The Speck to Flanagan's to Merhar's to Jim Dandy to the Tik-Tok, an endless circle which symbolized the decade.

On a Sunday afternoon you might see one or two of the cars parked at a neighborhood gas station, their owners moving around them, touching up the chrome with a cloth, attending to some minor repair while you stood respectfully by, waiting for just the right moment to make a comment or ask an informed question, to be a part of what was happening. Later, that night, when you were supposed to be asleep, you might lie in bed listening to the radio, the music of Little Richard, Lavern Baker, or a young Elvis Presley, thinking about those cars and the one you would own someday. The longing for adulthood and mobility, the juices of puberty, not to mention the girls down the street — mix these elements together and you've got a heady mixture, a memory of mind and body that's not easily exorcised even after 50 years.

I left the parking lot, filled with German, Japanese and American Uni-cars, each a clone of the other, and entered the Coliseum, yearning for the days when cars had an identity. Inside the building, the display area was filled with flashy show versions of the cars in the parking lot: Volkswagens with flared fenders, muscle cars with scoops and big rubber, vans with elaborate murals. There were molded fiberglass Model T hot rod replicas, all alike, one distinguished only by the roses painted on its starter!

Impatiently I made my way to the section set aside for cars from the past. There I saw a sharp '32 Ford five window with a hot flathead, and a lowered 1950 Mercury from California. They were classics all right, but I soon discovered that they had both been built the year before,

In 1957 the X-51 appeared on *High Time,* an early show for teens in Portland, Oregon (Pete Sukalac photograph).

to capitalize on the nostalgia kick, an off-shoot of the cars in "Happy Days" and "American Graffiti." They wanted to show what the 1950s were like to an audience that for the most part had not been born then. Fine. But I was looking for something more.

Then I saw it. Low, bright red, with elaborate fins—my heart did a small flip as I recognized it: The X-51, a radically transformed 1951 Ford coupe built in the mid Fifties by Ron Courtney, a McMinnville bodyman. The X-5I: the name suggested flight, an experimental rocket. I was amazed by the coupe's pristine condition, as if it had existed in a state of grace during the past 25 years. It was *exactly* like the version that lived in memory. The bright red paint unsullied by parking lot encounters, the red and white leather interior uncreased, the chrome flawless.

How had it not changed, I wondered, thinking of all that had happened since the first time I had seen it. It had been a simpler world in many ways, a world where a car, and especially a custom or hot rod, seemed to be not only interesting but of major importance.

I first saw the X-51 in 1957 at the Portland Roadster Show—the second annual show, and the first to be held at the Gresham Fairgrounds. I was 22 and for seven years had been working on my own car, a Model A V-8 which was on display. Because I'd brought it in early, I had time to look around before the show was open to the public.

Of the plethora of street and competition cars in the greater Portland area, the cars being shown were the *creme de la creme:* Don Fancher's Ardun dragster, Bill Peterson's red full fendered '32 roadster, Bob Knowles' blue '32 highboy roadster. Geno Ames' white '32 roadster from Spokane, and some 50 other chromed, bobbed, chopped and channeled machines. Also on display was the famous *Rod and Custom* magazine "Dream Truck," a chopped, channeled and sectioned 1950 Chevrolet truck built by Los Angeles' George Barris, King of the Kustomizers.

Into the midst of this pre-show activity came Courtney's X-51—it was driven, mind you, not pulled on a trailer — as if it were immune to the dangers of traffic, as if it were simply everyday transportation. People quit waxing fenders, spreading angel hair and arranging mirrors to watch the X-51 as it backed into its designated area. The car was a show stopper, even before the show began.

What Courtney had done to attract so much attention was to build an aesthetically pleasing custom, a more unusual accomplishment than one might expect. Most customs were built on a hit-or-miss basis, the owner's plans fluctuating with the amount of money he had in hand. Courtney had actually *designed* his radical car. He knew at the onset what he wanted the car to look like and he took two years realizing his dream.

What set the car apart from the other popular customs of the day was that it seemed sleek and light, not the usual "lead sled." Its roof was standard height and it rode regulation distance off the ground. The car was relatively practical. This was in marked contrast to other radical customs whose roofs were sometimes chopped to such an extent that the front windshield became a large slit, and which rode two or three inches off the ground. At least one car had casters mounted on the rear bumper to help it in and out of driveways.

The X-51 was so aesthetically pleasing, so well-proportioned, that it might have been mistaken for a factory prototype, a five-passenger Thunderbird perhaps or even a limited production Ferrari coupe.

To achieve the X-51's streamlined look, Courtney had sectioned the car, removed a five-inch section from the car all the way around, an extremely difficult task to do well. Refusing to rely on a mélange of factory parts as most customizers did, Courtney made his own grille and fitted it into an opening shaped from tubing and sheet metal. He also made his own taillight lenses, and the small scoops on the back fenders. There was hardly an inch of the car that had not been meticulously cut apart and reassembled to create the subtle changes that would complement his total design.

While the five-inch section job was the most difficult alteration, the rear fins were the most obvious. Fins symbolized the Fifties; they got bigger and bigger each year until some Detroit models seemed like cartoon cars—and the fins on the X-51 were the biggest and most exotic fins anyone had ever seen on a custom.

The car was the smash hit of the show, fins and all, and it was declared the sweepstakes winner. Courtney took home a trophy which stood a foot taller than the X-51. He showed the car in Seattle where it also took top honors, and at the same two shows again in 1958. It was a big hit wherever it went.

When the X-51 was featured on the cover of the October 1958 issue of *Hot Rod Magazine*, their caption suggested that the car could be a view of the future.

Now, 50 years later, I stood looking at the X-51 and wondering how it had lasted.

Custom cars do not endure. They represent years of work, they enjoy a brief moment of perfection, and then the paint, up to a quarter of an inch thick, begins to crack, lead pops out of old holes, and seams begin to separate. Normal bumpers override lowered bumpers, negating a blacked-out deck lid or custom grill. The fate of the exotic machine follows a typical pattern: the original builder labors to maintain the car, then finally sells it to someone who does not.

The X-51 fit this pattern, and would have been rendered into scrap iron except for two people, both of whom dreamed of turning back the clock and making the legendary X-51 perfect again. The car represented something important to them — important enough that one man would keep the car for 17 years with the dream of restoring it and the other would spend a year of his life obsessively searching for it. The difference was that one of them had the resources to do this—but the other man had the car.

It was 1974. Fifteen years had passed since the X-51 had last been publicly seen — it had dropped out of sight, could have been wrecked, junked, been processed through Schnitzer's shredder and already returned from Japan, reincarnated in the form of a new Datsun or Toyota.

Enter Portland grocer and produce distributor John Corno. Over the years Corno has built more award winning hot rods and customs than you can shake a long stick at. An avid collector as well, he's had to build numerous garages just to house them. The cars he's had constructed are prime examples of the tradition of Northwest rod building, cars that are imaginative, tasteful and well crafted. He has an obsession with fine machinery and he can't stand shoddy workmanship. People still talk about the Corno-Meeks' rear engined street roadster, a car that set California car builders on their ears almost 10 years ago.

A born administrator, Corno's method is to establish the divisions of labor. He has the money to hire the best people to do whatever needs to be done — welding, engine work, upholstery, paint. In this way he's able to see a car from conception to finish in a matter of months, unlike most builders who spend that much time daydreaming about their project.

He, too, had been at the car shows in '57 and '58 and the X-51 had left its impression. Corno is a practical person, but like most of us he likes to think about the past, recalling the things that were good, yearning for the things that have been lost. For some time he had been looking for the X-51. In the past few months, his efforts had intensified. Friends recall him following up leads on the car, climbing around in blackberry bushes, examining shells of abandoned cars.

Eventually his efforts began to pay off. He made contact with a number of people who said, yes, the legendary X-51 did exist. It was owned by a man named Willy. But no one knew where Willy or the X-51 might be. Later Corno learned that Willy drove a cab, and after a number of calls to cab companies, the year's quest brought results: he found Willy but Willy didn't want to sell. He'd bought the car from a used car lot on Union Avenue right after Courtney had sold it in 1959; he'd owned the X-51 for 17 years, and he intended to restore the car to the grandeur it had once known. There was a minor obstacle, money, and as soon as that problem was solved he'd have the X-51 in show condition again.

Corno continued to call Willy, offering cash for the car, trying to wear him down, but he got nowhere. Finally, weeks later, he got permission to *look* at the car.

As Corno recalls it, he drove to a garage near Franklin High one Saturday morning, arriving before Willy, and knocked on the door. The house and garage belonged to Willy's ex-wife, who refused to open the door to Corno's' knocks. When he identified himself as a friend of Willy's, she threatened to call the police; when he said he simply wanted to look at the car in the garage, she said she didn't want to hear about that damned car!

Corno pleaded with the ex-wife as he had with Willy, urging her to simply let him *see* the car. A long silence, and then the sound of chain locks being released, a chair being pulled away from where it had been propped against the door knob. A small girl opened the door a crack and handed him a key to the garage. He opened the garage door, and there it was. He felt the thrill of excitement known to prospectors who hit a mother lode, climbers who ascend to the peak. His excitement at finding the car caused him to gloss over its flaws. It didn't look too bad — the Fiesta Red paint had faded to a dull pink, the deck lid was smashed in, the right fin drooped a bit — a little bodywork and paint, he thought, and the X-51 would be as he remembered it.

As he squeezed between the car and the wall he noticed that the X-51 lacked tires and wheels; it was sitting on blocks. He glanced inside, then did a double-take: there was *mold* growing on the upholstery and around the windows! He looked up, where light came through a three-foot hole in the garage roof. A tree had fallen on the garage during the Columbus Day storm in 1962. He marveled that the car hadn't been flattened — one of several times it might have been destroyed — but it had been dented several places, and it had been subjected to 12 years' abuse by the elements. Oregon rain had poured through that hole, soaking the car, keeping it perpetually damp.

But Corno was excited now. He continued to call Willy, again offering cash, telling Willy that their goals were the same, to see the X-51 in show condition. Finally, Willy said he'd sell. The price was $1500. Corno said it was a deal.

Corno recalls the negotiations:

After they had agreed on a price, but before Corno could pick up the X-51, he got a call from Willy. "I can't sell it for $1500," he said. Corno said, "Well, Willy, you know I'm all set to come up there to get the car. What're you telling me?" Willy said, "I've got to have more than that." It's hard to know whether Willy wanted more money or if he really wanted to keep the X-51; parting with it must have been like parting with a leg. "How much more?" Corno asked. Willy said he had decided the X-51 was worth $2000. That was more than Corno had wanted to pay, but if there was ever any doubt in his mind about how badly he wanted the X-51, there was none now. Corno agreed.

When Corno arrived at the garage where the car was stored, Willy was waiting for him. "I've thought it over," Willy said, "and, I've got to have $2500 for the car." Corno had $3000 in his pocket. "OK, that's fine with me," he said. Willy balked, wavered, uttered a single word, "No—." "That's it!" Corno said, and started counting out money, a hundred dollars at a time, until he had a stack totaling $2500. "If you want it," Corno said, "pick it up; if you don't, I'm leaving."

Willy hesitated, thinking of a 17-year-old dream he had nursed through good times and bad. Finally he picked up the money.

Willy said he wanted to help Corno with the reconstruction of the X-5l, he knew where a lot of the missing parts could be found, he wanted to have a say in how the car was rebuilt, he wanted to be a *partner!* Corno agreed, but the implied partnership didn't work out. The two men operated at very different speeds, or so it seemed. Willy had let the car sit for 15 years; within two weeks Corno had the car apart and was coordinating the reconstruction.

He soon realized how much needed to be done to restore the X-51. He said recently, "I didn't realize the car was in that bad of shape, and if I would have realized the sonofabitch was that bad I wouldn't have taken on the project."

Willy, attached to the car but in need of money, had sold not only the McCullough supercharger and intake manifold but the exhaust manifolds, the generator, the water pump, the tires and wheels; he'd even sold the 1955 Chevrolet radio and the rear view mirror. Other parts had been lost or damaged: the chrome moldings had been removed, all the screws were missing: when the water pump had been removed, the radiator had been sculpted with a ballpeen hammer.

Corno contacted Courtney who came over and took a look at the long-lost X-51. To Corno's surprise, Courtney was only vaguely interested in the car and not at all interested in working on it.

"You know," he said, "I never did like this car. It represented a very unhappy time in my life." Courtney had, however, seen the car since he'd sold it. Only a few months after Willy had bought the car he'd had a wreck with it: the X-51 went over a small embankment and landed on its side on a double set of railroad tracks. He had difficulty finding a bodyman who would tackle the repair job and so he returned the car to Courtney who replaced the right side door, rebuilt the fin, and straightened the bent sheet metal.

The X-5l was made right again, but that wreck foreshadowed the inevitable. Willy seemed to have a love-hate relationship with the car. Eventually a large quarter window was knocked out, and an attempt to push the car caved in the trunk lid.

The car was driven in this condition, like a duck dragging a broken wing. When Willy recognized that the dream was going sour he put the X-51 in the garage, where it sat for the next fifteen years while Willy planned, plotted and dreamed.

What Corno had actually bought, he soon discovered, was the history of the car and some of its remaining metal. Virtually everything besides the sectioned body shell and the front suspension had to be replaced or rebuilt. The water-saturated fiberglass was torn off in chunks, another engine and running gear substituted, the window glass, interior, and wiring completely redone. Resurrecting the X-51 meant rebuilding it from top to bottom. The only thing left untouched was a small dent in the tirewell inside the trunk.

Corno hired the area's best craftsmen to do the job. Stan Jones was eager to do the upholstery work because he'd done the original work 25 years before. Gary Crisp and Harold Walton wanted to do the paint, and bodywork because they too remembered the car from the Fifties. David Kane built and installed the engine, Dave Dohenick and Vern White rebuilt the car's running gear and suspension. New trim and bumper parts were fabricated by Gilbertson Machine.

Only a few months after Corno had purchased the X-51, it was once again ready for the show circuit. But almost 20 years had passed and it would be seen by an audience which for the most part had not been born when Courtney had built the car. To illustrate the radical changes that had been required to create the X-51, Corno showed it along with a stock 1951 Ford coupe, a plain-jane model, stock height, small hubcaps, and black tires; the contrast was vivid.

A sign beside the car minimized John Corno's involvement in the X-51; he gave full credit to the people who had restored the car, and in large letters identified the X-51 as "The old custom of Ron Courtney..."

Willy's name was nowhere to be seen.

It's not clear whether Willy came to see the car or what he would have thought about it if he had. In a sense the display *did* show the changes the car had gone through, but there was much more that was hidden away, like the dreams and longings that were imbedded in its metal—an answer to the question of how anyone could ever be attached to a car.

In the view of some, Willy had nearly destroyed a legend. But a car out on Union Avenue is not exactly a gateway to historic preservation, and given the nature of an automobile's life, especially a car as fragile as the X-51, you might as easily say that Willy saved the car as best he could.

THE XM-800 DREAM CAR

Three years ago, when Dan Brooks ventured behind a barn near Manchester, Michigan, he found what he at first thought was a 1950s custom lead sled. It had hooded headlights, deeply skirted front fenders, a Dagmar front bumper, dual exhausts that exited through pods in the rear bumper. These were all typical custom styling touches of the period. It also had an unattractive grille that was "Obviously homemade." When the car was uncovered for a closer look he could see the body was made entirely of fiberglass and that it was beginning to "craze" all over. He knew that the car would require a lot of work, and yet he was still interested. He made the farmer an offer that was accepted and the XM-800 was his.

Over the years the car had sunk down to its rocker panels in "barn-mire," but when he and the farmer pulled it out with a tractor the tires were still inflated! They then noticed heavy steel rails bolted to the car's X-member. Since this wasn't usually done to custom cars of the 1950s, Dan began to wonder just what he had bought.

Research showed that he had become the owner of a genuine 1950s dream car—the Mercury XM-800 built by Ford Motor Company in 1954 as a styling prototype. The car was built on a 1954 Mercury chassis that had been lengthened to a 119-inch wheelbase. Overall the car measures 207 inches in length, and is 55½ inches tall. It has a stock 312 cubic inch V-8, rated at 255 hp, and a Merc-O-Matic transmission. Built at a time when power accessories were becoming popular, the XM-800 is loaded with them including power steering and brakes, power

Top: The XM-800 Dream Car was essentially complete but lacked grille bars and three of the special hubcaps. *Bottom:* The XM-800 Dream Car.

seats, and power windows front and rear, each with its own console. Unlike many prototypes, the XM-800 was fully operable and could be driven on the street.

The XM-800, as was the case with most dream cars, had an emphasis on styling rather than extreme engine or chassis developments. The body is made of fiberglass, a new material in 1954, and was hand laminated. The body panels are straight and solid, and the doors, hood, and trunk still fit tightly.

Fiberglass allowed the designers to mold and sculpt the body more easily than it would have been to do the same things in metal, and there were several places where they took advantage of it. The hood was "pancaked" below the line of the front fenders and it has a wide functional scoop. On each side the fenders cant forward and the headlights are deeply recessed. The front wheel openings have been minimized by the strong molding that extends back from the front bumper. The concave grille is simple and uses small bars within the spaces divided by sheet metal. The rear of the car is reminiscent of some of the old Studebakers with a rectangular "grille" made of anodized aluminum surrounded by one of the largest bumper overriders I've ever seen. The rear fenders have short fins along the upper edge tapering off above a pair of large taillights. The bumper is cleanly designed with, as we mentioned previously, the exhaust pipes exiting through pods on each end. Finishing off the rear is the radio antenna that, though stylishly raked, is mounted in the middle of the trunklid.

Inside, unlike most cars of that period, the XM-800 has red warning lights instead of gauges (except for a tachometer which is in itself unusual), and bucket seats. This was years before Pontiac first mounted a pair of those in a Grand Prix.

The car still has its original paint, a pearlescent white on the lower body, and a pearlescent bronze on the roof. This same color combination was also used in the car's interior.

What about those heavy steel rails that were bolted to the frame? They are part of a turntable that allowed the car to rotate when it was on display. In 1954 Ford took the XM-800 and another prototype, the Ford X-100 (a car that was a mixture of Turnpike Cruiser and four passenger Thunderbird) on a tour of the U.S. The reason for building the cars was to experiment with new designs, and the tour was organized to test the public's reaction to them.

Both cars generated a great deal of excitement. The 1950s were heady times for car builders and buyers, with body changes and engine developments changing rapidly. The factory dream cars did not seem light years away, but rather, they were right around the corner. *Motor Trend*, for example, praised the car saying that "The rakish lines of the XM-800 are highlighted by the futuristic grille, forward slanting corner posts, and reverse-angled rear end." Of course not everyone liked everything about the car. Some critics disliked the grille treatment, and *Motor* (a British publication) disliked the entire car, describing it as "a sharply contoured, overhung monster which seems to be Ford's nightmare answer to General Motor's Dream Cars."

Some of the styling features of the XM-800 were found on Mercurys and Lincolns in the following years. Bolt-on versions of the XM-800's headlight hoods were found on the 1955–56 Mercury models, and they also featured a vaguely similar taillight design. The ribbed chrome piece behind the side window resembles one found on the 1956 Mercury Phaeton four-door hardtop convertible. Overall the car looks a lot like the 1956 Lincoln, and the design of the molding around the front wheel opening was repeated in a larger size on the 1958 Lincoln.

What is really remarkable about the XM-800 is not so much that it represents an exciting period of automotive development, but that it is one of only two Ford dream cars that have survived. Other dream cars still exist today, but they aren't Fords. GM has saved most of their experimental and show cars from the 1950s, and have many currently on display. Other manufacturers sold their prototypes and show cars. For example in 1954 Packard built three examples of a promotional car called the Panther Daytona and those are now in the hands of collectors. On the other hand, Ford destroyed its cars, ostensibly for legal reasons, as it felt they couldn't warranty an experimental car, and in the event of an accident the company might be held responsible. Some Ford experimental cars have been accidentally destroyed, like the Ghia-built Ford that was on the *Andrea Doria*, along with five Ghia-built Chrysler cars, when the ship sank in 1956. But most have been destroyed by Ford. A Ford spokesman has said, "We go to great lengths to make sure they are scrapped after they have served their purpose."

Ford admits that the exception to this rule is the Ford Futura. It was sold to George Barris who painted it black, named it the Batmobile, and built five more like it. He's sold at least two of these, but still owns the original Futura. George Haviland, special assistant to William Clay Ford, has been quoted as saying that all other Ford experimental cars have been scrapped, "None have been sold to private buyers for on-the-road use, nor were any kept for museums."

How then did the XM-800 survive? Dan Brooks was able to learn that the car was given by Ford to the University of Michigan's School of Engineering in 1956, but no one seems to know how the car got to its place behind the barn, where it sat in manure for over twenty years.

Dan intends to rebuild the car, and although it is in remarkably good shape for a car that has been subjected to the elements and potential vandalism, it will still require a lot of work. The body is quite straight, but the finish will have to be stripped, and a lot of filling done. The fiberglass top is slightly bowed from the weight of snow over the years, but repairable. The car is basically complete and lacks only a radiator, grille trim, and three of the special hubcaps. A stock 1954 Mercury radiator might fit under that low hood, but the hubcaps will have to be hand made. If he were to restore the car to its original condition, even more work would be required. While it was at the U.M. School of Engineering someone changed the steering wheel and column, moved the dash knobs, and installed a padded dash.

It is a unique car, and the effort and money required to put it in first class shape would be worthwhile. Imagine pulling into your local cruise night behind the wheel of an original, genuine, 1950s dream car! Recently Dan offered the car for sale, although he would really like to keep it. Unsure of what kind of price to place on such a rare piece he asked $30,000. It didn't sell, but he did receive several substantial offers. That made it one of the fastest appreciating cars around as Dan got the car for storage charges—only $100!

Trophies

Because I haven't received a trophy for years, I'm the ideal person to talk about them. As an unbiased observer, I find current trophies to be too large, as if size alone equaled merit, and too flimsy. They seem to be made of aluminum, plastic, and other lightweight materials, all anodized or lightly plated to resemble genuine imitation gold plating. If you pick one up you find it's surprisingly light.

If that estimation sounds like sour grapes, it's not, I assure you. I love trophies—some trophies, anyway—but there have been times when I was happy not to win, because I'd have to dust that darn thing. The point of receiving a trophy is that it recognizes some level of superiority, that one has done something well. Therefore, it seems to me that the trophy ought to be superior too. It ought to be as well-made and attractive as the person, thing or event it honors.

Most trophies made during the Fifties had those qualities. Even the runner-up trophies were substantial. I won third place in street roadster class at the first Portland Roadster Show in 1956, and that trophy had a marble base and upper ring, creating a weight that secures the trophy to any shelf. It also had a lower cylinder, a loving cup and a winged female figure holding a crown; all were made of heavy brass. It's typical of trophies given during the Fifties: attractive, heavy, substantial, the kind of trophy you would put on a shelf in the front room.

In 1984 I did a feature on a car owned by Ollie Hines in Michigan. It was a 1934 Ford coupe that Hines had built in 1950, and it will forever be remembered because it had a distinctive Brewster grille. Ollie had a small house, and lots of trophies. He confided to me that the trophy he liked best by far was the one he got when he showed his coupe at the old Ford Rotunda in 1954. This was a big deal show, put on by Ford Motor Company, by invitation only, and yet the trophy seems modest at first glance. It is not large, perhaps eight inches high, and it features a brass sphere topped with a subtle fin, suggesting motion, mounted on a base made of a heavy, dark wood, perhaps walnut. The trophy has a presence stronger than that of trophies two or three times its size. I could see why Hines liked that trophy especially well. (Incidentally, the rods and customs in the Ford Rotunda show were primarily Fords; since Hines had a new Cadillac engine in his coupe the people from Ford made him keep his hood closed. A small placard said, "Powered by overhead valve engine.")

Unfortunately, not many trophies from the Fifties remain. I've talked with so many guys who said they dumped their trophies in a landfill or threw them in the scrap over the years. Usually when a hot rodder passes away, one of the first things a widow does is get rid of the trophies. I know of one case where the widow donated over a hundred old trophies to a trophy shop and got a tax deduction. If any part of those trophies got recycled, I never saw it. Even the parts, like the winged victory figure, or the cup, or those smaller American eagles, have a value. Karl and Veda Orr won many trophies competing at the So-Cal dry lakes during the Thirties and Forties, but most of them were broken when they fell from shelves during an earthquake. They told me that one well known rodder/writer desperately wanted even the broken trophies. I know that he didn't get them, but I hope someone got them after the Orrs passed away, someone who knows that the trophies should be saved.

It's better to recycle trophies than to throw them away. A long-time Oregon rodder, Ray Van Dorn, told me that he'd thrown away most of his trophies. But when he organized the first Columbia Timing Association reunion in 1991, he took the tops off his remaining trophies — usually a neat '32 style roadster at speed — and bolted them on to pieces of rare Oregon myrtle wood and added a brass plate commemorating the reunion. These new-old trophies he gave to deserving older rodders; the trophies were not only beautiful but also appropriate for this event.

I don't know anything about the economics of making trophies. Perhaps it's too expensive today to make a trophy like those made 40 years ago. And although you can easily find dozens of trophies given in recent years for bowling and golfing events, you won't find any old hot rod trophies, so forget about recycling those. But it ought to be possible to make a decent trophy using wood, a piece of metal, perhaps even a piece of clear or colored Lucite. The trophy doesn't have to be huge, but it ought to have a definite weight. It ought to be something that you could put on a shelf in the house and that you would enjoy looking at every day, and it ought to give you a warm feeling for having won it.

One of the trophies Ray Van Dorn made to commemorate the first CTA Reunion. The 1932 Ford roadster came from a trophy he won 40 years earlier.

The Zen of Nostalgia: Reflections in a Bullnose Strip

Hot Rodding 101: Back to Basics

How good was the 1932 Ford four-cylinder engine and car? Darn good, if Stan Ochs' hot rod is typical.

In addition to hundreds of miles of in-town driving, the little roadster has been driven thousands of miles on road trips, over mountains and across deserts, in all kinds of weather, and has never faltered.

Stan started out building a modern roadster with a Chevrolet V-8, automatic transmission and disc brakes—a car that would carry him long distances in relative comfort. He bought a Wescott 1932 roadster body, a reproduction '32 Ford frame, and assembled a chrome-plated front end with disc brakes.

Then he found a 1932 Ford chassis at a swap meet and his plans abruptly changed. The chassis had never been modified—it came with the original front and rear ends, mechanical brakes and a Model B four cylinder engine with an updraft Zenith carburetor.

Stan brought it home, sold the items he wouldn't use and assembled the chassis using the original steering, radiators, support rods and other parts. The car he now had in mind was the opposite of the high-tech rod he had intended.

Stan mounted the Wescott body on the frame rails. He dug out parts from his garage he'd had for years. He was building an era car, and the only criterion was that the parts had to have been available circa 1937 (of necessity, Stan decided that reproduction parts were acceptable if they conformed to the time period).

He already had a reproduction hood, grill shell and insert, parts that fit as snugly if they'd been made by Henry Ford himself, He also had 16-inch Kelsey-Hayes wheels that he powder-coated red. He mounted a set of Firestone blackwall tires on them; 5:50x16 for the front and 7:00x16 for the back.

The headlights were mounted the way hot rodders did before mass-produced headlight stands. Stan found a beat-up Model A headlight bar, cut off the center section and bolted the ends to the frame.

He could easily and understandably have fudged on the taillights and used the popular 1939 Ford lights (which actually came out in 1938), but he wanted the car to be true to the year 1937. He bought a pair of reproduction 1932 Ford tail lights—both right hand lights, without the license plate light—and made a pair of brackets from stainless angle. The lights are neat, simple and similar to what home mechanics made 60 plus years ago.

Two period pieces are the banjo steering wheel and the old four-gauge Stewart-Warner dash panel. The winged gauges, though, are readily available, as is the LeBaron-Bonney upholstery kit. These pieces combine to give the car's cockpit its old-time look.

What the car does not have is a four-bar setup, billet aluminum, chrome-plated running gear or speed equipment on the engine. Stan didn't even see the need to paint the chassis or body.

This is a car that looks amazingly like the funky, unadorned souped-up jobs of the 1930s.

Stan Ochs makes an adjustment on the original Ford Model B 4-cylinder engine.

Stan assembled the car in short time while on vacation. Late on a Thursday he got the car running and wired the lights. On Friday, he drove to the Department of Motor Vehicles and with surprising ease got it titled and licensed.

Early Saturday he threw his sleeping bag and a few other essential items in the trunk and, without even a shakedown cruise, he set out alone for the 50th Bonneville Speed Trials in Utah. The little four banger cruised at 2,000 rpm, or about 52 mph, mile after mile.

The car made the 1,800-mile trip without a glitch and rode comfortably, due to the original 1932 Ford buggy springs and four-wheel lever action shocks.

At Bonneville, it actually set a record of sorts, not for blazing on the salt, but for the number of admirers it attracted when parked with the high-buck cars in front of the Stateline Casino in Wendover.

The Slo Poks Celebrate 50 Years

The Slo Poks of Vancouver, Washington, celebrated 50 years of continuous fellowship and hot rodding fun in 2002.

Half a century is a long time. I suspect that there are only a handful of hot rod clubs in the entire nation that can claim to match that period of sustained activity. Even among those fledgling California hot rod clubs, some of which were started before World War II, there were periods of inactivity or morbidity. In most parts of the country, where rodding caught on, clubs were formed after 1954, largely, I think, because of the prodding of the new National Hot Rod Association (NHRA) which published booklets on how to form a club.

That was certainly true in the Pacific Northwest. When I joined the Road Angels during summer, 1951, there were perhaps 5 other clubs; at least 3 were formed during that same year.

I have spent too much time thinking about this subject, but I have learned while there were only a handful of clubs in the Portland, Oregon area in the early 1950's, by 1955, when the Multnomah Hot Rod Council was formed, there were 44 area clubs, 38 of which joined the council. I was astounded to learn about those numbers, and with a perverse tenacity I have pursued the subject for years and have found evidence or mention of over 100 area clubs that existed during the 1950s! But clubs formed before 1954 were rare.

I'm interested in how things got started, and I wonder why a club was formed. If it was the first club, what would be its model? Its goal? After, say, 1954 clubs were formed around issues of safety and unity, but were those early clubs simply extensions of high school social clubs, or like-minded guys gathering to enjoy their passion, like the early Christians who came together in darkened caves?

A major problem that clouds the formation of those early clubs is a lack of documentation. I've met a couple of guys who claim that their clubs were formed in the late 1940s, but when I inquired about some kind of proof like incorporation papers, a newspaper clipping, a membership card with the date, a photograph, anything, none was forthcoming. I'm not trying to prove anyone wrong, but if I put something in print, as actual history, I like to have some proof.

I have proof that the Slo Poks club has been around for 50 years. I've enjoyed the club's company for nearly 20 years; they encourage me to hang around as a designated observer and I've met and talked with several of the original members. But word of mouth is not enough and I'm happy to say that I have a couple photographs of Slo Pok cars that I took in March 1952 at the big show at the Expo Center in Portland. But the Poks do not need me, or anyone else, to justify their existence. They began meeting at Skeen's Garage at least as early as 1951. A plaque was designed by Roger Porter and Emery Strong, using, I was told, the Model T touring that appeared on the cover of *Hot Rod Magazine* in March 1950 (like the Poks, that Model T has survived the decades and is still a hot rod). Then Tom Pratt became the club's first president; he was elected, he told me "probably because the meetings were held in the basement of my mom's house."

The Slo Poks at first emphasized street rodding, but when the drag races began at Scappoose, Oregon in 1952, they were there. The club has always been active in drag racing, and in fact, during those times when street rodding declined everywhere, it was drag racing that kept the club active. Enthusiasts remember the quarter mile exploits of guys like Jack "The Bear" Coonrod, Doc Floyd, Wayne Harry, Tory Lea, Buz Peck, Nick Nicholson, et al. And I'm happy to say that all those guys are still active rodders and in Wayne Harry and Jack Coonrod's case, still active on the quarter mile. In this year's Portland Roadster Show the Slo Pok section had 38 cars! With the exception of a couple cool "rat rods," these were hi-dollar cars and the Poks could have mustered twice that many, if needed. The Slo Poks is, by any definition, a successful organization — it's active, it gets things done, the members have fun — and although I've seen the club's workings over a couple of decades I can't say how it works. There is some ingredient, more secret than McDonald's Big Mac sauce, that holds the club together. But I have some ideas. For one thing, roughly 15 of the members have known one another since grade school and high school. They, and the other members, live in the same area and run into one another outside of club activities. Since the 1950s the Slo Poks have encouraged social activities, and the club's annual bash, a picnic and sit-down banquet, involves wives and girlfriends.

Then there are clandestine activities, such as the balls out race from Vancouver to Long Beach (recently terminated) which I'm not allowed to talk about!

The most important thing is the membership. No one enters the club easily, and I'm told that the only way to exit is either by dying or by paying a huge amount of money. The secret,

I think, is that the members genuinely like and care about fellow members. If one looks at college fraternity photographs one is struck by the similarity of the people on display; guys were chosen because they looked like guys in the frat! This is not true of the Poks. There is, to use that popular catchword, a certain amount of diversity. But there is something, some old chemistry that binds these guys together, and has for 50 years. This is a club that has no rules, and yet for 22 years the club has staged the Ash Bash — one of the biggest and most successful events in the Northwest. The club has no meetings, but every Friday around 5:00 pm the guys gather at a different member's house for Alley Night (a traditional event that actually began in an alley!). There they eat, drink (mostly diet Pepsi these days) joke, laugh, talk, gossip, conspire, locate rod parts and plan future events. Somewhere within all that unplanned busyness is the secret glue that has bound the club together for 50 years!

STAN MOTT AND THE CYCLOPS SAGA

By the mid–1950s sports cars were dividing American drivers into two groups: horsepower vs. handling, us vs. them, macho drivers vs. tea baggers, and giving rise to several publications aimed at sports car aficionados. One fellow who was making the transition was Stan Mott, a So-Cal hot rodder who fell in love with sports cars. A big difference between Mott and most of the others is that he understands irony, and is a capable writer and artist. To have fun with people in both camps, and to make a statement about the U.S. invasion of all kinds of small cars, Mott created the Cyclops, an automotive icon.

The Cyclops was a really small car, resembling a diminished Citroën 2CV, with flat sides made from Cinzano signs, and featuring a single headlight, hence its name. The car made its debut in the March, 1957 issue of *Road & Track* in a piece entitled "Beyond Belief."

Two men, T. Tom Meshingear and Trebor Crunchcog, observe all the new Volkswagens and other small European cars on the street and smell money. They go to the Continent looking for a "cheap" car. In Italy they are introduced to the Cyclops II, which sells for $14.32 U.S. They buy a bunch of them, lash them together (they float), hook an engine to a propeller and sail the lot to America! In Los Angeles they locate a dealer, one Ernest Chumley, who is a lawnmower and Bugatti repairman. He sells a few, but it's not until people begin trading in

Stan Mott in Germany in 1962 during his 23,300-mile go-kart trip.

their VWs that Cyclops sales begin to take off. A final Mott drawing shows a city street filled with Cyclops.

What might have been the end of the story was the introduction, as interest in the car began to grow. In the April 1957 issue of *R&T* there was a letter from a reader who said he bought a Cyclops and was racing it. He'd bored it way out, to 7.8 cc, and hopped it up until it generated 0.08 hp. With a supercharger he got "a full 0.1 horsepower." On the editorial page there's a Mott drawing that shows a Cyclops II passing a Mercedes 300 SLR on the outside of a curve over a sheer drop-off. An editorial note says, "The Monte Carlo Rally organizers were so frightened by *R&T's* Cyclops II that the event was cancelled."

The May issue has several letters regarding the Cyclops, and a photograph shows a scale model resting in the palm of a hand. That almost convinced readers, but one requested that the magazine run "an actual photograph" of the Cyclops; that photograph appeared in the June issue. There were also two related letters, one from the Cyclops factory in Italy, and the other from a reader who applied some weird logic to understand the car's performance.

The point is that the Cyclops soon became "real" to the readers of *R&T*. The car appeared everywhere, including Le Mans, the East African Safari, the Nurburgring, and odd races such as the China Grand Prix! The car, as seen in Mott's drawings, was a lovable thing, the machine equivalent of Al Capp's Shmoo. It had a personality, and eventually took on a life of its own, appearing in 22 articles over a 33 year period!

The guy who had the most fun with the Cyclops was its creator, Stan Mott, who is a madcap genius. He got interested in cars in the late 1940s, in California, when he and his brother bought a 1930 Ford roadster, stripped it, shoe-horned in a 1928 Cadillac V-8 engine, then mounted a '27 T body on the chassis. That was followed by a '31 Ford roadster with a hopped-up four-barrel, then a chopped '32 Ford coupe and a chopped '34 Ford four-door sedan. The coupe ran in events at El Mirage, and Mott's first cartoon appeared in the event program in 1950.

Then Mott moved to two-wheel machines, and, as he told me, "I did social studies with the Galloping Gooses and Hell's Angels motorcycle clubs. Thus qualified, I worked as a GM car designer (I did the butt of the '58 Chevrolet) but redeemed myself by getting involved with sports cars."

The Cyclops on the "East African Safari" (*Road & Track*, June 1964). Here Crunchcog and Meshingear show their cornering technique (courtesy Stan Mott).

His life is more exciting than even that of most Cyclops drivers. He's a licensed glider pilot and ski instructor, has been a disc jockey on a Spanish FM radio station, where he broadcast as "Captain Stan" and has owned, lived on and sailed a 57-foot Turkish gaff ketch yacht throughout the Mediterranean, Caribbean, and Atlantic Ocean for 18 years. He currently lives on a boat in Germany where he is working on a book "designed to undermine political correctness and make a nuisance of myself during my golden years."

In keeping with that notion, I should mention Mott's trip of the early 1960s, which anticipated — perhaps caused — the nuttiness of that decade. During a period of three years and four months Mott drove 23,300 land miles through 28 countries on a go-kart! He fitted it with lights and road equipment to make it legal, got it licensed (in Florida) and hit the road. The adventure is recorded in the 1968 edition of the *Guinness Book of World Records*.

Young people, about to embark on an uncertain career, often ask Mott for advice. "I advise all young artists, outsiders and odd balls to follow their stars, and screw the rules," he said. "This secret formula eliminates stress, stimulates growth hormones, and leads to a long, happy, rewarding life."

His latest project is a 450-panel satirical graphic novel about sexual relations in the 21st century. Stan Mott is proof that he takes his own advice!

DAVE'S '37

There's an old maxim: "Those who can, do; those who can't, teach." Like most maxims, it has an element of truth. Dave Engemann, who teaches automotive shop classes at a vocational school in upstate Michigan, is the exception: he practices what he teaches. His pole barn is filled with cars he's built over the years. They include a 1935 Ford pickup he bought for $25 in August, 1956 when he was ten years old and a fenderless '23 T pickup he built from scratch in the early Sixties; both are powered by hopped-up flathead V-8s. He also has an all-steel '39 Ford convertible resto-rod that is excellent.

A couple years ago, feeling that Dave needed another project, some friends set him up with what he calls "a $35 blind date." It was a gutted, incomplete 1937 Ford tudor that had sat in the woods of northern Ontario since 1956. It was rusty, pitted, rain gutters gone, the driver's door had been torn off at the hinges, most of the floor had holes and the rest had been cut away and the metal below the decklid was gone. As Dave said, "On the positive side, the rear wheelwells were nice!"

Now if it were a 1937 Ford open car, it would have been worth restoring, but a common old tudor? Others might have salvaged some parts to take to a swap meet, but Dave saw a challenge here. He hauled the carcass all the way home and began the impossible. He had two goals in mind: to use up his inventory of flathead speed equipment and to see what he could built for $1000. As he put it, "I failed on both accounts." By hitting lots of smaller swap meets while building the '37, he kept coming across flathead speed parts until he's now doubled his original collection, and he spent a whopping $4000 to turn a hulk into a show-quality street rod. A third goal was to build it the way he might have back in the late Fifties — no late model parts, no aftermarket parts, no milled aluminum, no graphics. By today's building trends it's politically incorrect, but Dave thinks it's cute as a bug's ear and lots of people agree.

Dave rebuilt the stock frame, reinforcing it at strategic points with gussets. He used a '39 Ford front end and '41 Ford rear end with juice brakes, and mounted swap meet tube shocks all the way around with homemade brackets. At a swap meet he picked up a '39 Ford steering assembly, complete with banjo wheel. The newest things on the car, other than the big and little radial tires, are the '49 Merc wheels.

Top: Dave Engemann fabricated the floor, rain gutters and the section under the trunk lid that houses '46–'48 Chevy lights. Old running boards were filled and covered with black vinyl. *Bottom:* Dave Engemann painted his '37 tudor velvet green with tan wheels. He rebuilt a hopeless hulk into a clean machine using junkyard and swap meet parts — "no credit cards or 800 numbers."

The 1937 Ford V-8 uses Thickstun head covers from a boat. That cream separator is a 1939 McCullough supercharger, driven by crank pulley — a real period piece.

When it came time to tackle the body Dave had to fabricate a new floor, new body mounts and a new rear pan. He found a driver's side door complete with dents, rust and five bullet holes; as Dave said, "It matched the rest of the car perfectly!" He also replaced the rain gutters by using 5/16 steel brake line material tack welded along the drip rail line. Using a minimum of Bondo, he smoothed in the top and bottom edges until he had fashioned a gutter that closely resembled the original.

For power, Dave hauled out a 1937 Ford 21 stud flathead that he's owned since 1956! It's bored .060, has a Weber 3/4 cam with Johnson adjustable lifters, Zephyr springs, it's ported and has a Melling old style high volume oil pump. He milled the stock heads, then covered them with Thickstun covers originally designed for boat engines. He converted the ignition to a dual coil unit, then built tube headers and ran them back to glass pack mufflers.

The *pièce de resistance* is a 1939 McCullough supercharger. This unit, introduced in 1935, is a vane type centrifugal supercharger, and it turns at six times engine speed. Dave bought the blower in a box for the unheard of price of $25, and completely rebuilt it. He notes that "efficiency is very low"—factory claims to the contrary — as it puts out only three pounds of boost. He notes that it runs about the same as it did with dual carbs, and he estimates the output at around 125 hp. But it's a rare and authentic piece of Thirties speed equipment, and it really fits the car.

Celebrating the Low Buck and Beater

In 1984, at the Nats Northwest held in Salem, Oregon, I met a rodder from Idaho named Jim Lytle. Not to be confused with the guy who made famous a chopped '34 tudor powered by

Top: This '34 Ford coupe seen at a Lodi, California, run a few years ago was a beater with banged-up grille and homemade rear fenders. The racing red primer five-window was channeled, not chopped. *Bottom:* This channeled roadster seen at James Dean Run is low-buck. The glass body was made over a foam mold by the owner. The windshield frame is made from pipe.

an Allison engine, this Jim Lytle drove a '34 Dodge coupe. It was a good ride, and obviously dependable since it had made the trip across the high desert and over the Cascade mountains without problems. Jim was rightfully proud of his street rod, but he considered it more or less average, with a straight body, good paint and tires and a little chrome. Most important to him was the fact that the car was safe and dependable. Jim had a burning question to ask. How come magazines never did features on "average" rods, or even some that might fall below that mark? They always feature cars like that one, he said, pointing at Bruce Russell's Maserati-powered '32 roadster, a car that cost $125,000 to build and which sold a couple years later for $75,000.

I don't recall my answer, but I've often thought about Jim's question. Occasionally a magazine will feature a rod built on a slim budget. But from the beginning rod magazines have emphasized exceptional machines. That's because in the beginning most rods were pretty average. It was easy to buy, say, a '34 Ford coupe, pull the fenders and running boards off, and call it a hot rod. But editors wanted to show readers in South Dakota or Maine what a true California hot rod looked like, and so they chose cars that featured paint, tuck and roll interiors and hot engines. As rods evolved they got increasingly detailed, with better workmanship, and they got more expensive.

But let's face it, not everyone can, or wants to, own a show car. And that other tradition, the rod as daily driver, has continued. If you put your rod on the street with some frequency it's going to get dings and it's going to show wear. During the past 20 years, as rod runs have become increasingly popular, more people are driving their rods over longer distances. It's hard to keep a car perfect when it's put to use; many rodders are willing to settle for a driver that looks good albeit with imperfections.

Then there are the guys who either can't or won't mortgage the house to own a high-buck toy. They may, in flights of fancy, want a '32 roadster with a Maserati mill, but generally they know they're happier with what they've got. Chrome plating can wait, a new paint job someday, and machined aluminum isn't even in this dream.

Then there is the individual who has been struck by a vision of what he considers the ideal rod, or has had to work with what he could find. Maybe it's a 1937 Terraplane with a Chevy V-6, or a 1931 Durant coupe that has been made into a roadster. Whatever it is, it's different, and it stands out among the cookie-cutter rods. He might get some hoots from another rodder, but his rig goes back to the very roots of rodding, before a formula had been established or favorite models picked. Hot rodding was until fairly recently equated with ingenuity, and part of the point of building a rod was to make it unique. The reward reaped by the builder of the unusual low-buck/beater is to not see another rod like his at a major meet.

So, all you low-buck or beater builders, this one's for you!

Thanks, Tex

I was reading the Good Deals section of the *Gazette* when one really piqued my interest. It was a '25 T roadster on some kind of frame with a full-dress flathead V-8. That got me excited, but it also had a three-spring suspension and Buffalo wire wheels, things you hardly ever see anymore. The price was very affordable, but when the ad said that the car had belonged to Phil Weiand I picked up the phone. I'm no tire kicker; I wanted this buggy. I called the number, spoke with a young-sounding female and found that the car was available. However, the owner was elsewhere. I called again later the next day, and again the next day; this time a man answered. He said the car had been sold. I swallowed my disappointment, but I was still curious about the car. I knew that Phil Weiand had been paralyzed as a young man, the result of a street racing accident, and the only car I associated with him was a '27 T track roadster. How, I asked, did he know that this was Weiand's car? I've forgotten what he said, but as he talked small light bulbs began flashing in my brain. Is this Tex Smith? I asked. He allowed as how it was.

We talked for some time, but after I hung up I realized that I'd forgotten to thank him for saving my life.

It was winter, 1983. I'd gone to Oregon for Christmas and returned to Michigan, rattling around alone in the house where I'd lived with my family. Back then there had been five voices, music, homemade bread, a pot of soup on the stove and friends coming and going. The family had been like five spokes on a wheel, going out but always returning to the hub, this house. What had been unified was asunder, and I was lonely. My work helped to take my mind off of my problem, but my colleagues were no help; they were in the humanities, academics who had no sense of what it meant to be human, to be vulnerable. The weather grew colder, and the winter winds whirled. My house was built of pumice block with a flat roof, fine for California but all wrong for Michigan. The days grew darker and the walls grew colder. Every night when I came home I was reminded of Scrooge entering his house in the film version of *A Christmas Carol*— not the 1951 version with Alistair Sim, but the darker 1938 version with Reginald Owen. The house was bleak, cold and dark, filled with ghosts. A bit of distraction was a mid-weekly old car publication that I'd recently subscribed to; the new editor was LeRoi Tex Smith. Wisconsin seemed an odd place for him. I'd met Tex in 1977 at a rod run in Merced, California. I considered him a West Coast guy, as I was. I hoped that he was warmer than I was and did not feel displaced.

About the middle of January Tex offered a contest. He published an old photograph of a strange hot rod and asked the readers to identify the car, the owner, the body, engine, and top speed. This had to seem unusual to the readers who were interested in Doble Steamers and Dorts, but it was gravy for me. I'd been to El Mirage and spent years working on a book about the dry lakes, but all I had to do was recall what I'd read in a Trend Book around 1951. I knew this odd rod was a 1937 Lincoln Zephyr coupe with the top removed and a 1937 Ford truck grille added. It'd been owned by Charles Dimmitt and used a huge Cadillac V-16 that was mounted behind the driver. I knew it ran D class around 1950, but I had to guess at the speed, so I said 135 mph (another entrant, who seemed certain, said it turned 149 mph at the 1951 Bonneville Nationals). I dropped my answer in the mail right away and kept my fingers crossed.

I think two weeks passed before the issue arrived with the contest results. There were six winners, and I was happy to be one of them. The others ranged from old California rodders who'd raced at the lakes "way back when," to enthusiasts in Nebraska and Connecticut, guys who owned old iron and were hungry to talk. There seemed to be little interest in nostalgia in those days, except for guys like these. I felt connected, and their letters got me thinking about happier things. The next week Tex offered another contest, similar to the first, which I also entered. I thought about this contest for two weeks before I learned that I had not won, but by then the prize for the first contest, some car books, had arrived and I began reading them.

The contests helped take my mind off of the cold, empty rooms; by the time they were over and by the time I'd finished reading the books, the weather began to warm. Suddenly, one day it was Spring. Things looked better, and although my situation had not changed life seemed possible. I look back and think about the things that could have happened toward the middle of February, when walls and water pipes freeze, field critters die belly up in the ice, and the human condition creates an unbearable stasis.

THE PACIFIC GUNSIGHT SPECIAL

A few years ago, at the Goodguys West Coast Nationals in Pleasanton, I found myself attracted to a 1932 Ford roadster that appeared to have been built 'way back when. When I wrote a piece about several of the cars at that event, I noted that this '32 had all the right stuff: steel body, big 'n' little whites, filled shell, chrome front end and a dash full of S-W gauges. I also noted it had a stock flathead with chrome headers, the maroon paint was time-worn and the white interior and the whitewall tires had yellowed. No criticism implied; rather those places showed the patina of time.

Then I met the car's owner, Jim Palmer, who filled me in on the car's history, which is documented back to the mid–1940s, when it had been used as a work vehicle by a Chinese gardener in Menlo Park. It became a hot rod in 1946 when a young sailor named Roy "Mack" MacKinney bought it; Jim knows all the details of the car, as well as the Bay Area hot rod scene since World War II, and he told me the names of all the owners and drivers who drove it in competition. It became the Pacific Gunsight Company Special in 1952, when Leo Juri bought it, put in a very hot flathead V-8 and took it to Bonneville, where it turned 124.82 mph.

The car had four more owners over the years, and it's notable the car was always driven but, unlike so many rods, was never altered. Then in 1971, Jim Harvey replaced the flathead with a Chevrolet V-8 and drove it to Andy's Picnic that year. That's when Jim Palmer bought it, traded the Chev back for the flathead that had been in it and swore that he would keep the car as a traditional hot rod. That was not an easy promise in 1971, when most rods were being updated with fat tires, wide rear ends, huffed OHV engines and lace paint jobs!

Jim Palmer has owned the '32 for nearly 30 years. The first few years he averaged 10,000 miles per year on the car. Then he tore it apart for a rebuild and, well, with business and family obligations, ten years passed. Eventually it was rebuilt, with new paint and chrome plating. He had Paul Gommi build a 286 cid flathead using really rare items, such as a SCOT supercharger and ELCO twin-plug heads. In 1984 Jim drove the car to the Western Nationals, where he won the "Stroker McGurk" award.

The roadster was driven many miles over the next 14 years. Then, in 1998, Jim decided to restore the car to the way it was when it competed in the 1952 Bonneville trials. The plan was to have it ready for the 50th Oakland Roadster Show, just a year away. Fortunately, Jim has some very good friends, and he insists they get credit for their efforts, "The body and frame were finished and repainted by Brian Hill…. The engine was assembled by my racing partner, Neil O'Kane. The engine features the same equipment as (it) had in 1952. The wheels were built by Gary Nubback. They are chromed, 16-inch units, the same type the car had when it was first built, and when it raced in 1952. The tires are Firestone Deluxe Champions. The chrome work was done by High Lustre Plating of Hayward, CA. Tri-Valley Interiors of Pleasanton created the interior upholstery. Great pains were taken to ensure the car is as close as possible to its 1952/53 character." Jim also names Tom (Tip) Tyler, Dave Wilkerson, Kent Walton and Mike Pauselius as guys who gave a lot of time, talent and effort in seeing the car through to completion.

Working together, they got the car to the 50th Oakland show where it was awarded First Place in its class: Vintage Race Car, and also Outstanding Overall Restored Antique Vehicle. Then the car was invited to be one of a group of nine historic hot rods exhibited at the posh 1999 Pebble Beach Concours d'Elegance, a major honor. Today, Jim reports, "The car is back on the streets and roads of California." Exactly where it should be, don't you think?

Mystery

There's no mystery about where or when: I took this photograph in Merced, California, in 1977. It was at a major rod run, and we'd traveled hundreds of miles to see a bunch of street rods. It's not a mystery as to why, but a puzzle of remembering how exciting it was to see rods everywhere, in parking lots, outside restaurants, and on the street, after a winter of denial. It was like a mammoth fireworks display, celebrating true independence of spirit with explosions and starbursts in every color imaginable. That's all fairly clear.

There's no mystery as to who the lad on the far side of that roadster is either. That's my son, Moss, now six feet two, and with a pair of boys approaching the age he was in the photograph. Did I pose him there, or was he naturally interested in whatever he's looking at, some construction technique on the car or an exotic insect smashed flat on the sidewalk? I know he's there, in part, because he loves his father and wants to accommodate me on this mini-odyssey around parking lots in the hot sun, but also because he digs old cars. I think that was the year we saw Tom McMullen's '32 Ford phaeton, and Moss was fascinated by the way all functions of the car could be activated by a card inserted into a slot in the dashboard.

So, Moss and I are out looking at rods, and where are my wife and daughters? Back at the motel, I assume, probably enjoying a dip in the cool water of the swimming pool. The previous year I'd talked the family into going to both the big Lodi and Merced runs, and came prepared to camp. My wife complained, and rightfully so, about the California summer sun burning a hole through her hat and into her skull, and she was not too keen about going from a hot parking lot to a showerless campground. At Lodi, the nearest place to camp was along the Sacramento River. We ended up at a campground called Terminus, a name that filled my wife with foreboding. I was grooving on the cars I'd seen, and those I hoped to see, and also the region.

The mystery rod, my son, Moss, and in the background some high-tech rods showing 1977 trends.

I like the rural quality of the area, the dry heat, the vineyards and olive trees, the Greek and Italian names on the mailboxes. I often thought, while driving through, that this part of mid-California was a place where I could be happy. But at that particular moment the year before, as we unpacked the car, I realized that where we intended to camp was beside the levee that contained the river, and we were about 20 feet below water level. Then my wife became really upset: the ground nearby was on fire! A layer of peat slowly burned beneath the topsoil, releasing smoke and occasional sparks. I think it was at that point that my wife said that Terminus was an apt name for this place.

After that we always got a motel, so my wife could cool her heels beside the pool while I looked at cars. I was like a man possessed: I could look at rods all day and still not be sated. How I kept from exploding, from experiencing spontaneous combustion, like a character in a Gothic novel, is beyond me. I was 30 years younger then, with immense energy, at least when it came to hot rods, and I was determined to see them all and to talk to everyone who would talk to me. And since this was California I was anxious to discover an old timer, a rod or custom that I'd seen on the pages of a magazine 20 years earlier. At breakfast one morning we emerged from a Denny's and there in the parking lot was a black '32 Ford 3-window with a '40 Ford dash, an unusual touch then, and I was sure that this was an old hot rod that had been upgraded, with fenders and paint. I also looked for flathead powered rods, but there were few to be seen, and that made me wonder what was being done with all the old speed equipment I saw advertised. As a teaser, at one meet I saw a tall, black '29 roadster, fenderless, with a Rajo OHV conversion: it turned out to be a Chevy II engine with a reworked rocker arm cover.

Of course there were fewer old time rods: there was also little interest in nostalgia. Rodders were concerned with the existential now: the result was a high-buck, high-tech resto-rod, with a modern engine and drivetrain, capable of covering great distances, and affording comforts such as a soft ride, leg room, heat, music and air conditioning. New and different mag or spoke wheels were being manufactured, and guys wanted them to mount radial tires on. The reproduction industry began producing obsolete parts that had gone to the scrap yards years before; things like cowl lights, banjo wheels, gauges and grilles. As fiberglass fenders became available, fenderless rods soon looked like Uncle Daniel stockers, but with chrome plated Jag rear ends. Soon backyard builders formed mini corporations and began an assembly line that turned out stainless steel parts. All these changes created a trend that drove up the price of a nice rod considerably.

In contrast, there was this odd rod parked at the curb near a major motel, on a towbar hooked to a late model station wagon. Why any rodder would want this old rod is part of the mystery. One only has to look at the rods in the background to see the trends and the desired finished product. In the parking lot are a pair of '32 roadsters, a Victoria and a phaeton. Presumably those are all steel bodies, full-fendered, with fine paint jobs, complete with cowl lights and luggage racks.

What hope did this old rod have in this world? It was from a distant and long ago galaxy: the Washington plates had tags that read 1956, as I recall, although I suspect the car had been built years before that. It's a 1930–31 Model A roadster, an uncommon model to rod, and it's been channeled several inches, enough to require mounting the fenders at the top edge of the body. In addition, the top has been chopped several inches. It dates from a time when guys wanted their rods low, and riding comfort be damned. This rod is low for a fendered car; my boy was tall as a kid and of course he's standing on the curb, but the rod's beltline is even with his.

The mystery deepens when one considers the old time styling tricks: that homemade shell and mesh grille, the odd top, which is designed so that the tonneau cover can be used with the top raised, the welled front fenders with dual spare tires and tire covers, the hint of an odd rear bumper and taillight. The full moon hubcaps covered with old wax as a preservative, date from the mid–1950s, but the overall design suggests the car was built much earlier. It seems longer than a Model A, and I have a feeling that that body was channeled over a 1932 or later Ford frame. At first I thought the front fenders were 1930 Ford with the leading edge filled in, a style seen on a number of nice rods built in the Portland area around 1950, but then I thought they were 1932 Ford fenders, given their length and shape. Now I'm uncertain whether the fenders are from a Ford. The rear fenders a have a pronounced curve on the outboard edge. There's no doubt about the hood, which has been lengthened and is definitely homemade. I wish I knew what kind of engine it covered.

I usually made notes, but I didn't make any on this car, so the above observations are based on what I can see in the photograph. If I knew more, I've forgotten whatever it was in the past 30 years. But it's safe to say that long ago some forgotten hot rodder had a vision, and he labored long and hard, using whatever junkyard parts he could find, to build this rod. And his goal was not too different from that of the builders of those high-tech rods in the background: to be able to cruise around town and on long-distance journeys in comfort, with the benefit of a top, fenders and a couple of spare tires.

Now here's the real mystery: who built the car and when, who towed it to Merced and what happened to it? I lived in the Northwest during the 1950s and I never saw this rod on the street, at a car show or in a car magazine. It appears to have been in storage, perhaps since 1957, but where and why? And what happened to it after this 1977 Merced meet? I continued to read rod magazines for the two decades that followed, and I never saw anything that resembles this car. Perhaps it was unbodied or rebodied, the fender wells filled in, a different grille and different wheels used, but it would have to have been changed considerably to be unrecognizable. Because the car was so unfashionable, perhaps it was parted out. Or perhaps the California owner was towing the rod back to Washington where, even now, it resides in a barn or garage, waiting to be again discovered so this mystery can be solved.

A la Recherche du Temps Perdu

It was 20 years ago when, landlocked in frigid Michigan, I wrote *Street was Fun in '51*, the first book on historical hot rodding. It was my way of remaining sane; to reflect back on the cars and people I'd known 30 years earlier was a way to combat loneliness and the cold. I didn't write the book for money. In fact, there was almost no interest in hot rodding's past, and I wondered who would want to read the book.

I'm happy to say that over the past 20 years, *Street Was Fun*, has achieved something akin to a cult following. In fact, the graph line for "nostalgia" has risen sharply and is holding steady. In 1987 Don Montgomery published the first volume of four handsome books about rodding in the 1940s. Andy Southard Jr., has reached into his archives and pulled out a treasure trove of slides; the resulting books showed us some neat 1950s, 1960s, and 1970s rods and customs in color. There were other titles and authors, and all contributed to help us understand rodding's history.

A certain amount of time had to pass before anyone could discuss hot rodding history, or for many to admit that it had a history. A benefit of this realization is that older rodders began to document what had happened in their own world when they were young. Two good examples are *Cool Cars, Square Roll Bars*, by Arnie and Bernie Shuman and the early years of Gary Meador's book *Goodguys, Hot Rod Chronicles*.

In what almost seems like a parallel universe situation, similar activities were happening in far away places like New Zealand. My kiwi friend, Paul Gilbert, tipped me off when he handed me a book entitled *30 Years of Hot Rodding in New Zealand*. Paul, a superb panelbeater, knows more about American hot rodding, past and present, than most Americans, and of course he's hip to what's happening in New Zealand, where he was born and grew up. The book, he explained, was written, compiled and published by a hot rod club, the East Bay Rods of Auckland, to celebrate the club's 30th Anniversary about three years ago. That book found a market and quickly went out of print.

To fill requests, the club got busy and published a second book, *Looking Back*, which goes back to the beginnings of hot rodding in New Zealand. Both books are soft-cover, professionally done and loaded with photographs of rods that have to interest any car guy. In spite of the cultural differences, the economy, the problems of finding suitable rod material and speed equipment, the photographs of New Zealand rodding reflect similar cars and activities that took place in America during the '50s. That's because they were directly influenced by us. In fact, the writer points out, the three major influences were: American rodding magazines, American films, American rodders who were in the military and who talked with New Zealand servicemen.

The three influences came together around 1958, and the result was a huge increase in the number of hot rods in New Zealand. Some rods resemble the best rods seen in the U.S., while others have a unique, almost foreign quality—and not just because of the RHD. There's a special pleasure in looking at photographs of early rods, including those that are imperfect (those existed in the U.S. too!). Such photographs are hard to find, and when we see one, it reminds us of where we came from and also what we have lost.

While the first book is no longer available, the second book, *Looking Back*, is still in print. This 112 page softbound book is nicely done and contains approximately 200 black and white photographs of rods, customs and the lifestyle. They can be bought on-line: at the *NZ Hot Rod Magazine* website: www.nz-hotrod.com

HOT RODDING DOWN UNDER

Sometimes I think it's a bit odd that many rodders and customizers celebrate the Fifties, but other times it makes perfect sense to look back at that decade of peace and prosperity when the car craze was booming. It's part of our history, after all. But how to explain the interest in the Fifties in England, France, Sweden and other countries? It's *our* Fifties that attracts them, not their own. They're nuts about American cars, rock 'n' roll and movies of that period and go to great lengths to recreate what they understand happened in American 50 years ago.

The Fifties are big in Australia too. I've recently been corresponding with Geoff Rea, an Australian hot rodder who digs American Fifties hot rodding as do some of his mates. A boiler maker and welder, he's able to do much of his own work, which is characteristic of Australian rods and customs. Most are owner-built, which was the situation in this country, way back when. He owns a 1967 Camaro and a 1972 Corvette, a 1956 Ford F-100 project, a 1950 Chev Fleetline and is a partner in a dragster and a salt lake car. He's an avid builder of model cars, and has an extensive collection of some 3,500 rodding magazines from which he gets a lot of his ideas. He belongs to the Slingshots Rod & Custom Club, a club with a 26-year history, the Dry Lake Racers Australia, Antique Drag Racers Australia and the Australian Street Rod Federation.

While he appreciates the work that goes into any modified car, he says he much prefers a Fifties-style machine over a high-tech job. His pride and joy is a 1932 Ford five-window coupe which he bought as a project six years ago. It had already been chopped and when Geoff painted it he followed the example of an America cover car, Larry Stacey's '32 coupe. For power he chose a Ford 289 mated to a C-4 driving a nine-inch rear end. Although he's driven it over 25,000 miles during the past four-and-a-half years the interior is still stripped except for the bench seat which was done in brown and cream tuck and roll Naugahyde.

For years he had read of the cross-country trips taken by rodders in the U.S., and when the coupe was finished he took a two month vacation and drove across Australia, a 7000-mile trouble free trip! He describes it as one of the greatest experiences he's had with a hot rod, and he was constantly amazed at the reception the coupe got everywhere he went.

In 1990 the first time trials were held on Lake Gairdner, and although it's a 1900-mile round trip from Geoff's home, with the last 100 miles being a rough dirt road, Geoff made the trip in the coupe. He was hooked, and a couple of weeks later he became partners with his mates, Chris Weir and Wayne Munsford, in a car for the salt. They cleaned out their garages and found they had a pair of 1928 Chev rails, a glass '24 T bucket and steel turtle deck, a quick-change rear end, chopped '32 grille, some Model A crossmembers and a '39 transmission. Just about everything else the guys built themselves. Chris and Wayne put together the Merc flathead, using Kong heads, a four-barrel intake with a 600 Holley carb and a Lucas magneto. They were ready eight months later and made the trek to Lake Gairdner where on a very wet course the car turned 100 mph. The trials were rained out the next two years, so the guys rebuilt the T and powder coated the entire chassis orange.

Nostalgia drag racing is big in Australia, and last year the three partners bought a 12-foot dragster, complete less engine and transmission, for $2500. They plan to run an injected flathead mated with a Powerglide transmission next year.

In his spare time Geoff has been practicing striping, and he's not only become very adept, he's developed a distinctive Von Dutch style. His work is in demand, and now when he attends a rod run he spends most of his time hovering over a brush. This came about by chance. He striped the dash on his coupe and went to the Port Fairy rod run to show it off. Others wanted

Alan Sherman's roadster is powered by a flathead and went 98.33 mph on Lake Gairdner (photograph by Geoff Rhea).

Top: Geoff Rea's '32 Ford five-window, with four-inch chop, yellow paint and red scallops. It definitely has the Fifties look (photograph by Geoff Rhea). *Bottom:* This Australian '29 phaeton has right-hand steering (photograph by Geoff Rhea).

their cars done, but Geoff was reluctant because he didn't think he could do it; he finally decided to give it a try, and during the next six hours he striped four cars. He gathered a huge audience, only a few of which had ever seen a striper at work.

Geoff's close buddies also have Fifties-style rods. Chris Weir has a '32 Ford highboy roadster running a flathead, early transmission with Lincoln gears and a quick-change rear end. Wayne Munsford is in the process of building a Niekamp-style roadster with a Model C four-cylinder engine. When they all park at the petrol station it's like a scene from So-Cal during the Fifties ... except for the kangaroos hopping in the background.

IN PRAISE OF ORIGINALITY

During the many years I spent under the sheltering boughs of academe, I earned the epithet of "car lover." If I were introduced to someone, my name would quickly be followed by "He's a car lover," as if to sum up my life. It was also a pejorative remark, as if someone who appreciated fine machinery was incapable of appreciating other things, such as people. My colleagues all owned cars, but, believe me, they did not love them or, so far as I could tell, even find them interesting.

Actually, my interest in machines is quite narrow, something I never tried to explain because my colleagues wouldn't have an inkling of what I was talking about. For the record, I do love pre–World War II Mercedes and Auto-Union grand prix cars, the Indy 500 roadsters of the 1940s and early 1950s, Indians, early fat-bob Harleys, most British cycles of the 1950s, but especially AJS/ Matchless singles with the sleek tank and huge fins on the cylinder. In rods I love clean traditional roadsters and coupes, chopped and dropped '36 Ford roadsters and phaetons, '40 Mercs, et cetera, on to the customs that epitomize the 1940s and early 1950s. I also like originality, cars that sometimes defy a category, where the builder follows his individual vision. When done nicely, I'm more than enamored—I feel lust!

A lot to notice: stepped frame, hood shaped to match, the windshield, with cowl molding, capped header exiting through frame, Allen head bolts to secure hood (plus stock catches), etc. Dodge six flathead has triple intake, headers, and is very detailed.

Such a car is Stewart Campbell's '29 Dodge roadster from Australia. Geoff Rea sent me photographs of the car, and I immediately fell in love with it. It's a good-looking car, done in traditional black with red interior, plus red wheels, scallops and running gear. Second, it's an unusual car — I don't believe I've ever seen a 1929 Dodge roadster — with unusual power plant and running gear. It has a flathead Dodge six coupled to an automatic and early Ford rear end running a quick change.

Third, it's clear that Campbell is a meticulous craftsman, with an eye for design and detail. Every area reveals his touch, and everything blends beautifully. Check out that DuVall-style windshield, which may be owner-built; to get a good fit it appears Campbell had to build up the cowl. He apparently built the removable top, complete with the molding that matches the one on the cowl. Check out the dual gas caps, the neatly reworked stock hood panels, the stepped frame rails and Auburn-style dash.

Although hopped-up MoPar flathead six-cylinder engines were not uncommon years ago, it's been years since I've seen one and I don't think I've ever seen one this nice. It uses the stock head, perhaps milled, owner-built headers, a three-carb intake and finned side plates that appear homemade. The manifold resembles a Tattersfield or Nicson, but I don't recall anyone making a triple for a MoPar six, so Campbell may have built that also. Everything is painted red, with lots of chrome accents.

I love it, and should Campbell decide to bring it to this country it's safe to say he won't see another rod like it unless this column inspires some builders who share my appreciation for this original rod.

This roadster has RHD steering using modern column with automatic, Bell-style wheel, neat column support, Auburn-style dash insert with S-W gauges. Interior is red Naugahyde, rolled and pleated.

BRUCE GEISLER AND THE CHIPMUNKS

When I saw the club plaque I thought it was a joke. I was at a Slo Pok Alley, held that night in Gary Vail's shop. There were several car club plaques on the wall above the workbench and I noticed one from the Chipmunks club. Somehow the name struck me as funny. A couple animals below the Gophers, a well-known old hot rod club, yet not even a squirrel, a term once used to describe erratic drivers. It also showed a guy from the rear driving a very low hot rod with an oversized head topped with a tam (the funny flat hat with a ball on top). "What's the story on that plaque?" I asked Gary. He looked up from whatever he was doing and said, "That's Bruce Geisler's old club."

That *really* struck me as funny. I've known Bruce for twenty years and never heard him mention the Chipmunks. He's a modest guy, not given to bragging about his many accomplishments, but over the years I've learned some of his history. He's been a rodder for over five decades and his GMC truck, built in the early Fifties, was featured in *Rod & Custom* in 1958. The editors said that his truck was the inspiration for the famous "Dream Truck." Bruce still owns this original truck and drives it often. Bruce started running at the El Mirage dry lake in 1956 and set a record right off the bat, turning 120 mph in a Corvette. He's been a regular at the lakes and Bonneville since then, becoming a member of the 200 Club and holding 99 land speed records, more than any other person ever.

From other sources I've learned that Bruce was president of the SCTA three years in a row (the only guy to do that) and has served as VP. He won the Meb Healey Sportsmanship award and has been voted into the SCTA, Dry Lakes and NHRA halls of fame. In addition to building and racing cars, he's been involved in numerous administrative activities. For example, he was a key figure in bringing SCTA and Rusetta together years ago and was instrumental in forming the inline and flathead classes at Bonneville leading to a revival of interest in these seemingly obsolete engines.

Bruce is also a street rodder. He and his wife, Diane, own nine rods and use several as daily drivers. His wife has two, a big block 1956 Chevy Suburban on an Impala chassis that rides like a car, and a 1987 McClaren Mustang convertible with 56,000 miles. Bruce recently sold a '29 Ford roadster pickup with 140,000

Top: Bruce Geisler has been running at El Mirage and Bonneville for fifty years and holds 99 records, more than anyone. The Chipmunks plaque is where it all began. *Bottom:* Bruce Geisler and the Chipmunks club ran this '29 roadster with Chev V-8 power at El Mirage dry lake in 1956 (photograph by Bruce Geisler).

miles on it; it had a supercharged small block and was used to tow their trailer all over the United States and Canada. Bruce once told me, "I've been in hot rodding all my life. That's all I drive is hot rods. I don't have a 'normal' car."

So when Bruce walked by I asked him about that plaque, the start of fifty years of hot rodding. He said yes, he was a Chipmunk. Bruce added, "Back in the early Fifties the car clubs were always fighting, drag racing and bad mouthing each other. In East L.A. where I lived there was a real rivalry between guys from Garfield High and Montavilla High. A bunch of us car guys decided to start a club. We used to go to Lake Arrowhead to go water skiing and hang out. My father had a cabin there that we spent at least a week at each summer. We decided that our club should be removed from the L.A. area so we chose Lake Arrowhead so no one would bother us. Then, of course, we had to come up with a name. There were a lot of chipmunks at Lake Arrowhead so we called ourselves the Chipmunks." Bruce saw the puzzled look on my face. "Well we didn't want to be called the Squirrels of Lake Arrowhead," he said, laughing.

"Was it a real club?" I asked "Sure," Bruce said. "We had perhaps 30 or 35 members. When we had the plaques cast each guy chose the number he preferred. (That cost more but it was a nice touch). My mom and dad sponsored the club, so they got plaque number one. I chose number 13. I ran my plaque in the back window of my Jimmy pickup from 1951 to 1961. The club was really active. We even put on one-day outdoor car shows at Montavilla High School. We had some neat cars on display."

There it was: the beginning of a lifetime of hot rodding. When I asked who designed the plaque, Bruce said he did and that the early Chipmunks' plaques didn't have a car on them. "This is the later version," he said. "I like this plaque, I want a tattoo like it." I looked at him but I couldn't tell if he was serious.

THE ZEN OF NOSTALGIA

As it pertains to hot rodding, nostalgia is a recent term. It almost overwhelms us now, with several new publications aimed at the past, a fleet of new rods being built in an earlier style, people in their twenties caught up in the music and clothing styles of 50 years ago. I do not recall people using the word nostalgia a couple decades back to describe things that happened in the 1940s or 1950s. I do remember conversations that focused on a particular car, such as the Matranga Merc or the Dick Flint roadster, cars that had seared our souls, but none that discussed a way of life.

Perhaps that's a slim distinction, but it's one that seems to me to sum up the very nature of nostalgia. The event happens and might be discussed, but a certain amount of time has to pass before it could be considered nostalgic material. It relates to the Zen teaching question: "If a tree in the forest falls unseen did it make a noise?" There is the event, and then there is the audience; both are required for the event to have meaning.

A possible example of that: in 1985 I had an old roadster in the Portland Roadster Show, and I met a young man with an unusual last name. I said that the guy who had painted my car had that same name; he said that guy was his uncle and we were both surprised. On Sunday he brought his uncle to the show, and although 30 years had passed since I had last seen him, I recognized him immediately. The same could not be said for him: he did not remember the car or me. I couldn't imagine how he could not remember the car at least; he'd worked on it for months! I assumed it was because he'd swallowed gallons of paint over the years, and it had put layers of lead in his memory banks, but his speech and movements were unaffected, and except for a dull, gray pallor he seemed normal.

I pressed him, reminding him that the black paint on the frame had been a new kind, a paint that, he had said, would withstand the flame from an acetylene torch. No response. The paint he shot on the body was Sierra Gold, a new 1956 Chevrolet color and it must have been the first time he used that color. No, he didn't remember. I pointed out the rear nerf bar, and the gas tank, items he had fashioned himself. Nope. The car did not inspire even the smallest memory from 30 years earlier.

So much for nostalgia, I thought. Another question I ask myself: does nostalgia automatically imply sweetness and fun? Can one wax nostalgic about a painful reminder of the past? Or is a subject like that simply part of the burden of memory? A possible example: One evening in 1956, I fired up that same roadster and scooted off to the Jim Dandy Drive-in. When the roadster had been my only transportation, I thought nothing of jumping into it and zooming off to places around town, and I even left it parked on the street when I went to a movie. But now the car had a new full race flathead, new Sierra Gold paint, new leather interior, new whitewall tires, new everything and therefore I drove it infrequently.

So it was a big deal to pull into the drive-in, the overlap on that cam thumping away, and to park near the front door. The car absolutely glowed in the neon light, and within a few minutes I began to feel very uncomfortable. In the roadster I was fully exposed to everyone, and because I was alone, all I could do was sit there. I became aware of my hands, and there seemed to be nowhere to put them. Hang the left one outside? Hold onto the steering wheel? Put an arm over the top of the seat? The awkwardness I felt made me wish I had taken up smoking.

About that time the car hop came out the door with a tray of food in each hand, and then she tripped, began to fall, the twin trays of food also falling, and the milkshakes creating a splash in mid-air. When they hit the ground the thick shakes cascaded against my roadster, bonding to the warm engine, the frame, the chrome plated front end. I'd like to say that I handled it well, even laughed it off, but I probably swore and yelled and I certainly blew my cool. I hit the starter button, revved the engine and got out of there, feeling uncool, depressed, upset and knowing as I drove home through the warm summer night that it was more than the crusted milkshake spattered on my car, which, after all, could be hosed off. So much for nostalgia!

A Classic Memory

Who among us has not said: If only I'd bought that '34 Ford Woodie (or B-400, or M-B 300 or whatever) back then and held onto it I could now sell it and retire? Although I've hung onto various cars for years, I never did it because I thought it'd be a good investment. If I'd been thinking, I would've gotten a genuine classic, back in the days when they were selling for a few hundred dollars. Check out the classified ads in early *Motor Trend* magazines, where Cords, Auburns, Pierce Arrows, etc., are for sale at bargain prices. Oh, the benefit of hindsight!

But I was always a hot rodder, with plebian tastes. Besides that, I never had any money. In 1952 I had my roadster torn apart at my father's service station. It was about 20 miles from home, and because he was seriously ill and everything seemed to be falling apart, I had to walk and hitchhike from my lower-class neighborhood to Oswego, the affluent suburb where the station was located. Some days, hitchhiking in the rain, I felt a sense of despair.

One Sunday, after working on the roadster all day, I left the station and within a block I got a ride with Paul Hebb, a kid who came in often for gas. Like me, he was nuts about cars. Unlike me, he had money. He said he'd take me to the Sellwood Bridge, but then he turned into a long, secluded driveway where there were some cars he wanted to show me. The house was a mansion, with a detached garage far larger than my parents' house. The fellow who emerged was perhaps 25. His taste in cars was different from ours, as we saw when he opened the garage doors. In the last light of day I could make out the huge chrome headlights and stainless radiator shells, and beyond them the massive bulk of truly classic cars.

The first was a Rolls Royce limousine; the roof over the driver and over the rear section folded back, leaving a solid section of roof in the middle. I think it was a 1930 model, and perhaps maroon. I remember little else about it, except that the owner started the engine. It was so quiet I could hardly hear it, even within the confines of the garage.

The second car was a 1930 Cord, big and black with a white top — a magnificent car! The third was the one I remember best. It was a 1928 Mercedes-Benz SSK model, a roadster, with massive headlights and radiator shell, a long hood and chromed pipes coming through the side panel.

He'd bought all three cars from the Convoy Company, a trucking outfit; he said that they'd come from California, and had been used in movies. I tried to place them in something like *Sunset Boulevard*. We stood around and talked for a while, then Paul said I needed a ride home. The other guy said hop in, he was looking for a reason to drive one. I was excited and amazed as the owner started the engine of the Mercedes, which was noisy. I climbed in, and while the engine warmed up I checked out that incredible dashboard, thinking how all those gauges would fit in the dash of a hot rod.

Then we were moving down the wide driveway, like a scene from a movie, and onto the road leading to Portland, traveling in style. There was the sound of that powerful exhaust along the river and then, as the driver let up for the bridge, there was a loud backfire. He downshifted and it backfired again, the sound of a cannon. He said that it backfired because the impellers in the supercharger were shot.

On we went, the air rushing past, exhaust rumbling, and occasionally the engine backfired, until it seemed perfectly ordinary. We drove through fashionable neighborhoods, past the golf course, past Reed College. Whenever the car backfired, there was a flash of light, bright enough to illuminate one of the great houses for a second. As we continued eastward, the houses grew smaller, plainer, and eventually we got to Lents, my neighborhood, where there were poor houses, empty fields and unpaved roads. The Mercedes seemed out of place in this landscape I thought, as I got out and thanked him. He waved, bounced down a section of my street filled with mud puddles, then turned and disappeared in the darkness. I heard the car backfire twice, in the distance, a sound like gunfire.

False Memory

In recent years the term "false memory" has been in the news. It usually refers to a person who remembers something that may have been forgotten, repressed or maybe never even occurred: the process of answering that question often requires a psychiatrist and a good deal of time and money.

In my case I can think of some examples of memories that were not repressed, but simply wrong, and it has required many years for me to recognize the truth. It's funny what one remembers, how clear the memory is and how doggedly one hangs on to that memory, unwilling to let it go. For example, around 1952 I saw a chopped '39 or '40 Mercury coupe. I remember exactly where I saw it; I can see it in my mind right now, coming toward me as I drove on a certain street in Portland. At that time or later I somehow knew it belonged to Red Bliven; we were both in the same club, the Road Angels. Years later I mentioned the car to Red and he said he'd never owned such a car. I guess I didn't want to believe that, and recently again asked Red who

In the 1950s this Bantam panel was on the roof of Mecca Motor Sales in Portland, Oregon.

was adamant. So I had to rethink things: I saw the car only once, and if it had belonged to Red wouldn't I have seen it again? I could not have confused it with a similar car because there was not a chopped '39/'40 Merc coupe in Portland until the summer of 1956. In fact, in the early Fifties I was aware of only three chopped hardtops in Portland. I admit I was wrong, but what did I see on the day long ago? A mirage?

Over the past fifteen years I have become friends with Don Krueger, although I actually met him in the late spring of 1951. He's a few years older, and at the time of our meeting he was a mechanic at Montavilla Garage, a hot bed of hot rodding in a neighborhood loaded with rods. Don had four rods and I was impressed a with all of them: a '36 3-window, a '36 tudor, a '28 roadster and a '25 T roadster, all Fords. The '28 roadster was full fendered with a Riley two-port and was very white. One thing I have always remembered about the car was the rear bumper, which was a '37 DeSoto ribbed bumper cut down until it was about two feet wide; it served as a capable push bar. A couple of years ago the car came up in conversation and I mentioned that bumper. Don said that the roadster never had such a bumper, nor did any of his cars have one. He showed me a couple of photographs of the car, and sure enough, he was right. Then where did I get that idea, and how could I have carried it around in my head for fifty-five years? To the best of my knowledge, I have never seen another car at an event or in a magazine with a whacked '37 DeSoto bumper, so I could not have confused Don's car with another.

In 1952 I bought a cute '29 Ford roadster body mounted on a '37 Willys chassis and powered by a Jeep engine. I got my first ticket in that car, and when the cop said he never wanted to see that car again, I knew I had to get rid of it. I kept a few pieces for my other roadster, and traded the rest to a young guy in Oswego for a complete 1930 American Austin tudor. I had that for a while, and when a neighbor kid said he'd trade me a rebuilt '41 Ford flathead for the Austin I agreed. Looking back, I now think I was lousy at trading stuff, but that's not the point here. The guy who got the Austin pushed it to a local garage, where the mechanic got it running. The kid drove the little car around his yard and up and down the street beside his house until he got tired of it and sold it to a used car dealer, who parked it on the roof of his building as an advertisement. The lot was near my house, and I must have driven by it hundreds of times; every time I'd think, there's my old Austin. Even after I moved away I thought about that car. About five years ago a friend and old car fanatic, Steve Sauer, showed me some photographs from an American Austin/Bantam club that existed in the Portland area around mid-century. Among the photographs was one of a used car lot, Mecca Motors, at 82nd and Holgate, and it had an Austin on the roof. I instantly recognized the place and my Austin. Except it wasn't my 1930 Austin sedan; this one looked newer, perhaps a 1937 model, and it was a Bantam panel! I was shocked, and it took a few minutes for the reality of the photograph to sink in. I still have to rearrange my thoughts when I consider what I thought I knew. The car is gone, the car lot is gone, and I suspect that the people connected with the business, as well as those who were in the club, are all gone, so there is no one left to explain this false memory to me. But regarding all the other cars and events I've spent years researching and thinking about, I'm sure I'm right. I must be!

THE GLENN JOHNSON COUPE REVISITED

Some magazines are like old friends: you remember where you were when you met them. That first issue of *Hop Up* I read in the kitchen, summer, 1951. A photograph of a Dodge bucket and a caption that said the car wasn't built for beauty; I thought it was beautiful! A copy of *Cycle* bought about the same time after carefully deciding which magazine I could buy, since, even at two bits, I could buy only one. An early *Hot Rod*, bought used, with a low '32 coupe on the cover, memorable because it was from South Dakota. A copy of *Road and Track* that I did not buy but read on the stands, memorable because it had a fascinating article about the new Citroën DB-19, which the author described as a plumber's nightmare!

Then there was the April 1952 issue of *Hot Rod Magazine* which I clearly remember reading on the city bus on my way to school. I was on the bus because my roadster was apart, and as the bus rocked onward I built cars in my head. The cover showed an almost futuristic looking car, a low and lovely red coupe, and the caption read: "We channeled and chopped our car at home." One thing I thought odd was that both the man and the woman washing the car had bright red hair! Another thing I found odd was that the builder chose a 1937 Ford as the basis for the project. I loved '36 Fords, and then my mind skipped ahead to the 1939 models. Others apparently felt the same way. I can recall only one extra nice '37 Ford rod in Portland during the 1950s. However, in 1953 I bought a '37 Ford coupe that I became fond of, but I bought it because it was, most of all, affordable, not because I thought it was beautiful.

The '37 Ford in the article looked good even before the serious work began. The owner, Glenn Johnson, had blacked out the trunk lid, inset later taillights below it, added skirts, solid side panels and dual pipes. These modifications, even in a '37, would have made it a neat car in my neighborhood. The reason the article was in *HRM* was because the car was chopped and channeled, and the job had been done at home by the owner. I have to stop and think to remember how remarkable that was: in Portland, Oregon, my home town, in 1952, there were, so far as I knew, no more than half a dozen 1933 or later coupes and sedans that had been chopped. Oh sure, there were lots of roadsters and phaetons with lowered lids, but it took a great deal more skill, fortitude and money to chop a hardtop.

So there I was on the bus, my car torn apart, no money, little time, and yet that article gave me ideas and hope, for a day at least. It suggested that I could buy a mid-1930s coupe and I could start cutting and leading, like Glenn Johnson did. If not a Ford, then a Plymouth or even a Terraplane, something expendable, so if I made a couple bad cuts and things didn't line up

Glenn and his wife wash the coupe on the cover shot of April 1952 *Hot Rod Magazine*.

the loss would be minimal. The thought of chopping and channeling a '36 Plymouth coupe was on my mind all day, when, of course, I should have been thinking about school matters.

Flash forward 50 years, when I became pen pals with an East Coast rodder named Marv Silverstein. I wrote a *Gazette* column about a 1938 Ford coupe that he had owned in 1954, and when I saw a photograph of Marv's chopped '38 I was reminded of Glenn Johnson's '37, and I wondered whether somehow the latter had influenced the former.

Glenn Johnson's '37 Ford coupe as it appears today outside his home in Las Vegas (photograph by Glenn Johnson).

Marv remembered the article. Moreover, he said he'd been in touch with Glenn Johnson, and he told me that Johnson still owns the same '37 Ford and that he'd restored it. I was astounded, and asked for Glenn's phone number. I had to discover where that car had been all these decades, and whether his restoration had been true to the car on the cover of that 1952 *HRM*. I called Glenn twice and we had long conversations about that coupe, then and now. I told him I wanted to write something about this amazing time warp story, but before I finished my article I picked up a copy of *Hop Up* #5 and discovered an informed article on Glenn Johnson's '37 written by Drew Hardin. There were also neat photographs of the car, and I was especially interested in one that showed the coupe after 40 years of sitting outside.

My first question to Glenn was where had the car been? He said he'd owned a ranch outside Las Vegas, and in the late 1950s, when he quit driving the coupe, he'd simply parked it beside a building, where it stayed for four decades; when he retired and sold the property he took the coupe with him to his new house. Now, he told himself, he had time to restore it. The car survived well in that hot, low humidity climate; it's also amazingly complete, down to the spotlights and hubcaps.

My second question was, why a '37 Ford? He said, "It was a dog! I thought the '37 Ford was the ugliest car there ever was, until I saw a '41 Willys. The reason I chopped it up was because that's what I had." Were there other chopped cars or customs in town; where'd he get his ideas? "Las Vegas was a little bitty cow town then — only 20,000 people. The only other chopped car was the coupe Carl (Gratz) had." That car, a '36 coupe, came from California, and although Glenn studied the top carefully, the chop was done so neatly it did not supply answers. Glenn had to figure out how to chop a top on his own.

He did a beautiful job. The article in *HRM*, which Glenn wrote and illustrated, is primarily devoted to how he chopped and channeled the car, and it's so well done that others could tackle the same job, and many no doubt did. Glenn made it look possible, even easy, but I cannot recall ever seeing another coupe like this. The angles of the cuts and the amount of metal removed — 4" in the front, 4½" in the rear — are just right. The way the front and rear end taper, with the fenders moved up and back, make the car seem longer, although, according to Glenn's 1952 drawing, it is not.

The ideas involved in building a custom were to make it look newer and different. If no one could figure out the make and model you started with, that was even better. Even though it's clear that certain styling ideas worked best, and have therefore become the standard for new old customs built today, there were almost no rules back then. So I was surprised in 1952, and again now, to find that Glenn used a 1947 Cadillac grille, turned upside down, in his coupe; ditto regarding the massive 1941 Cadillac front bumper and the massive '46 DeSoto rear bumper. They seem too heavy for the car, but when we see the finished product, with its ruby-maroon paint and reshaped front sheet metal, they work perfectly; all the parts are nicely integrated.

Glenn mentioned that the coupe had been his only transportation, and that he had to drive it every day during the building period, which covered the years 1947 to 1951! "During this period," he wrote, "I was traveling 60 miles daily, to and from work, six days a week. At no time was I ever able to have the car laid up for more than a 24 hour period." Imagine driving a car day after day with the top removed, or tack-welded on, but no glass, no fenders, no hood, almost no interior, driving it long distances to work and back, and then, after dinner, going out and working on the car until bedtime.

I'm not surprised that Glenn became an architect. The coupe reveals he has an eye for design. The car is solid, sleek and uncluttered. There are no louvers or flames or gizmos to break up the car's smooth lines. The interior was done in rolled and pleated ivory and red Naugahyde. An unusual feature is the way the gauges have been removed from the dashboard to the area above the windshield. Although the coupe originally had a V8-60 engine, Glenn replaced it with a 1947 Mercury, and by 1952 he had it hopped up. Currently it has the same engine, enlarged to 286 cubes, with a full-race Iskendarian cam, Offenhauser heads and an Edelbrock dual manifold with a pair of chrome Stromberg 97s.

Today Glenn Johnson enjoys driving and showing the coupe, and occasionally he meets an old timer who remembers the car from the 1952 *HRM* article. Oh sure, the guy says, you did it at home. Three times, Glenn replies.

BRIDGE TO THE FIFTIES

Way up in Michigan, at the northern end of the five mile long Mackinac Bridge, is the village of St. Ignace. It seems like it's in the middle of nowhere, a lovely, unspoiled area, but each year it is the site of the Straits Car Show and attracts some 2,000 registered vehicles and a crowd of some 50,000 people. For that three day weekend the town is jumping! The show welcomes cars of all types — antiques, classics, special interest, rods and customs — and you'll see everything from an Allstate to a Zephyr.

But because the chairpeople, Ed and Mary Ellen Reavie, really dig the Fabulous Fifties, the cars and personalities of that decade are in St. Ignace in abundance. Stock iron of the Fifties is everywhere (the Reavies own a super sharp '55 Chev hardtop) as well as Fifties-style rods and customs. People, too. I grew up on the West Coast, saw George Barris in 1957, but I had to go to St. Ignace to meet and talk with him. That was in 1985. This year I met a bunch of neat people from the Fifties, and saw some machines I never expected to see.

A prime example is the Hirohata Mercury, or rather the recreation of this most famous Fifties kustom: The original was built by Barris in 1952 for Bob Hirohata. It's a radical kustom 1951 Mercury, chopped, with the posts removed to make it into a hardtop convertible. I'd read

Top: This 1950 Ford tudor was built in the late Fifties by Hal Hutchens and was in *Hot Rod*. The car is now owned by Bob McCormick of East Hartford, CT. *Bottom:* This is John Abee's first custom, and he did good. The 1952 Ford came to his wrecking yard a few years ago and he reworked it. The paint is yellow, with green scallops.

Top: Smooth! This 1949 Cadillac was nosed, decked, lowered, has reworked '53 "sombrero" hubcaps, spotlights. Looks super! Let's bring back the mild but elegant ride! *Bottom:* Jim Stockton owns this 1950 Chev convert — chopped and padded top, one-piece windshield, dual carbs and pipes on 216 CID six engine. The car received the Joe Bailon Award of Elegance at St. Ignace.

The "Polynesian II," a clone of the old Valley Custom job of the Fifties, was built by John Ballard. It fooled me!

about the car in magazines in the Fifties, but then it dropped out of sight. When it was found, the owner refused to sell it; he recently refused an offer of $50,000, I've heard. Jack Walker, of Belton, Missouri, had seen the car in magazines and had fallen in love with it; when he was unable to buy it he commissioned Doug Thompson to help build a kustom that is identical to the Hirohata Merc down to the license plate number. It is a super gorgeous kustom — not "typical" of the Fifties kustoms but identical to the best.

Another car I never expected to stand beside is the "Arctic Sand," a radically customized '46 Ford coupe built in Detroit in the mid Fifties. That car, which I'd also seen in magazines, was created by ClarKaiser (spell it with a C) Custom Shop of Detroit. It disappeared, was perhaps eaten up by Michigan roadsalt, but Tom Philpot asked Bob Kaiser, one of the original builders, to build an exact duplicate which he calls "Arctic Gold." It is an unusual kustom, and it took first prize in the Nostalgia class.

I took some pix of "Arctic Gold" and got to talking with a tall, slim, energetic guy standing near the car. Turned out that he was Bob Kaiser, the builder of both "Arctic Sand" in the Fifties and "Arctic Gold" in the Eighties. He was also half-owner (along with Ron Clark) of ClarKaiser Custom Shop of Detroit; it was the earliest kustom shop in Michigan, and between 1948–58 it turned out some terrific machines. Bob Kaiser is still into cars — his latest is a "gull wing" Yugo concept vehicle — and brims with energy and ideas.

He pointed to another kustom that was built by ClarKaiser back in the Fifties; it too was a famous show and magazine car, called the "Utopia." It's a 1950 Ford with Olds quarters and a wild purple/orchid paint job. I needed a few minutes to remember the car, because when it was in magazines it had been two-tone green and had less trim. It's now owned by Tom Liechty, who loves Fifties kustoms and has spared no expense in restoring this authentic pan-dragger.

Top: The "Forcasta" was built in the early Sixties by Daryl Starbird. It uses a 1960 Corvair chassis. The car is owned by Rick and Shelby Klibenski. *Bottom:* Joe Bailon with two of his cars: the 1965 El Camino is "The Golden Gate," and the 1951 Mercury is "The Widow." Both are owned by Richard Crane.

Top: Famed car builder Doug Thompson's personal ride is this '50 Merc. Doug, and his wife, Nita, are behind the car. *Bottom:* Mild or radical? This 1950 Chev has stock grille, chopped top, bubble skirts, and bright yellow paint.

People were going nuts over all this kustom metal; for some it was a way to relive the Fifties. A man came up to me and, very excited, told me that he had ridden in both cars when he had been in high school. He had known Kenny Nicholson, who had footed the bill for the original "Arctic Sand," and Al Reason, who had had Clarkaiser build "Utopia." That was the kind of day it was!

There were lots of other era pieces in St. Ignace. Spike McMurtrie drove a very sharp full kustom '53 Buick. Dick Styles motored around in a '39 Ford coupe that captured the flavor of the Fifties: nosed and decked, '49 Plymouth bumpers, skirts, sports, Fiestas on the front, Plum lacquer and — somewhat unusual — Frenched headlights. In the spirit of the Sixties there was Elaine Pawlowski's 1965 Buick kustom, originally built by KKOA Hall of Famer Lee Pratt. And in the spirit of the Eighties there was Ken "Posie" Fenical's high tech '38 Ford phaeton, a neat rig that people will be recalling thirty years from now!

There were many others who made the Fifties (and early Sixties) come alive. Paul Hatton was there; he began building hot rods in 1949, he learned kustom painting and pinstriping in the 1950s, and opened "Hatton's House of Crazy Paint" in Detroit in 1957. He was kept busy striping dashboards, doing scallops and painting creatures on quarter panels and bubble skirts. Then he moved on to do special paint jobs on cars, trucks, boats, trains and planes. He also did work on cars owned by the Smothers Brothers, Don Nicholson and Connie Kalitta, and over the years he worked for all the legendary Detroit kustomizers, including the Alexander Brothers, Chuck Miller and ClarKaiser. During the Fifties he was the Midwest version of Ed Roth and Nick the Greek.

Chuck Miller, owner of Styline Customs, was there. He's built many well-known machines, including the "Red Baron," "The Fire Truck," "Crater Raider #1" and "Sonic Cuda." Down on the dock, in the Nostalgia Section, cartoonist Dave Bell was talking to people who thronged around to buy T-shirts and posters with his wild artwork. His stylized rods really capture the flavor of the Fifties, and his work is so detailed that every time you look at one of his drawings you see more. Beside him was a wild '59 Cadillac lowrider owned by Terry Cook, Mr. Fifties himself. He's the creator of Lead East, and promotes about eight events around the country that celebrate the Fifties.

Ronnie Dove scored big in the early Sixties with hits such as "Right or Wrong" and "Little Bit of Heaven." He racked up twenty-five chart singles and nine albums, and was voted number one male vocalist in North America in 1965. On Saturday afternoon he sang on the main street, renamed "Memory Lane," to a huge crowd. Then he invited a man from the crowd to join him onstage. The man was Tommy Durden, who in 1955 co-wrote "Heartbreak Hotel," the song that shot an unknown singer named Elvis Presley to fame. Durden sang that song, and it was a moving experience.

The Straits Show was a gathering of luminaries from the Fifties, but one person many had hoped to meet was absent. Henry Gregor Felsen was scheduled to appear but had to cancel because of poor health. Felsen is the author of several books that two generations of car nuts have enjoyed, including *Hot Rod, Crash Club, Street Rod, Rag Top* and *Road Rocket*.

Friday and Saturday nights the Fifties were relived at the Cruise-Ins at the Big Boy. The parking lot was filled by 2:00 P.M., and by 5:00 P.M. the crowd stretched for 1½ miles to the west. Unable to get into the Big Boy, cars cruised up and down the highway. Two years ago the crowds were almost as large, but the traffic was crazier — first the cruisers rapped their pipes, the next pass they laid rubber and finally some hot dogs were doing burnouts! This year the police kept things under control — you could cruise, but nothing crazy.

If you could find a parking spot, you could walk to the Big Boy parking lot that was filled with fine rods and customs and a large crowd of energetic dancers who were rolling 'n rocking back in time. They danced to records and commentary supplied by legendary Chicago DJ Dick

Biondi. Known as the "Wild Italian" and "The King of Nighttime Radio," Biondi was to the Midwest what Wolfman Jack was to the West Coast.

On Saturday night a Fifties dance was held at the local high school. The music was supplied by the Laradoes from Detroit, a group that was originally formed in 1955 at Dearborn's Edsel Ford High School. Prizes were given for the best D.A. haircut, beehive hairdo, best leather jacket/T-shirt/Levis combo, and prizes for poodle skirts, prom formals, white sports coats, high school sweaters and bobby sox. For young and old, the Fifties lives!

My final image of the show came when things were breaking up and people were heading for home. Posie had mentioned to me earlier that he did not plan to build another car — at least not for a while. But as others were pulling out Posie and Dave Bell were head to head, and Bell was sketching some wild French curves on paper while Posie got increasingly excited about building a street rod resembling a Delahaye, with enclosed front wheel coverings. We'll have to see what emerges from his shop next spring, but it does prove that the St. Ignace Straits show can build for the future while venerating the past.

THE GREAT UNWASHED DEUCE

At the Goodguys meet last year in Salem, Oregon, there was a beautiful high-tech '32 Ford roadster with super paint and billet everything, a real rod of the Nineties. The owner was rightfully proud of his neat ride, and totally confused when people went past his car to gawk at another '32 Ford roadster parked nearby. This car was tall, with room to stick your head between the front tire and fender, and looked as though it had never been washed. In fact, the color under the dirt suggested that the paint had slowly been worn away by time. The car had apparently spent most of its life in a barn, probably one with a poor roof, and had recently been exhumed. And the owner, the guy beside the car, looked like a farmer with bib overalls and a long gray beard. Both car and owner were incongruous among the sleek high-buck rods and hip people, but it was a surprise only to the owner of the high-tech '32 when the great unwashed '32 received the Best Beater Award, and the perfect high-tech '32 got — nothing!

The owner of the unwashed '32 is Mike Foster, and during the twenty years that he's been driving his roadster he's had to put up with mild abuse from people who stop him and want to buy the car. It's dull, it's dirty, the canvas cover on the spare tire is torn and what they see is a big dollar sign. They assume it's a gennie steel '32, and they also assume the graybeard owner can't know what it's worth so they offer a couple thousand bucks, just to take it off his hands. Mike has to politely decline the offer and, with a chuckle, tell the prospective buyer that he's got to be on his way, got to get the eggs to market or put the cows to bed or whatever it is they assume he does. Mike zips away, leaving the guy standing beside the road, checkbook in hand, thinking how he could've made a few thou if the graybeard had at least wanted to *dicker*. All the car needed was a paint job, or maybe even a good cleaning — hell, it looked like it had never been washed.

In fact, the roadster has never been washed. Mike should know; he built it in 1974, has owned it for all those years, has driven it thousands of miles all over the United States and, for reasons unclear to me, he has just never washed it. But that one fact gives you an inkling of the kind of guy Mike Foster is: unique, quirky, perhaps eccentric. But Mike loves '32 Fords, and does not mistreat them. You should know that in 1952 Mike got a '32 Ford three-window coupe that had been in the family since it was new, and turned it into a beautiful rod that was featured in *Hot Rod Magazine*; the amazing thing is that forty-five years later he still owns it (no, it's *not* for sale)!

The great unwashed roadster possibly got its start during the 1960s when Mike was driving across Montana. He saw a '32 Ford tudor behind a house out in the middle of nowhere and stopped to take a look. The owner was using it for a doghouse, and he didn't want to discuss selling the car. But apparently the people living there were starved for company and they did want to talk about other things. Mike stayed with them for three days, and he said they fed him so well he was getting fat! Finally he said he had to move on, and would they please consider selling the '32 tudor? The rancher thought a moment and said he'd probably want too much — $40! Mike drove into town, bought a new doghouse and fifty pounds of dog food and gave those to the rancher plus $40. Then he trailered the tudor back to his rural property in Oregon. There's some confusion about whether that particular chassis was the one used under the roadster because Mike also bought tons of '32 Ford parts from a man who had seven 1932 Ford tudors sitting beside the Hillsboro, Oregon, airport. That guy was nuts about Willys-Knight cars, so naturally he wanted to get rid of the 1932 stuff.

There's no confusion over the '32 body. Mike helped build the giveaway '32 Ford roadster that Dee Wescott donated to the 1974 Portland Roadster Show. Mike's wife thought that the car was "pretty cute." so Mike struck a deal with Dee to build his own body using Dee's molds, jigs and fixtures if Mike would represent Wescott at the Mini-Nationals in Lodi, California, and the Grand Nationals in Tulsa, Oklahoma. Mike's a computer expert but he's also good with his hands and with the assistance of Bob Butler, who built the mold, and Homer Campbell who built the jigs and fixtures, he soon had a body. As Mike recalls, the body was completed, mounted on the '32 tudor chassis, wired and essentially ready for the road in something like thirteen days. Mike believes that this is Wescott body number five. It has a number of trick touches, such as the rear frame horn covers that Mike reworked to cover the shackles on the elliptical springs. Kay Wescott made the top and curtains and on the latter she used the special wind lacing found on the original 1932 Ford roadster curtains.

For power Mike used a 1969 Corvette engine and backed that up with an aftermarket magnesium case using a combination of gears from the Chevrolet pickup, Buick Special and Olds F-85 transmissions; it's been a super gearbox over the years. In back he used a Pontiac rear end, and later replaced it with one from a Granada.

Mike met his deadline and drove the roadster to Lodi and Tulsa and he's been driving it for twenty years— to Texas, to Michigan, from Portland. Maine, to Portland. Oregon. His pal, Pete Hirschberger, who purchased the Wescott '32 roadster body number one, built Mike a matching trailer which sports deuce pickup fenders, bumpers and taillights, and Mike has often towed it behind the roadster on long trips. The body has been subjected to temperatures that have ranged from well below zero to well over a hundred degrees, and the glass body has withstood it all. Mike never painted the car because he felt if he were representing the factory, he wanted people to see what they were getting. Nor has he washed it in twenty years! Once he *almost* washed it. "I went to a four-by-four meet sponsored by the Sons of the Beaches at Seaside where my friend Tony (Marino) was driving and I got down to the axles in the mud and the announcer says ... look at that beautiful car in the slop. They had to pull me out! I just drove it through a creek and got a brush and got the mud off. That's the only bath it's ever had — just the underside." Nor does he intend to wash it — why break a perfect record?

JAMES DEAN RUN

Fairmount, Indiana, is located smack dab in the middle of the state, and it embodies the best middle-class, Middle America values. It's a sleepy, peaceful town, the kind of place made famous by Norman Rockwell, with narrow streets bordered by huge shade trees. Beyond the town, in every direction, are cornfields.

It's also the town where James Dean grew up and where he's buried. Once a year, on the last weekend in September, the anniversary of his death, the town echoes with the rumble of dual pipes. On that weekend Fairmount is the site of the James Dean Memorial Run, an event that attracts car enthusiasts from several states away.

The occasion is both festive and solemn. On the main street there are amusement rides, concession stands and craft vendors. In the cemetery north of town people stand beside the movie star's grave to mourn his passing. And at the other end of town, in Playacres Park, car buffs gather for the annual James Dean Memorial Run.

While the event is open to cars of all types, including antiques, sports and special interest cars, the majority are street rods and customs. This year 1,677 cars registered, up from last year's total of 1,189 and the 1985 total of 967. That's a heckuva jump, and the numbers reflect the meet's increasing popularity. The reasons for its popularity are many: The town's proximity to major population centers such as Indianapolis, Chicago and Detroit; the continued interest in James Dean; the friendliness of the townspeople; the organizational skills of the host club, the Magic City Street Rods of Muncie; and the location that allows a couple thousand cars to park together with ease. Overall, it's an exciting and yet comfortable meet, without the traffic hassles of a big city.

The increased numbers also reflect the increased interest in rods and customs in the Midwest. Things are booming here, and customs are big; I suspect there are more custom cars per capita or square mile in the Midwest than anywhere else. There's certainly a bigger variety. I'd been on the West Coast before the Dean meet and I can honestly say I felt I was running into a different breed of custom car. The Dean run attracted chopped and dropped machines of all types. Imagine a chopped 1950 Studebaker convertible, or a chopped 1953 Studebaker coupe. How about a chopped and dropped full custom 1973 Lincoln, or a chopped Henry J? I saw those and more, ranging from mild to wild. Then there were cars that could have been from Dean's days, '50 Chevs and Fords, nosed and decked, duals, whites, flippers, spot primer, the works. Because Dean drove a 1950 Mercury in his second film, *Rebel Without a Cause*, Fairmount has become a mecca for 1949–51 Mercs. There was a new feature called the Merc Corral sponsored by "Mr. Merc," Sterling Ashby; it contained 104 Mercs of all types. The Merc Dean drove in the film was a mild custom. Many in the Merc Corral were wild—chopped, dropped, molded, with super paint. In the Fifties I recall seeing one chopped Merc coupe—an Oakland Show car—and two chopped Merc convertibles; now chopped Mercs are plentiful. The big trick now is to rework a Merc *four door*, a model that no one would have bothered with a few years ago. Lee Witt drove a beautiful black chopped four door, and Paul Pittard drove an outstanding green '49 four door that was chopped and had the rear door glass filled in.

Another new feature was MoPar Country, an enclosed area featuring 76 Chrysler products of various years and types; many were street rods or customs, such as Hugh Anderson's '37 Plymouth which won the Best Custom MoPar trophy. Across from the marque areas was the swap meet; it was much larger than last year, with lots of Merc and custom parts, such as hard-to-find '53–'55 Packard taillights.

There was not a dull moment all weekend. Everyone, kids and adults, could keep busy playing games or cruising or eating. A continuous drawing for door prizes kept everyone on his toes. In the evening there were flame contests, and dancing until late to the "Free Ride Express" band. While the weather was a little warm during the day, the nights were beautiful; all in all it was a perfect weekend.

THE PAN DRAGGERS REUNION

In the early 1950s hot rodding spread across the country from California, and soon hot rods were found everywhere, in cities large and small. The fictional versions of this phenomenon, as chronicled in novels by Henry Gregor Felsen and *Clint Curtis* comic books, were generally true, because the writers used events that were happening all over the country. Teenage boys rebuilt an old car into a hot rod, they formed a club, they made plans to get or build a strip where they could hold legal drag races or timed speed trials. If anyone doubts how extensive this activity was, one vendor has a stock of over 5,000 different plaques of clubs that were formed during the 1950s. A club brought together like-minded young men who helped one another build rods, and collectively it promoted safe driving. Because, although we don't like to think about it today, there was plenty of street racing going on back then, and when you put a teenage kid behind the wheel of a fenderless, hopped-up roadster you have a potential for trouble.

In 1950 in Lansing, Michigan, some teenagers banded together because of their interest in hot rods and formed the Pan Draggers, the city's first hot rod club. These guys were the pioneers in the area and because there wasn't much information available about how to channel a car or hop up a flathead V-8 engine they had to learn by trial and error. As the club grew it began to stage events new to rodders, such as road rallies, poker runs, reliability runs, timed runs on Highway 43 and gravel pit runs (the latter, which was like a gymkhana with cars being timed individually, might be peculiar to this area). The club also held drag races at Capitol City Airport, and three members, Noah Canfield, Charlie Johnson, and Jim Van Horn, went to an early Bonneville meet in Canfield's Studillac.

In short, it was a very active club during the good old days when rodding was new and exciting, when Michigan's economy was booming, and legions of consumers wanted the hot machines that came from the Lansing Oldsmobile factory where a number of the boys worked to get the bucks to modify their own cars. In the 1950s, Lansing, the capital of Michigan, had a bustling downtown and on Friday and Saturday nights the Pan Draggers would cruise up and down Washington Avenue or out Michigan Avenue before heading to Benny's Drive-In on East Michigan. Benny's and Sully's drive-ins were the places to be seen. The boys would kick a tire, trade stories and perhaps arrange an impromptu drag race between two cars on Highway 43. These were responsible rodders, but a contemporary, Roy Petersen, who was not a Pan Dragger, recalls that Benny's was located across the street from Sparrow Hospital and that in spite of the posted "Quiet Zone" the area of Michigan Avenue next to Benny's was perpetually black with rubber marks for 200 feet in either direction!

When I lived in the area years later I heard all kinds of stories about the Pan Draggers. Someone told me that often in good weather several guys would pile into a stock touring car and pick up another Pan Dragger, Roger Huntington, who was already a noted automotive writer; he was a quadriplegic, so they'd put Roger and his wheelchair in back and cruise the Michigan State College campus and ogle women. I'd read in *Hot Rod Magazine* about the decidedly different roadster designed by Huntington and built by another Pan Dragger, Warren Tanzola. It had a T body, aluminum frame, Pontiac engine and had the radiator in the rear. I met Ollie Hines, a Pan Dragger who built a super '33 Ford coupe in the early 1950s using a brand-new Cadillac engine and a Brewster grille; that car is now owned by Ollie's son. Two Pan Draggers, Charlie Johnson and Noah Canfield, owned Capitol City Speed Shop, a Lansing landmark for decades; their "Glass Chariot," a blown Olds fuel roadster, was a contender against cars like Ray Godman's "Tennessee Bol Weevil" and the "Speed Sport Special."

The Pan Draggers formally disbanded in 1956, after a tragic accident. The club had held an endurance run that day, and afterward some of the boys were horsing around. The details were sketchy, but at least four cars were street racing on Miller Road south of Lansing; for whatever reason, two were going north and two were going south, and the four cars met at the crest of a small hill. One driver was the late Bill Waddill, a member of the Genesee Gear Grinders from Flint, and a life-long rodder who was well known in 1952, when his purple '32 roadster appeared on an early Trend book. Waddill's car and another car narrowly missed each other, but the other two rods collided head on, killing Don Hunt. After the club folded, the president, Bob Fisher, and another rodder, Dave Crowner, formed the Headers.

Flash forward to the present: Duane Allen, a staff member of the R.E. Olds Museum, thought it'd be interesting to have a reunion of the Pan Draggers, to celebrate the forty-fifth anniversary of the formation of the club. He mentioned the idea to members of the Mid-Michigan Street Rod Association, an active club with its own long history, and the club agreed to organize and host the reunion at the museum. MMSRA members designed fliers, event T-shirts and advertised the event. The club worked with Dick Harrington, a past Pan Dragger president and still an active rodder, to locate club members which, after forty years, took some work. Although a dozen Pan Draggers still live in the Lansing area, others were all over the country. A couple guys were in the hospital, and at least seven had passed away, including Roger Huntington and Ollie Hines.

On July 22nd, a beautiful Saturday, twenty-three of the original Pan Draggers showed up at the museum, and many had traveled from as far as Florida for the reunion. The MMSRA bunch parked cars, handled registration, controlled the crowds of spectators, videotaped and photographed the event and tended to what needed to be done to make things run smoothly.

For the Pan Draggers there were some frankly emotional moments, since many members had not seen one another for many years. Some were amazed that anyone cared about what they'd done as young men, so very long ago, when the world was very different. They'd changed, some waistlines had grown larger, some had hair that had turned white, and some had less hair, but these were superficial changes. All the original Pan Draggers wore large name tags so they could be recognized, and soon everyone got to talking, remembering when, and it seemed like only yesterday that they had cruised Grand River Avenue in a fenderless '32 Ford coupe or a Cad-powered '53 Studebaker. All the years of working, going to school, raising a family, were compressed into a small calendar and for this day they were back in time, young again, thinking only of the joys of working on rods and hanging out with their buddies.

For the record, original Pan Draggers in attendance were Otto Blossey, Tom Gallagher, Noah Canfield, Jim Van Horn, Roger Innes, Bob Krueger, Charlie Johnson, Kermit Jensen, Chuck Baxter, Bob Dilday, Joe Guylas, Dick Harrington, Ben Hutchinson, Jon Lundberg, Gordie Maurer, Ron McQueen, Bruce Moening, Tom Snider, Chuck Sweet, Monty Thocker, Roy Grubb, Gordon Klotz and Gary Knight. Former president Bob Fisher was in a nearby hospital. Some of the guys quit rodding years ago, some dropped out for years, then got back into it again, and some, amazingly, never quit being hot rodders. Bob Krueger, for example, still owns the channeled '29 Ford roadster he built in the 1950s. Five Pan Draggers had cars on display at the reunion: Joe Guylas' '34 Ford coupe; Ron McQueen's '32 Plymouth coupe; Dick Harrington's '40 Ford Coupe; Gordie Maurer's '34 Ford coupe and VW-powered mini Jeep; Chuck Sweet's '40 Chev coupe; and Roy Grubb's '57 Chev.

Roy Petersen of the MMSRA took the mic, welcomed the Pan Draggers and invited them to come forward. Each was presented with a copy of a videotape of Bob Krueger's color films of the early drags at the airport and the local gravel pit runs. Then another original Pan Dragger, Jon "The Voice of Drag Racing" Lundberg, took the mic and interviewed each of the guys.

From left: Gordie Maurer, Jon Lundberg, Noah Canfield, Monte Thocker, Joe Guylas, Charlie Johnson behind Dick Harrington, Chuck Baxter, Kermit Jensen, Ron McQueen behind Roger "Ozzie" Innes, Tom Snider, Tom Gallagher, Gordon Klotz, Otto Blossey, Bob Krueger, Roy Grubb, Chuck Sweet and Gary Knight (photograph by Roy H. Peterson).

There was lots of nostalgia as guys remembered specific cars, people and area landmarks. There were detailed memories of how to put juice brakes on an old Ford and how the first torque converters were modified. Several mysteries were solved, such as where the club name came from. Joe Guylas said that the oil pan on the flathead V-8 in his '34 Ford was about an inch from the pavement, and everyone told him it was a real pan dragger. In 1950, when the club was trying to decide on a name, Dick Harrington hollered, "Pan Draggers," and the others agreed.

The day went on like that, with everyone telling stories, most of them true, renewing old friendships, and looking at rods in the parking lot and the display of Pan Draggers memorabilia until, in the later afternoon, clouds gathered and soon a Midwest summer storm hit. Then the Pan Draggers and the MMSRA folks retreated to a local eatery where, during the conversations that went on into the night, it was agreed there should be another reunion in, say, ten or twenty years.

Coming Home: Back to the Fifties

COMING HOME

A couple days after I returned to Oregon, I got a call from my friend Stan Ochs, who said he's coming over. We'll go cruising in my new coupe, he said.

I looked forward to seeing Stan and his new ride, but I was a little surprised. Stan lived quite a distance away, it was already around 8:00 pm and the thermometer was lingering around 39 degrees. It was winter! But I've known Stan for a dozen years, and I've always considered him an enthusiastic hot rodder. He grew up in rural Idaho, and learned about rods through the magazines. He got into cars around 1960, and between high school and the military, he'd owned, by his count, 72, "some for only a few days:" In the years I've known him, he's owned about a dozen, some that were bought in running condition, some that he built, some that were sold in various degrees of the project stage.

But our friendship is special, I feel, because Stan is one of those guys I really enjoy talking shop with. He has a photographic memory, and can discuss at length a car he saw in a magazine years ago. He can remember minute details, and then cross-reference the car with others on points of similarity. A lot of this is the kind of stuff I have to look up, and whenever I do go to the source I find he'd always right. I not only enjoy talking with him, I always feel I learn something from the conversation.

Maybe half an hour later, I heard, over the sound of the TV, the rump of dual pipes coming down the street. I threw on my jacket and went out to meet Stan. Under the arc light was a dumped '32 Ford five-window coupe. It was chopped, channeled but full fendered, and with the gray primer, big 'n' littles, steel wheels with Ford caps, it looked old-timey. Stan found the coupe in the paper, and got it for $8000. It's all steel, and came with a built flathead. The car was built in Portland in 1952, driven a while and then garaged. Stan chopped the top 3½ inches, and recently substituted a 283 Chev for the flathead.

Otherwise, it's got all Fifties stuff, from the dropped axle to the S-W gauges. It's not a show car, Stan pointed out as we sat on antique seats, but it is a driver, and Stan has put a lot of miles on this Deuce. He turned the key, hit the starter and the roar of short-pipe duals filled the car. Stan put the '39 floor shift into low and we moved down the street.

I was back in the Fifties, and I loved it! At first I could see my breath, but then the coupe's interior warmed up. There was the faint odor of oil blow-by from the engine, and I love that smell. When we got to Foster, a wide, one-way street, Stan wound it out in low; the engine and gears screamed. He shifted quickly into second and caught some rubber and wound it tight again. I'd done this so many times on this same street 40 years before, and the movement through time was instantaneous: the sensation of speed, the smell of blow-by, the flickering headlights and pounding exhaust sound. Yep, I was back.

We drove around for a couple of hours. I never got over the kick of pulling up to a light and looking at John Q. Public and family gawking at two middle-aged geezers in a radical street coupe. Stan took it easy for the most part, kicking it through the gears occasionally, and although we saw several police cars, we weren't even followed. The coupe has a small radiator and grille, but the engine never heated up, and this is true with the Chev even in summer. It's just a good driver, with all road equipment, and the fenders do their job in the rain.

Stan Ochs stands head and shoulders over his '32 five-window, which has been chopped and channeled.

Moreover, it's a car that Stan feels fairly comfortable in parking on the street when he goes to dinner or to a movie. This isn't true of his other rod, an all steel '29 A roadster pickup that was a magazine car in the late Fifties. It has new paint, chrome and interior, and he has to keep an eye on it. The coupe will no doubt get a new coat of primer this summer, and that's all.

Finally, it was time to head home. When Stan got to the corner near my house he shifted from second to low at about 15 miles per hour and popped the clutch. The engine roared, a tire screamed and porch lights went on in every house. It was very satisfying. I could see heads popping past screen doors, and I imagined the older neighbors thinking: Drake's home again!

LES AMIS DE ROUTE 66

When the French speak of the Fabulous Fifties, it's the American Fifties they refer to. Even during that decade, the French were more hip to cool jazz, William Faulkner, the Beats and our *cinema noir* than the man on the street in Des Moines. James Dean was an instant idol, with Jean Paul Belmondo rushing in to fill the void; Elvis, Jerry Lee Lewis and Little Richard were big in France shortly after their debut here. And as for cars, the French have long had a love affair with those big beautiful boats built in Detroit during the Fifties.

So it should not have been a surprise to receive a package from France, sent by a group of Frenchmen who are nuts about rods, customs and American cars of the Fifties. I was surprised, however, by the layout of the long, marvelous letter, with the handwritten text surrounding cut-up color photographs of guys clowning around in and with their cars. There was also a tape

Top: Three of the Route 66 men with a rare French 1937 Ford. *Bottom:* Fabrice, Jean-Michel and Pascal "Bodie" Bodet show the club logo and a favorite book!

Fabrice's customized Citroën 2 CV had wide whites, red rims, light blue paint and detailed engine. Wild!

of T. Texas Tyler singing "Hot Rod Rag" circa 1953, which they asked me to translate, and a hand-embroidered jacket patch of their club logo, "Route 66."

The wonderful letter was the work of the club president, Jean Hernandez, who was kind enough to call me their "Walt Disney of hot rodding"! He said that the club had been in the planning stages for two years, and it has been official since June 13, 1989. It was inspired, he said, by the article in *Nitro* about the "Low Flyers" of Brittany and my book, *Street Was Fun in '51*, plus a dedicated interest in cars, especially American cars of the Fifties, and rods and customs of that period.

Jean's ride is a 1955 Ford sedan, with the original green paint and wide whites. It's interesting to see how American movies have influenced the world's car culture. Jean plans to remove all the trim on his Customline and to make it into "a slightly customized copper car," an idea that came to him after watching *Rebel Without a Cause*; the LA police cars in that film are '55 Ford Mainline models. He added, "If I had the money and could afford a '56 Ford convertible, I'd take the entire hood off, and paint her white with red flames like Elvis's mechanic's car in *Viva Las Vegas.*"

It must be costly to buy, own and drive an older American car in Europe, but they are in demand. The club's treasurer, Jean-Michel Dajon, spent over a year searching for the car of his dreams, an immaculate 1956 Olds Holiday hardtop. Jean Hernandez is right when he wonders whether such a car "must have been a daydream for the teenager of the mid Fifties." Some of us older cats still have those daydreams!

Some of the members dig native material. The secretary, Pascal "Bodie" Bodet, has a Simca Ariane and a Ford Vedette. The Vedette looks like a downsized 1949–50 Mercury sedan, and would lend itself to traditional customizing. Moreover, it has a European version of the Ford V8-60 engine — a flathead that generates 66 hp and can easily be hopped up! That'd be a neat rig to bring to a Nats or KKOA meet! Merve "Veve" Dajon, Jean-Michel's brother, has two

Renault Dauphines, and "one-and-a-half for parts." Fabrice "Ptit Fab" Gilbert owns a two-tone Simca Ariane. He had a neatly customized Citroen 2 CV — light blue, big 'n' little wide whites, red rims and full wheel covers, and a very detailed engine compartment. Neat ride!

As Jean said, "Everybody's got his jolly jalopy" now and the club's work is moving ahead. They have rented a garage for their cars, and "Things are going to rock for our rattlers," said Jean. When the cars are ready, the gang plans to take to the road. Of course, they hope someday to bring a car to the U.S. and hit the "nostalgia drags, to run on the dry lakes, to run in the Panamericana Mexico," etc. I think they'll do it, and I can guess which route they'll take across the U.S.

I wondered how they chose the name "Route 66" for the club. Jean said he'd suggested "Toits Ronds," which means "rounded roof," but the others objected. All agreed they did not want something like "The Friends of Peugot, or "Custom Cars of Toulouse." Jean felt it had to be a French name, it should deal with cars or roads, and they all had to accept it. He saw an article in *Nitro* about Route 66, and the rest is history (they're still amazed that we use the French word route rather than road!).

Now, with lots of enthusiasm and a few francs, they want to build a low buck roadster as a club project. So, if you're heading across America next summer, and you see a rat gray, primered A-V8 roadster running the tri-color and packed with wild and crazy rodders follow them to the next rest area. Hum a few bars of "La Marseillaise," open a bottle of Gallo vintage '90 and give them a warm welcome.

DALE MOREAU: ACE PHOTOGRAPHER

Usually when I think of the good old days I have to go back 50 years. But occasionally there have been good old days in recent history. Some that come to mind are the times I worked with Dale Moreau covering the Portland Roadster Show. Dale took photographs of the cars as I followed him around taking notes, and together we created a photograph-essay for a magazine. Those were good times. We'd work some on Thursday, then arrive early Friday, before the displays were set up, and work hard for four hours. Then we'd head for the VIP room for a great, catered three-course lunch, with real silverware and crystal, and food served by a waiter. There would be other automotive journalists there, such as Gray Baskerville, David Marin, Eric Geisart and writers from the local newspapers. After lunch the main floor of the show was cleared of people, and Dale and I would have the place to ourselves until that evening, when the show opened to the public.

Dale and I worked together on several Portland Roadster Shows, and it never seemed like work. Hot rodding in Portland was on a high; there was a sense of alacrity, less friction, fewer factions, less acrimony. We had a job to do, and with Dale's connections we knew when and where the article would appear and we knew when we'd get paid. Most of all, we loved our work! Dale is a high-energy guy; he works quickly, with an artist's spontaneity and a technician's control. He has been taking pictures for many years, and knows what will make a good shot; he would take two or three shots, then we'd move on. After several hours of this the show would open and we would stand around talking with the participants. There was no end to the guys who hoped Dale would get their car in a magazine. Then we'd go to dinner. Eventually, I'd get home, happy but dog-tired — and the show would go on for three more days!

I don't think Dale ever got tired. He is a veggie guy who works out in his basement gym and stays healthy, in part, because he never did the things that so many others did in the 1960s. I mention that because I'm amazed at his stamina and his perpetually positive attitude; I keep looking for the source of his strength. He has been a photographer and car nut since the age of fourteen, and his enthusiasm for both is unflagging. The secret, he says, is his passion.

Dale was raised in Lockport, New York, home of the widest bridge in the world, and of Brock Yates, noted automotive journalist and TV personality. He grew up with cars, his first being a '51 Ford convertible painted red using an Electrolux vacuum cleaner. Dale's father was an airbrush artist and commercial photographer. He grew up spending time with his dad on photograph shoots and in the darkroom, and although his dad passed away when he was eleven, the seed was planted that would give him his life's career.

Although Dale majored in art in college, it was photography that drove his artistic eye for composition. He attended AUS in Massachusetts then took advanced photography classes at the New York Institute of Photography, and the University of New York at Farmingdale. In 1992 he earned a Master of Photography Guild degree from the Professional Photographers of America.

But by then, of course, he had been a working photographer for many years, primarily as the staff photographer at Freightliner Corporation. That job took him on the road to numerous locations to photograph Freightliner trucks at work, for advertising and for the people and manufacturing facilities that built them. A typical assignment might see Dale fly from Portland to Chicago, then get on a smaller plane and head to Bemidji, Minnesota, to shoot cold weather testing in below zero weather. Then he might fly to Dallas, Texas, to photograph almost the entire Fort Worth fire department personnel with their new Freightliner fire trucks, shooting from a bucket two stories up in the air! From there he'd fly to Nebraska to photograph the principal dealer in Lincoln and one of his best customers. Dale calls trips his "happy hops," as he was hopping from one plane to another for days at a time. He did that for years. Therefore, it was not surprising to see Dale at Bonneville Speed Week an few years ago as the official photographer for the "Joint Venture" Freightliner diesel truck, the fastest in the world in its class, setting a record at over 225 miles per hour!

As with many car nuts, Dale has had quite a few different rides, from hot rods to muscle cars. He moved to Portland, Oregon, in 1969 and got mixed up with a bunch of hot rodders. In 1972 he joined the Rose City Street Rods club and has been a member off and on since then. That was a time of transition for street rodding: the large associations were formed, established publications ended and new ones were started. Bruce Miller started *Street Rod Magazine*, and Dale went to work on the side as an unpaid photographer. By 1972 John Slaughter owned the title, and he sent Dale to the 3rd Annual Street Rod Nationals in Detroit, Michigan. During that event Dale again got hooked on old cars, and he formed several life-long friendships. The first was Gary Will, of East Aurora, New York, and the second was Brian Brennan, well-known editor of *Street Rodder Magazine*. Several weeks later, back in Portland, Dale was riding his young son, Jay, around the block on the handlebars of his Schwinn and two blocks from home he found a '37 Ford coupe for sale. He bought it for $850; he had it painted and put it in the Portland Roadster Show the next spring.

Photographing street rods followed naturally. His first two published articles appeared earlier in *Hot Rod Magazine*. In November, 1966 he won an amateur photograph contest sponsored by *Hot Rod* and won $25, and a little later he placed his first feature, on a customized 1962 Chevy SS, in the magazine. Then a growing family and the move west meant he had to put his interest in photographing cars aside until the early 1970s. Since then he has worked full time as a corporate photographer. After getting an "early out" from Freightliner during one of the industries downturns, his work has appeared frequently in most of the leading automotive publications.

Dale continues to garner awards for his photography. The list of awards and prizes won would be as long as the list of cars he's owned. A crowning achievement was being named Nikon

Dale Moreau wheels his roadster around a turn on the backroads of Oregon. His planned epitaph? "He Had Passion!" (photograph by Dan Brouillard).

Corporate Photographer of the year. For this competition, in which he was competing with the larger photograph departments of major companies like Hughes Tool and Kraft Foods, he had to submit a comprehensive portfolio of his work and a résumé. It took Dale several years to earn the award. This past spring he won sweepstakes, the Fuji Award and Best Commercial award at the annual Professional Photographers of Oregon convention.

Dale could be described as the consummate photographer. He photographs not only cars, but advertising projects, industrial settings and portraiture. Dale said, "I see beautiful images in many subjects other than automobiles." He also claims that his profession has never really involved hard work. "It was too much fun taking pictures to ever be called work. I usually had more fun on location in the desert, or shooting trucks at John Wayne airport than going on vacation!"

From the street rod Dale drives, to his long-time friends, to his attractive home, there is a poetry to his life. His wife, Kathy Willburn, is an accomplished illustrator, specializing in children's books and greeting cards. She started out at Hallmark in Kansas City, and has had her own studio for most of her career.

Dale's primary concern is to record the beauty he sees everywhere. He keeps making images because of the passion that drives him. The light changes momentarily, shifts, the sea mist softens it, and he has to make one more shot to capture the mood. It is the same passion for light that drove Degas, Monet and the great Impressionists.

THE AMAZING STORY OF TAD WINIECKI'S SAFERCYCLE

Tad Winiecki is a scientist, engineer and inventor. A long-time motorcycle rider, he got tired of hearing people say that he was crazy to ride a motorcycle because they're unsafe.

Using his engineering background, he decided to build a motorcycle with remarkable safety features that would encourage even the faint of heart to give motorcycling a try. The result, after many years of experimentation, is a bike that Tad calls the Safercycle.

Winiecki defines the Safercycle as a "street-legal two-wheeled motorcycle with convenient crash protection." He says that it will protect the rider, when other vehicles hit the front, back or sides of the Safercycle or when the Safercycle impacts an object.

Winiecki worked in the aerospace industry. He was able to gather data on how well the human body can withstand impacts, as well as on advanced restraint systems and methods of providing some kind of shock absorber to minimize injury. He also studied the crash protection used in race cars and motorcycles that run at high speeds on the Bonneville Salt Flats.

In a 1986 technical paper, written for the Society of Automotive Engineers (SAE), Winiecki outlined the design goals he had in mind when he started this project in 1976. They were as follows: that a rider wearing street clothes and without a helmet would not be hurt in a simple upset; that the rider would be able to get back on the bike and be underway in less than twenty seconds; that the rider would be able to ride again two days after being hit by a car from the side or the rear, at 16 m/s, or head-on, with both vehicles going 20 m/s (the Safercycle would be wrecked, of course); and that the safety features cost less than $1,270 (in 1986).

In 1976, Winiecki bought a new BMW R90S motorcycle and fired up his welding torch. He extended the frame (and drive shaft) six inches, to give the rider more space in which to move forward before striking anything under impact. Next, he added steel tubing around the outside of the motorcycle — for side protection — and built a kind of cage around the rider (with a roll bar that extends above head level). Tubing at the front converges to a point, behind the headlight, to create what he calls an "anti-somersault front end."

Winiecki's research — as well as that of others — showed that, in a head-on crash, the motorcycle tends to somersault and crush the rider between the cycle and the colliding object (which is why seat belts are not used on motorcycles). His front end lowers the center of gravity, thus absorbing some of the impact and theoretically, keeping the bike from flipping over.

To keep the rider from being ejected during a crash, Winiecki devised a unique seat and restraint system. Using a fiberglass dune buggy seat, he cut notches in the bottom, so that the rider could put his feet on the ground (required by the California Vehicle code). He cut the top of the seat off, and replaced it with an adjustable headrest. He then built a restraint that fits around the rider's stomach and lower chest. It's made of fiberglass-reinforced plastic, with a steel structure. It attaches to the seat bottom with a quick-release latch, and to the sides with catches. Padded nylon belts go from the restraint, over the rider's shoulders, and connect to the headrest and to a cable. The result is akin to a child's safety seat for an adult.

To lessen some of the crash energy — and to absorb the impact the rider would be subjected to — Winiecki built a huge shock absorber that is a central safety feature of the bike. It's actually a steel tube, with a mandrel at one end that attaches to a cable. The cable is attached to the seat. Should the bike experience a head-on crash, the mandrel is pulled through the tube, allowing the seat and rider to move slightly forward, with the cable absorbing some of the initial impact. The device has a force of 3½ tons. A series of ropes and pulleys pull the rider back to his original position within the safety of the roll cage. This shock absorber design was adapted from that used on the seats of the Convair 880 airplane. Another safety feature is the padded handlebar, which breaks away in the event of a major frontal impact.

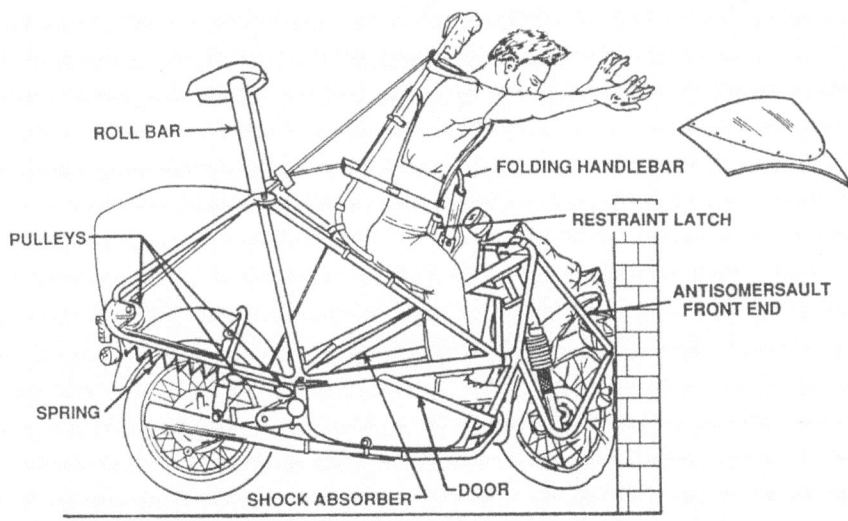

Top: Although Tad Winiecki is a very religious person, he feels he needs additional protection when riding a motorcycle. *Bottom:* This illustration shows the Safercycle's design and what might happen in a front end crash (art by Tad Winiecki).

Winiecki worked with motorcycle designer Craig Vetter in developing a fairing. They did not have the benefit of a wind tunnel, but designed it using computer drawings. Tad had a fiberglass fabrication shop make a mold from his plug. He did the finish work on the mold and had the shop make the fairing. The doors were then padded with aluminum honeycomb and polyethylene foam to absorb side impacts. When open, the doors also serve as side stands.

Over the years, Winiecki put many miles on the Safercycle. He has found it to be very road worthy. The longest trip he's taken on it was from San Diego, Calif. to Cape Canaveral, Fla. and back. This was accomplished without incident, although the large fairing was buffeted from the turbulence of large trucks. It's aerodynamically stable at speeds over 30 mph and Winiecki has never had any control problems. The Safercycle's top speed is 109 mph, and fuel economy is 45 mpg at 60 mph, in spite of the bike's 700 lb. weight

Winiecki describes this version of the Safercycle as an engineering model. It is one step below a prototype, and he knows he'll make some changes if he builds a second Safercycle. One change would be in the doors, which currently open from the front. Winiecki now considers this a design flaw.

Although the bike has fallen over several times, the only accident happened when a mechanic took the Safercycle for a test drive. He wasn't wearing a helmet; and didn't put the body restraint on. He also did not get the door properly latched. The door flew open at 40 mph, throwing the bike out of control. The rider fell down, spun around, and slid into a car — at about 25 mph — breaking his collarbone.

Although there are micro-switches on the door latches, with an indicator light to show if the door isn't closed, the light may not have been working when the accident occurred. Winiecki has now installed engine interlocks, so the engine won't start if the doors aren't properly latched.

Winiecki has four patents on the safety features of the Safercycle. Although he's offered his inventions to the major motorcycle manufacturers none has shown an interest. Winiecki is realistic, though. He realizes that the Safercycle would probably appeal to only about two percent of the potential motorcycle-buying public — those who would love to own a motorcycle but consider them unsafe.

CTA Reunion

I'll be the first to admit that much of the past is murky, but some things are clear as crystal. That's especially true of my early days of hot rodding, before my head got filled with stuff. I vividly remember the sense of June 1951, when my father and I got my A-V8 roadster on the road, and that Sunday in July when we drove it to Eugene, 120 miles south, for the only legal drag races in Oregon. In August I joined the Road Angels — the only thing I've ever joined — and I found myself living the life I'd read about in the rodding magazines. As the warm evenings of late summer headed into fall, as high school once again started, I went to club meetings, hung around with older guys who were building hot engines and street rods. After the meetings we'd head for Bart's Drive-In, where we'd stand around, kick tires and talk.

Things were happening, and quickly. The Road Angels plaque I put on my roadster had the acronym N.W.T.A., for the Northwest Timing Association, the outfit that put on the drags in Eugene. The Portland guys thought there should be a local drag strip, and so in the fall of 1951 two clubs, the Road Angels and the Ramblers, formed the Columbia Timing Association (C.T.A.).

I barely got my plaque on my roadster when I had to turn it in to get a new plaque with C.T.A. on it (those marked N.W.T.A. were melted down, and how I wish I had kept mine!).

The first thing the group did was secure the use of an emergency airstrip near Madras, Oregon on which to hold timed one-mile speed runs. (Later the distance was ¾ mile, then ½ mile.)

On September 21st the first run was held; although an October rain date was set, the weather was gorgeous, and the cars ran all the way down that strip and tripped the clocks, flat out! In early March, C.T.A., still comprised of only the two original clubs, put on a car show in the Portland Auditorium. By June 1952, C.T.A. held organized drag races at the Scappoose airfield west of Portland.

This was like a dream for a high school kid who lived and breathed hopped-up cars! I suffered through classes, watching the clock until the 3 o'clock bell sounded and I could jump in my roadster and cruise around, stopping at someone's body shop, garage or service station, dreaming of building a flat out race car. Of course, I was just a kid, and could offer little except enthusiasm. I shared a dream with rodders all over the country, even those in So-Cal who had the dry lakes, who wanted a timing strip. Look at the old magazines, or Felsen's novels, where young rodders keep hoping for a paved strip that would be long, safe and fast, their version of Bonneville. Or even a drag strip, where a guy could go through the gears. Drag racing had gotten a good start on the West Coast, but there were places that would not have a drag strip for years.

The Portland area had both a drag strip and a timing strip, primarily because among the hot rodders there were personable young men who were articulate. Armed with a copy of *Roberts Rules of Order*, they could form a group of guys into a club, and a couple of clubs into a timing association. They were natural leaders who were able to conduct meetings, draft proposals, meet with the city fathers and speak eloquently. Most of all, they were able to convince the powers-that-be that it would be a good idea to let some wild-eyed kids race side-by-side in stripped machines down their air strip.

That all happened 50 years ago, when it seemed impossible to top 100 mph in the quarter and two carburetors were a lot. One of the guys who made it all happen was Ray Van Dorn, who is still a hot rodder. He thought it'd be a good idea to have a 50 Year Reunion of the old C.T.A. guys, their families and friends. In addition, he wanted to invite anyone who digs the good old days. It'll be a chance to see vintage iron on display and talk with guys who are hot rod history. It'll happen August 18, 2001, at Woodburn (Oregon) Drag Strip.

Going, Going, Gone!

The two old cars were always there, part of the landscape, like cows nuzzling each other as they nibbled on the towering laurel bush that grew out to meet them.

Over the past two decades I've usually managed to return at least once a year to the city where I was born. Each time I'd drive around, noting what had changed and what had stayed the same. Mostly things had changed. During the past twenty years, growth had occurred at a terrific rate. Skyscrapers dominated the skyline downtown, and every formerly empty lot in the suburbs now had a house on it. Traffic was crazy, and the joys of driving had become greatly diminished.

Nevertheless, I'd drive around, trying to capture memories or feelings of past years. Sooner or later I'd drive along Foster Road, near the city's edge, the area where I grew up, and I'd glance down 100th Street, down the road that used to lead to Dwyer's Mill and Indian Rock. The mill, which I thought would last forever, was now shut down and the machinery scrapped; Indian Rock, an old quarry with stones as big as boxcars that I was certain would never change, had been filled in and a road built over it.

Now the only reason for glancing down the road was to check out the two old cars parked there. They had been there forever, or at least since the early Sixties. They represented constancy, in a crazy world that was changing too quickly for me.

The two cars had become old, but otherwise they were not especially interesting. One was

The '49 Chevy and the '48 Frazer had stood together for years, like two patient cows. Both cars were complete, solid and easily restorable.

a 1949 Chevrolet Styline sedan with a couple of dents and a broken side window. The other was a 1948 Frazer four-door in similar condition. These cars were not rare or exotic or valuable — but they were *there,* year after year, growing old gracefully.

They were in the same old place when I returned again this year. I had never stopped to check them over, but one day I was visiting the body shop next door, a shop that turns out some nice custom cars and muscle cars, and because I had my camera in hand I wandered over and took a couple of photographs of the Chevy and the Frazer.

It's fortunate that I did, because a couple weeks later the cars were gone: I found their disappearance hard to believe. I stopped, but there was nothing to see — only the two brown outlines on the grass where they had stood, like the tracings that police draw around a homicide victim.

The next time I passed by I automatically looked up the street, expecting to see the cars. Instead I saw the laurel bush being decimated by an elderly man with a bow saw. I stopped and, out of curiosity, asked about the absent cars. He was friendly, and volunteered the information with some chagrin. He had stopped driving the cars years ago — he couldn't recall when or why — and had them parked for many years in the back yard. Then he had moved them to the front. The city had bugged him a couple times about doing something with the cars; he had not done anything, nor had the city. Someone — kids, he supposed — had broken a couple windows, but otherwise the cars were not bothered. Nor were they bothering anyone — there were, after all, a good many cars parked along the street — but finally the city had presented him with an ultimatum: move 'em or lose 'em. He had allowed the cars to be taken to the crusher. He was not angry, but he would not have given them up if he had had a choice, he said.

My amazement must have been obvious. I had assumed that the cars had gone to a collector, or at least a parts scavenger. Neither car was highly desirable but both had possibilities. Both cars were solid, with a minimum of surface rust, and both could easily have been restored. Or they could have been customized; because of the scarcity of coupes and convertibles, four-door sedans have been getting the treatment lately. The Frazer was pre-1949, and would have made a cool sled for both NSRA and KKOA events.

At the very least, the cars could have been reduced to parts. The annual Portland Swap Meet is huge, and brings together buyers and sellers of every imaginable automobile part. I don't know what the market is for Frazer hubcaps, grille, fenders, etc., but I know that a 1949 Chevy front license plate guard is going for an easy $50. I would've hated to see the cars parted out, but at least something would have remained. It seemed inconceivable that the cars had been reduced to two bales of metal that were now, no doubt, in the mid-Pacific, en route to Japan, to return as econo-box uni-cars.

When I passed the house months later it had not been painted, but the laurel bush was putting forth new leaves. Except for the loss of the two cars, the street was the same. Other cars were parked in front of other houses, cars on blocks, some without wheels, some missing windows. They were all fairly recent, but already derelicts. Perhaps in twenty or thirty years they would become interesting, although I have doubts.

Mr. Motor Manners

Because of my age and sagacity, from time to time I receive personal letters asking for advice. This I'm happy to give. Acting under the assumption that the problems I hear about no doubt affect others, 1 share these letters with you; perhaps you see yourself or your soul mate here.

Dear Mr. Drake:
My husband, Sylvester, has some clothes and a car club jacket from the 1950s. The problem is that he won't let me wash them. Whenever we go to a Fifties dance others stay away from us because the clothes smell of sweat and the jacket reeks to high heaven of mothballs. What should I do?
Edna C. Pittsburgh, PA

Dear Edna:
Do nothing! He's being authentic!
Clothes were seldom washed back then. Sweat and mothballs — that's what I remember from the Fifties!

Dear Albert,
Please help! The mantle and sideboard shelves are covered with trophies my husband won with his street rod. The problem is, they gather lots of dust and I'm tired of dusting them. I think he should dust them, but he refuses. Who is right?
Leonora Smith Danville, CA

Dear Leonora:
In the Fifties you can bet your booties you'd have that duster in hand. In this liberated age — for better or for worse — the rule of thumb is: the person who won them dusts them!

Al,
Settle an argument, okay? I own, free and clear, six cars from the Fifties, including a couple 300-letter Chryslers, and also an assortment of rods, including a couple Deuces, a T-bone

and two A-bones, a show-winning '35 Ford pickup, a neat-o '36 3-window and some other stuff. Okay, I have some parts cars too. The thing is, I think fat is where it's at (I don't seem to be able to shuck any of it — ha ha) and I now have my eye on a neat-o '48 Ford coupe. It's unfinished, but so sweet. It's full custom and pro-street, so it's not cheap. I want to take out a second mortgage on the stump farm, but the better half says no. I tell her it's a good investment; she says it's another toy. Who's right?
Big Eddie Big D, TX

Dear Eddie,
If you're really big, of course you're right! If your wife's bigger, then she's right! Seriously, I can see it both ways. That fat fendered thingamabob is going to give you a lot of pleasure; so I say yes. On the other hand, you do have lots of toys, so I'm siding with the wife. How many is enough? The Bhagwan Rajneesh, the spiritual man who got kicked out of the country, had 96 Rolls Royces when the law came down on him. They were somehow supposed to get him into Nirvana. He died recently, and I was thinking about those cars. The guy who bought them was in his early 40s, good-looking, rich, flew from Texas to Oregon in his own Lear jet with a snappy-looking girlfriend and took them all. They were still trucking Rolls Royces down to Texas when, a couple months later, he keeled over, the victim of a brain tumor. There's a lesson for all car nuts there somewhere.

Dear Mr. Drake:
Why do car people feel the need to own so many cars? A friend likes Corvairs. He started with one, now he's got 24! Please explain this sickness!
Arthur A. Athson

Dear Art:
See above.

Dear Al Drake:
For a couple years now I've been trying to buy a buddy's '40 Merc Kemp. He wouldn't sell it, but now he's got an offer from a guy in Japan. That guy'll pay $5000 more than the car's worth — and it's $5000 more than I've got! I can't match the offer. But this guy's my best friend. I say he ought to sell it to me. Right?
Danny Salinas Seattle, WA

Dear Danny,
Absolutely! It's more than a question of friendship. It's more than making a tiny dent in the balance of payments deficit. I don't think one more old car ought to leave the US of A. Appeal to your buddy's sense of patriotism!

Dear Mr. Drake:
My husband brought home a 1939 Plymouth as the basis for a street rod. Now he's got two more parts cars. We live in a typical suburb, have a small yard, and the neighbors are complaining Any suggestions?
Debbie Salazar
Des Moines, IA

Dear Debbie:
Thirty-nine Plymouths make excellent planters. Who can complain about a flowerbed on wheels? Not even LadyBird Johnson.

Dear Mr. Drake:

My fiancé is a rodder, and he insists I accompany him to every swap meet, rod run and car show. Frankly, I don't give a darn. I love him but I think chromed, over-powered cars are macho, phallic and akin to many of the sexist attitudes that plague our society. How can I get him to make a distinction between the person I love and the life-style I detest?

Bonnie LaBelle Chicago, IL

Dear *Bonnie:*

I think you two should have a long talk before you take that short walk down the aisle. I see your point; and agree with some of what you say. In the Fifties, hot rodding was enjoyed by young men in their late teens and early twenties, mostly single. Now it's become a family activity, which is good. I suspect, however, that women are often superficially interested. It's probably a case of the nesting instinct (female) being incompatible with a balls out engine (male). In the last few years I've seen too many divorces that were the result of this situation.

Dear Mr. Drake:

I have an odd problem that I don't dare write Dear Abby about. My husband insists on keeping an open can of Castrol under our bed. He claims it's an aphrodisiac. He's a wonderful lover, but afterward he falls asleep and makes noises, like an accelerating engine and squealing tires. My question is: can the odor of Castrol help our love life?

Betty Vidan Boise, ID

Dear Betty,
It can't hurt!

THE TRUE MEANING OF CHRISTMAS

Christmas means gifts, whether spiritual or material, and we give what we can, what we have, hoping to please. There is the gift, the intent behind the giving and the receiving. To give a gift implies clarity of mind, an open heart and nobility of character. But if a gift is not well-received is the giving diminished?

It was two weeks before Christmas and I was lying on the ground, on three inches of snow, staring up at crank journal number one. A rod bearing had begun to knock, and simply by listening I decided that it was either the first or second rod, or possibly the third. Now, in the late afternoon light, I strained to see anything that would indicate that a particular bearing was the culprit. I removed the caps on the next two rods, keeping nuts, lock washers and caps in correct order on the shop rag I'd spread in the snow.

In spite of the snow the weather wasn't especially cold, somewhere in the mid-thirties, well above freezing, and there was no wind. But I was wet, greasy and uncomfortable. It would have been better if I could have tackled the job a couple of months earlier, but of course the rod was quiet then. It began to rattle around Thanksgiving. I had stacks of term papers to read, and tests to give, read and grade, then days of conferences and so on. One morning I turned in the grades, hit the parts store and around noon I jacked up the front end of our International Travelall. I had the pan removed, the rod caps off and a decision made by 3:00 P.M. I put the new insert bearing in, hoping I'd chosen the correct rod, and I buttoned things up. In the last light of day I scraped off the old pan gasket, got out the Permatex and put on a new gasket. I unjacked the Travelall, put in new oil and crossed my fingers. When it fired, the engine ran smoothly without a hint of rod noise. I was ecstatic! The rig had 160,000-plus miles, and all I hoped for was another 5,000. Okay, 2,000. Just keep running until spring, I prayed. I was proud of my ability to fix the problem. This was not precise work, but it did the job. Although I have never been the kind of mechanic I once hoped to be, I have largely been able to keep the family cars running.

I was standing beside the Travelall, the hood raised, listening for any odd engine sound, when my wife loomed out of the darkness, her arms filled with sacks and boxes, her boots slipping in the snow. "You could have met the bus," she said, sliding toward the house. She apparently thought I'd spent the afternoon leaning on the fender of the Travelall. I tried to explain. "Just open the door," she said. I moved toward her and tried to take some of her load. I was a mess, my pants and jacket wet, my hands and arms black with the grime peculiar to old engine oil. "Just open the door," she repeated.

The argument went on for some time. I should have helped her shop, I should have driven her into town, or at least met her at the final bus stop on her return to save her the long walk home on the snow-covered shoulder. I countered that I had spent the day fixing the Travelall, thereby saving money that we could use for Christmas. "I did it for the family," I said. A Christmas present! But there was no mirth in my voice when I said it. Nor any in hers when she said "Big deal!" I had had a feeling of euphoria when heard that engine purr, but now my temper was rising and my thinking was confused.

Much later, months or years later, I thought about how dopey I had been to buy a bearing for only one throw. A reasonable person would have bought two or three sets, thereby bettering the odds. A much more reasonable person would have taken the Travelall to a repair shop. I should have been guided by the manifold meanings of the part replaced: to have good bearings, to know specifically your location and direction, or one's personal bearing, meaning the manner of conducting or carrying oneself. Replacing that bearing, and all the other repairs made on the family's failing machines, was irrational thinking. I said that I was doing it for the family, but the work in the long run was a series of warped gifts. It took me a long time to see that.

But no one wants to read an unhappy Christmas story. With the exception of "The Little Match Girl" every story I can think of about Christmas has a happy ending. The happiness of Christmas often depends on excessive behavior: people eat too much, drink too much, sing too much and spend too much money. Most of all, people remember too much: the splendid tree of one's youth, the gaily wrapped gifts, the wonderful turkey dinner, the illicit taste of a Tom and Jerry, the odor of cigar smoke, the talk, the laughter, the perfect day. Christmas is a time of good intentions and confused thinking.

My thinking gets confused too, but I know I remember when the true meaning of Christmas was as clear as an icicle. It was long ago, our first Christmas in Michigan, far from our families and friends. We rented a crappy house with a basement that usually had three inches of water on the floor, an unfinished upstairs and a septic tank that was often full. On the other hand, I think we were extremely happy. My wife worked to make things nice, as she always has: she baked cookies, made Christmas cards, tree ornaments and socks to hang on the mantle that we didn't have. She made some presents, and shopped with skill. There were toys, treats, art supplies, clothes and educational games for our two small children and a third soon to be born. Although we lacked a TV, the radio pumped out holiday songs at a fever pitch — songs the kids echoed endlessly. Bowls of nuts, fudge and brightly-colored hard candy sat on tables, along with fresh fruit and, for adults, a bottle of decent brandy. The kids lived on the edge of expectation, wondering when, if ever, Christmas would come.

On Christmas morning I woke to a noise. Light from a major star came through the window, illuminating the unfinished rooms, a place as crude as that original manger, and through the wall that was simply a skeleton of studs I could see our son Moss climbing out of bed. Slowly he made his way into the space where my wife and I slept, he woke his sister, helping her from her crib. He took her hand and led her through the darkened room to the stairs; little red slippers covered their feet, and their steps sounded like whispers. Then they were out of sight, but I could see them in my mind: Moss, only three, led his sister, Monica, half his age, down the steps, taking care of her as he now takes care of his own children. So do Monica and her sister Bellen, all caring people who were genetically imprinted to always do the right thing. Moss led Monica through the darkness until they could see the tree, and his voice, clear and honest, carried upstairs: "See Monica, he really did come!"

Aussie Hot Rodder Finds Good Tin

David Waight is an Australian who loves hopped-up Model A Fords and '50s-style American hot rods. The trouble is, there's a dearth of Model A coupe and tudor bodies in Australia, and most of the available cars have already been modified. When David completed fifteen years as a bank auditor and was eligible for a fifteen week "holiday," he decided to spend the time in the United States looking for old cars to take back to Australia.

David and his two brothers, Les and Bob, all own Model A Fords, and they're active in the Australian swap meet scene. In addition to buying, selling and swapping parts they also make fiberglass "guards" (fenders) for Model A Fords. So David had a good idea of the kinds of things he wanted to pick up in the States; he knew what he wanted for his own use, and what kinds of things would sell when he got back home.

He made the arrangements for transportation for himself and for the cars he would buy over here before he left home, and paid the bill; that left only expenses such as food and lodging during the trip which he paid by credit card. He arrived in Los Angeles early in the summer and was soon met by two "mates" (friends) who came over shortly after. They did a "fly around" from LA to Tucson, Las Vegas and San Francisco, sight-seeing and always on the lookout for old cars. In San Francisco they rented a car and went to a swap meet. David bought Ford hydraulic brake setups, 1934 Ford axles, finned Buick brake drums, steel Model A fenders, and other "trinkets." With the car overloaded, David drove to Los Angeles, parted with his friends and left the car parts at a secure place on the dock.

David's plan was to buy a 1955 Chevrolet, drive it around the country, sleep in it, then take it back home and sell it. But he got the use of a late-model Chev van that another Australian leaves in Los Angeles for his use when he's over here. In a few short weeks he drove the van 16,000 miles, traveling alone, over the western states, into Canada, and as far east as North and South Dakota. He attended the Antique Nationals, the LA Roadster Show, swap meets at Pomona and Long Beach, the Oldies but Goodies drag races in Boise, Idaho, saw the motorcycles at Sturgis, South Dakota, back to Boise for the Night Fire Funny Car Nationals, then down to Pleasanton, California, for the big Goodguys rod run. He covered a good deal of the United States in a short time, and as he put it, "I've built a lot of cars in my head while traveling."

All during his travels David was on the lookout for cars and parts to take home. How does one find old cars in this vast region? "By word of mouth, basically. From the coffee shop in the morning, or getting petrol, I ask people about any old cars in the area. Then I have to clarify and ask about Model A Fords. Some of them think an old car is a '72 Datsun. And I bought the local papers." Often he'd find an interesting car in the paper, take a look at it, and find that it wasn't exactly what he wanted or that the price wasn't right. But he'd ask the owner about other Model A Fords and sometimes that would lead to a more desirable car. The rod runs were another source. He'd hang around the Model A's, approach an owner and ask questions. As a result, he found excellent, unmodified Model A coupes in San Francisco, Fresno and Portland, and bought all three.

He used the same method to find old junkyards. In a yard in Boise he found an excellent 1936 Ford coupe body and chassis for only $300. I asked David how in the world he could move a hulk from Boise to Australia, since I'd have trouble getting it to the West Coast. At the same yard he bought a 1964 GMC pickup, complete, but not running, for $300 and loaded the '36 Ford into the bed. Then he filled both vehicles with finned Buick brake drums, wire wheels and other parts. Then he got on the phone and called until he found a trucker who'd take the load to LA for a reasonable price, in this case $300. So David had $900 invested, and he's certain he can get $2,500 for the '36 Ford back home. The only Chevrolet and GMC pickups in Australia have been imported, and they're very rare and in demand. Although the 1964 GMC David bought needs restoration, it should sell for $4,000. Any vehicle over 30 years old brought into the country is duty free, but he will still have to pay a 21 percent sales tax on the purchase price. On anything under 30 years old the duty can amount to 60–70 percent of the sales price.

In addition to the '36 Ford coupe and the GMC pickup, David bought four original Model A coupes, a 1953 Chevrolet Bel Air two-door, a 1965 GTO convertible, and a 1949 Chevrolet two-door fastback (only four-door fastbacks were imported). These vehicles will be loaded into a huge container and shipped to Australia. The insides of the cars and other vacant spaces will be filled with various "trinkets" he's picked up, such as the ten sets of finned Buick brake drums he got from the wrecking yard in Boise. He's also bought several sets of white wall tires; he can buy and ship new whitewalls for a fourth of what they cost in Australia. Another hot item is riding lawn mowers; he can triple or quadruple his money on them.

I asked if he had met any Americans who resent seeing their old cars going to Australia. "Only one chap," he said. "Everyone else has been very open, friendly, and helpful. Perhaps it's the novelty of meeting an Australian car enthusiast who's coming over and buying cars. Besides, if I weren't doing it someone else would be."

In fact, others are, as David noted; even within his Model A club there are four members who come to the United States every year for a combination vacation and buying spree. "They buy a bunch of stuff," David said, "clean it up, take it to the swap meets and after a year they've made enough money to pay for the trip and perhaps enough to come a second time. It's much more attractive than spending your holiday in the U.S. and not having anything to show for it at the end."

Said David of others who make a business of buying and importing old car parts, "They'll buy up bunch of cars, and then, to cover the cost of the freight, they'll throw in a larger quantity of a single item, such as fairly new V-8 engines, to cover their profit margin. If you put, say, twenty Chev V-8 engines on the bottom of the container and stack all the other stuff on top, the money you'll make on the V-8 engines will pay for the transportation of the whole container. Then what else you've bought goes back for free."

David added, "I'm only batting around with nickel and dime stuff, but others are taking back Corvette fuel injections, Corvette front and rears, and they can charge probably ten times what they pay for it here." While anyone can take back old car parts, only three people in Australia have been licensed by the government to import Corvettes. David knows one of them, and said that the fellow bought a 1988 Corvette here for $10,000 and sold it there for $80,000. "But he had to convert it to right hand drive, make it comply with all Australian standards, get registration on it and present it as a finished car, with good paint and interior. So it pays to buy a good one here. We don't get Corvettes over there; there are no dealers who sell them new. So it's only these three guys who convert them who can bring them in, and that's their business. Really, they are Corvette dealers. If something happens to the car, people are going to go back to them to get parts. That's why they're licensed by the government, so there are no backyarders getting into the business. It also ensures a market—if they let a hundred people do it they'd probably all go broke. If only a few are doing it under license the government is getting its taxes and a few more people are employed."

While many Americans take the seemingly infinite supply of old cars in the U.S. for granted, David was astonished by what he saw over here. "We've grown up on the American Dream, read all the American books and seen the films, and so we have to come over and take a look. It's like a little kid in a candy store. Every corner I turn, every book I open there's something I want and things are so much cheaper than at home—if you can even find them there." David plans to return next year, but for a shorter trip. He says he now has leads on nearly 1,000 cars that interest him, and he'll check them out later. He'd also like to bring some cars from Australia to sell, such as Model A phaeton bodies and the 1936-'48 Utes (utility pickups) that are available in quantity there. Right now, he plans to rod a 1940 Ford "sloper," bring it to this country, drive it to our rod runs and then sell it to pay for the trip.

HOT RODS AS A BELIEF SYSTEM

I confess I have never been a spiritual person, preferring the pragmatic. I believe in the weight of a Stromberg 97, a banjo steering wheel, a '39 Ford taillight. These things are not only desirable, beautifully shaped, tactile, they're also real. I can see and hold them, and so I believe in them. And we all have to believe in *something!*

I'm reminded that I stopped attending church, the Lents Evangelical United Brethren, late in the spring of 1952, so I could attend the drag races, which were always held on a Sunday. I suppose somehow I could've done both, but as a teenage hot rodder I had to arrive at the drag strip early and see and experience everything. Although speeds then were nothing like the speeds turned today—fewer than half a dozen early rail jobs turned over 100 mph—I was fascinated by the cars, the engines, the noise of open exhausts. In those days I'd seen perhaps 50 hot rods, primarily at the fledgling car shows, and at the drags I could see that many on any Sunday. How could church compete with the panorama of the pits, the cacophony of the starting line? Besides, church was primarily my mother's idea of what we should be doing. I have no idea what I thought about church, except that I probably saw it as an obstacle thrown up to keep me from the drag strip.

I know it's politically incorrect to mention Christianity—we've just got through a holiday season where Christ was not mentioned at all—and this is not a sermon, I assure you. Rather, with the start of a new year just around the corner, it seems a good time to pose the overwhelming question: in what *do* you believe? Hot rodders by definition believe in themselves; they believe they're capable of improvising, fabricating, making parts fit in a way that the factory never intended. I hope that you harbor that belief, and a strong belief in your family, community, country, the future. Of course you believe in your rod—that roadster cowl is real, and somehow comforting.

And perhaps that's enough. But to go further requires a terrific leap. You not only have to have faith, you have to believe in faith, and you have to sustain that belief, which is asking a lot. Unlike that beautifully curved cowl, which is a concrete thing, faith is an abstraction, something you can't touch, taste, smell or see. It's difficult to believe in that which we can't see, just as it's difficult to comprehend concepts that are beyond our understanding, concepts such as infinity and eternity. As a kid I sat on the front steps at night and listened to the radio that played from the front room; the prologue to a particular program mentioned the Egyptian pyramids, the mysteries of time, and days numerous as the sands of the desert. I looked up at the sky and began counting stars; when I counted past a hundred I realized I'd covered only a small area of sky, and I felt dizzy, my head reeling as I tried to imagine how many stars were in that vast panoply. At that moment I had some insight into the concept of eternity.

But the rodder who decides to build a car must have faith, or he'd never begin to gather parts. At the onset he must believe that one day he'll be able to drive a finished car, or else why do it? We can make a distinction between mechanical and spiritual faith, but in the end both require desire, belief and commitment. Both imply that if we have those qualities, and carry the project through, that we will be a better person.

Not only is this not a sermon, it's not a simple car/religion analogy. But in either case, if you believe in something and sustain your faith, the end result — whether car or person — should have integrity. The cars I admire are usually simple, unadorned by doodads or distractions, but with utterly smooth metalwork and paint that would reveal the smallest imperfection. It's true that less is more, a variation of the last shall be first and the sum of both dicta is a matter of integrity, something I keep striving for. If the car and the driver have integrity, then there's something beyond that burnished radiator shell.

OLD DOGS AND NEW TRICKS

Here's proof that either hot rodding is on its last legs or that it will never end.

Or as a topic paragraph for this piece I should include something about the values of old friendships, old cars and the idea that if that if one lives a long time life takes on some of the intricacies of a Russian novel. It might also hint at those people who told us, when we were youngsters, light years ago, that our interest in old cars was a "phase" that we would soon outgrow. None of that was on my mind when I took my friend, Bob DeFehr, to see another friend, Larry Deyoe. They've both recently bought restored Model A Fords, and I thought that they should meet. In addition to owning similar cars, Bob and Larry were born and raised in Portland, they're both retired and they both have car histories, so they have a lot in common.

Bob is a good friend. We met in 1996 at the Portland Roadster Show, where Bob was showing his unique Buick, a 1953 Skylark to which he's added a steel top. The Skylark is a rare car, and in the 1960s Bob had two of them which, for whatever reason, he dismantled and then stored the parts. Some 30 years later he assembled the best pieces into this gorgeous, one-of-a-kind car he calls "My Little Margie." He shows it often, and attends as many rod runs as possible, sometimes hitting four or five on a weekend. Bob is a dedicated family man, but I think he's happiest at a rod run, showing off his car, having a hamburger and talking to people.

Since 1958 he's owned a 1928 Model A sport coupe, bone stock, which for years was a daily driver. Recently he bought a beautifully restored 1928 A-bone sport coupe for far less than it would have cost him to restore his old one. The new one has a few amenities too, such as juice brakes, Mallory ignition and turn signals. It runs like a dream, and so we cruised through my neighborhood, Lents, avoiding hookers, muggers, cut-throats, drug-crazed scumbags and indifferent cops, and as I focused on that unique Model A exhaust noise I was transported to an earlier, more gentle time.

We got to Larry's house, and as the guys began kicking tires I thought about all the years I've known Larry. We met in grade school in the 1940s, a time so long ago it makes me dizzy. The first time I remember seeing him outside of school he was about 12 and was riding a Doodlebug scooter with a pair of water pipes sticking out the back like duals. I was so envious! I thought if I had a ride like that I could conquer the world! A few years later, in 1953, he had a

Larry Deyoe and Bob Defehr look at Bob's '29 model A sport coupe.

1951 Ford a new car really, which I drove to the garage where I worked and fitted with real duals; it had a flathead six, and those pipes were beautifully wicked!

Only recently did I realize how many cars Larry told me to buy in the 1950s and I did; they included a Jeep-powered '29 roadster, a weird custom I called "The Beast" and his 1937 Ford coupe which I enjoyed through the entire summer of 1953. Then there were all the other cars that he owned that I never saw: a full custom 1940 Merc convertible, three Corvettes and a bevy of others. Years passed, and now Larry and, his wife, Valerie, have retired after driving an 18-wheeler (yes, Valerie drove that big rig too). Larry bought a restored 1929 Model A roadster, bone-stock, a car that needs nothing, and that's what he and Bob were discussing. That and their 60 plus years in Portland, who they knew, and where they'd lived, etc.

Then Larry said he really wanted a hot rod, and he was thinking of getting some flashy new wheels, and maybe putting a V-8 under the hood. Bob and I tried to dissuade him of that notion. It's usually a mistake to take apart a perfectly good old car in order to make something else out of it, and neither of us wanted to state the obvious, that the two or three years it might take to build a rod could be a lifetime at our age. Just enjoy your Model A, we said. As we left, Bob and Larry vowed to meet at rod runs this summer, to park their A-bones side by side, kick a tire, enjoy a couple Big Macs and talk cars.

I thought everything was settled, when to my surprise I got a call from Larry a couple weeks later saying that he intended to build a hot rod. He'd owned nearly a hundred cars but had never built one, and now, at age 70, he said he wanted to build a hot rod. No, he was not going to touch his roadster; instead, with Valerie's blessing and support, he had bought a Model A tudor and was ordering a rollaway chassis. He had plans, and lot of questions, one being whether I thought he would have the stamina and determination required to complete the job. I said yes.

The Suicidals Car Club

"Junkyard Jim" Creighton is a serious rodder from Albany, Oregon who likes to have fun with cars. Several years ago he developed the idea of "yard art," by using his leftover parts as lawn sculpture and planters, and encouraging his buddies to do the same. The local authorities couldn't object to an old hulk in the yard if it was deemed "art." Then Jim and his lovely wife Janeen, created an "art car." They got a 1949 Chevrolet, painted it white, and took it to car events where people were encouraged to use magic markers to color the car, named Picarso.

Now Jim has unleashed his vivid imagination to create his own hot rod club. It's called "Suicidals," and is limited to hot rods with "suicide" doors. The idea came to Jim while he was working on his 1934 Dodge pickup (which earlier had been an attractive hulk of yard art). The truck has suicide doors, and he began wondering whether any other truck came from the factory with doors that opened from the front. There were cars, of course, including the Murray-bodied 1932 Ford 3-window coupe, the 1933-34 Fords and a bunch of others, such as Terraplane, Lafayette, and also expensive cars such as Duesenberg, Auburn and Cord. There are plenty of potential members for Jim's club.

The manufacturer never used the term suicide doors. The reason for the front-opening design was clear enough: such a door offered more leg room and made it easier for people to enter and exit the car. But — and here's the weak link! — it also made it easier for people to exit the car during an accident! That door could spring open on impact and the person beside it would be hurled from the car! Or even without an accident, if the door were opened, intentionally or not, the wind would catch the door and fling it back.

So why are they called suicide doors? Apparently the term contains a bit of "urban legend." People felt that you must be suicidal to drive something that dangerous. And as Jim thought about the doors he wondered about other associations of the word, such as the "suicide" front end used since the 1920's as a way of lowering the front end of an early Ford, or the "suicide" clutch found on certain motorcycles, or the "suicide" knob guys attach to their steering wheel.

Those questions and others are addressed in the club's "unofficial" by-laws. I should say that Jim sees the club as a "firm tongue-in-cheek parody of elitism among car clubs," and as an indicator of that he's drawn up a list of articles and "rules" that is as long as my arm. The name "Suicidals" sounds terribly serious, but Jim is having fun with the concept as well as the club.

For example, "cars are members of the club, not people." That's a different notion; it means that the people (caretakers) are owned by the cars, and while the members (cars) can display the club plaque the people cannot wear club jackets, T-shirts or caps! Also, a club meeting is in progress whenever two or more cars are parked in close proximity. Then things get more anthropomorphic, e.g., how do the members communicate, what do they "talk" about and how do the current members induct new members? And those prospective members must have, in addition to the suicide door, "a certain attitude, spirit or state of mind.... The true criteria for joining the club is mysterious and known only to the cars themselves." For more details talk to Jim or, rather, Jim's truck.

Should your car have what's necessary for membership, it'll be in good company. There are seven charter members, and they have histories to tell. The founding charter member is the 1934 Dodge pickup whose caretaker is "Junkyard Jim." It was an old hot rod with a colorful history. Another charter member is a 1933 Dodge pickup but with a different personality; this one, which owns Jerry Kruger, is channeled, fenderless and flamed.

Communing with those members is a 1933 Plymouth coupe/roadster. Its caretaker is Bill Kruger, the "honored builder/fabricator." A fourth charter member is "in-progress" but is able to communicate. He's a 1932 Ford 3-window, chopped and channeled, that was originally built

The logo for the Suicidals club was designed by Randy Rhoades (Paul Smith collection).

in Portland at mid-century. Its caretaker is Randy Rhoades, the "Awesome Artist" who named the club and designed the logo. The final three charter members are 1934 Ford coupes, all receiving care from Paul Smith, who knows the rich history of each car. That is an impressive line-up.

Jim tells me that I can tag along, but I'll believe that when I hear it from his truck!

Paul Smith's 1934 Ford drag coupe has suicide doors (photograph by Paul Smith).

WENDOVER

On Monday of Speed Week I returned to my motel room after having a U-joint in the truck fixed, and as I was about to head for the salt I heard the strangest noise. It sounded like gravel being thrown against a long sheet of metal. I turned off the TV (all three channels were in Spanish anyway) and opened the door. Balls of ice bounced on the balcony, collecting in a pile by the door. Hail! Sheets of hail fell from a gray sky that had, shortly before, been blue. Hail collected along the curb, then melted, creating a wave of water that swept down the parking lot and crested when it met a larger wave that swept down Wendover's main street. This was a real desert flash flood. Within minutes the water in the street was several inches deep.

The first car back from the flats was a cute red '25 T street roadster; water flew in every direction, and the back tires spun twin rooster tails twenty feet in the air. He pulled into the parking area next door and jumped out, soaking wet, exclaiming that everyone was racing to get off the salt flats before it became impossible. Soon the main street was busy with open-wheel traffic searching for a dry place.

Within half an hour the rain and hail had ended, and the sun broke through in places. But the force of the storm was still apparent as a steady wave of water broiled down the hill from the casinos at the state line; each parking lot contributed its flow. The water ran past my budget motel, flooded the Taco Burger across the street, and flowed down a side dirt road to the poorer part of town, following a prehistoric geological route.

At six the next morning I drove out to the flats to see if the storm had affected course conditions. It had rained hard the previous Saturday night, but a strong wind had pushed it away from the course and had dried the salt. The result was an excellent course, and the racers had been able to make eight mile runs on Sunday and Monday.

Bonneville is a unique place, and so are the Bonneville racers. Most build a car only to go fast in a straight line, which means Bonneville, which means they can race that car one week of the year (or somewhat more often if they live near the So-Cal dry lakes). In recent years the Bonneville meet has been cut short due to rain, and I hoped that wouldn't be the case this year. Too many racers had too much at stake to have the meet aborted.

I followed the paved road that extended five miles onto the salt and stopped at Land's End, to join a small group of people and vehicles. All around us, for miles, was water where yesterday there had been salt. Slowly the sun rose, and the water reflected the orange and pink glow. It was a beautiful sight, but it was not one we wanted to see.

I met a couple of racers from Chicago who showed me Polaroid photographs they had taken on Monday when the storm hit. One showed a long wave of water enveloping the salt, the result of rain and hail in the mountains. They said that there had been a mad scramble to get off the salt, but that some cars were still on the course.

I saw Jim Lindsley, a guy who has raced at Bonneville since the first meet in 1949. I knew he'd know whether there'd be any racing today, so I asked him. He looked at me, swept the wide expanse of water with his hand, and growled: "What the hell do you think?" I took that to mean no.

I talked with Multy Aldrich, "Mr. Hospitality," whose camper is always first in line so he can greet hot rodders. We talked about the good old days of hot rodding, and I bought a program and a couple of Bonneville posters from him.

Then I walked toward the people clustered around a neat little '27 T street rod fitted with a late model Chev in-line six. I searched the crowd, figuring that if I couldn't get on the salt I might meet some interesting folk. LeRoi "Tex" Smith was holding forth and I went over and reminded him that we'd met a couple times years before. He's a super friendly guy, and conveys excitement. We had a nice talk about his new publishing ventures and about hot rodding in general.

"Here's what Bonneville is all about," he said. "A guy from Georgia came here last year, then went back home and built a neat competition roadster. He was in touch with some Bonneville racers, and said he was having trouble getting tires. They wrote back that they had tires waiting for him. That's the spirit of Bonneville!"

As we were standing there talking, a tiny green Honda slowly cruised past, a video camera out the open window. The letters on the door said Ed "Big Daddy" Roth. Wow! I grabbed my camera and autograph book and moved toward the car but it kept moving, slowly, down the asphalt, into the brine, sinking until the water covered the lower body line, and it kept moving, following the double row of pylons that led toward the horizon, the camera still cranking.

Later I returned to town, wondering whether I wanted to pay for another night in the motel if racing had been halted. But most of the rodders had driven back to town too, and there were neat cars and people everywhere. In fact, it was easier to strike up a conversation in town than it was on the flats because people weren't concentrating on going fast.

I was hanging around Petersen's Garage, a small place on a residential street, and hot rodders came in a steady stream. Petersen said that Speed week really kept him busy, but that it was mostly small stuff. One guy I met there was Danny Iandola, a name I'd heard for years. He's a founder of the 4 Ever 4 club, and has been running ancient Ford engines almost since they were new. This year he again had a four barrel in his belly tank. With him was Andy Jenkins, who had designed a new OHV head for the old four cylinder engine in the tank. Jenkins is a native of New South Wales and has managed to attend the last four Bonneville meets—that's dedication!

The S&D Supermarket is in the middle of town and, like the casinos, is open 24 hours a day. It serves as a central meeting place for rodders—or for the women, on days when the men are racing. It's busy! Almost everyone comes in for beer and ice. I asked the guy working for Moschetti & Sons, the ice people, how much ice was sold during Speed Week. "About ten times the usual amount," he said.

After buying my ice and beer, I stood beside the truck watching traffic. It was like a car show that kept moving. A late arrival came past with an old belly tank on the trailer. A guy and a woman got into a gorgeous orange '34 coupe and motored up the street. There was a gaggle of neat custom cars in town, including a '41 Studebaker coupe and a low '53 Chev hardtop with scallops.

One thing I love about Bonneville is seeing all the old stuff. Out on the salt the racers are running Ford flathead V-8s, Chev and GMC in-liners, old Hemis and weird things like Rangers, Allisons, Hispano-Suizas and Lord knows what else. The same people often have neat tow cars. I saw a '48 Ford pickup that must have been built years ago; an old time touch was the taillight treatment—two '49 Merc lights on each rear fender. 1 haven't seen that done in years!

Then into the S&D Supermarket lot came this fenderless '29 A roadster pickup. It looked as though it had been built in year one: The red paint was faded and chalky, oil streamed through the louvers, and the interior—well, there wasn't any! The owner, Chuck Sharp, said he had owned the truck since 1947. When he lifted the hood I saw a Model B block capped with a Cragar OHV set-up, a pair of Stromberg 97s and home-made headers that ended in a capped lake pipe. Then I began to see many trick items on the truck: the genuine 1930s Auburn dash with S-W gauges, the fuel pressure pump and 1940 Ford emergency brake handle under the dash. The A steering post mounted a 1940 Ford column shift, which meant that Sharp had mated the old B block to a V-8 transmission. This was a real old time California hot rod! Sharp admitted that he used to drag the car regularly in the early 1950s, but since then he had used it as transportation.

That evening I ate in the restaurant whose sign claimed "the best Mexican food in Utah!" In the booth next to me two hot rodders were extolling the virtues of the older motels in Wendover. They probably stayed at the one next to the restaurant, a long-time hangout tor SCTA racers; I know they weren't staying at the new Casino motels.

"The new ones, you get lost in the hallways:' one said. "It's more friendly under the veranda."

"Jeez," the other one said, "remember last year, that guy drove his roadster under the veranda, ran a trouble light from the room and pulled the pan, put in new bearings right there?'"

"Hell," the first guy said, "I remember when we pulled an engine and took it *into* the room and rebuilt it!"

"Yeah, phooey on these new motels," the other guy said. "How you gonna carry your battery up three or four flights of stairs to charge it overnight?"

I decided that that, in a nutshell, was the spirit of Bonneville. I finished and walked back to my motel—neither new nor old—and watched a couple of TV shows in Spanish. When I woke in the morning the sun was out; by noon the course was dry, and the racers were on the salt, revving for the records.

Tyler's Tales

Tyler James Hoare designs restaurants and drive-ins in Northern California. He's also a sculptor who has won a number of awards; perhaps his most famous public works have been a series of World War I biplane and triplane replicas that have been placed in People's Park in Berkeley and on pilings in the bay.

It's no surprise then that Tyler sees custom cars as rolling sculpture, and has since he was a teenager in Joplin, Missouri, in the mid Fifties. At 16 he owned a 1952 Chevrolet Bel Air that was lowered, nosed and decked, had Olds Fiesta hubcaps, sometimes scallops, sometimes primer spots. By 1959 he was corresponding with noted Midwest customizer Daryl Starbird, and he was asked to exhibit the Chev in Starbird's first show.

His hometown is on Route 66, and a popular saying among the young men was that you had to get in your custom and head for California. After several false starts, Tyler got to California in 1966 — by plane, and with a wife and daughter. This was during the period when custom cars were out of fashion, and muscle cars took over. Tyler never lost his enthusiasm for customs, however, and as soon as he was established in his twin professions, he knew he wanted a lead sled. He built a 1941 Ford coupe into a mild custom but found it lacking performance and reliability; he wanted a custom he could drive on the freeway at freeway speeds, which, even in Northern California, means you have to have some beans under the hood.

His answer was a 1967 Dodge 440 RT Coronet that was chopped 3½ inches and used parts from a dozen other cars including a '67 Merc, a Datsun 280Z, a Corvette and Mercedes — he did his junkyard parts picking, just like in the Fifties except now he was choosing from a plentiful supply of late model stuff. With its low lid, louvered hood, lakes pipes and handmade hub caps, it was a distinctive ride.

His current car is a 1985 Mustang that has been chopped 4½ inches, with working hatchback and tempered split back window. The rear quarter windows have been filled in and replaced with metal louvers, and the roof has been peaked. It's had two dozen modifications, including functional 30-inch lakes pipes, redesigned Moon hubcaps and louvers punched everywhere. It's show quality, but Tyler uses it as a daily driver, attracting attention wherever he goes,

At some point he began writing short articles for *Cruisin,'* the West Coast Kustoms' newsletter. These were titled "Louvers," "Frenched Headlights," "Chopped Tops," etc, and combined how-to-do-it information with personal reminiscences of what it was like to be a kid in Joplin in the Fifties, nuts about customs. Each piece ended with the refrain, "Still looking for that first custom out on the freeway," because he believes customs should be driven. But soon the custom resurgence occurred, and customs began to be seen everywhere.

He became the historian for West Coast Kustoms, and his column was expanded under the new title "Tyler Tails." He has made an effort to seek out the old-time artists, and he's written about Tommy the Greek, a striper from Oakland; Sal Alesse, San Jose striper; the late Sal Guerrero, a Berkeley striper: and King George II, a Midwest striper. He's also discovered customizers who have not yet gotten their deserved recognition, such as the late Paul McElley of Hayward.

In 1988, at an exhibit honoring 30 Bay Area artists, Tyler got artists to autograph their photographs and artwork. He felt that car customizers were also artists, so he began to have them autograph photographs of their custom cars. He bought a 100-page bound sketchbook that he used to hold the photographs; he began to have customizers write comments in the book. Ed "Big Daddy" Roth filled a page with commentary and a Rat Fink drawing. Soon he had photographs and notes from known and unknown customizers; the known included George Barris, Tommy the Greek, Herb Martinez, Rod Powell, Frank DeRosa, Bill Reasoner and many others.

To show how this project has grown, Tyler finished that first book in 1989; he's now working on book number 13! That, he figures, is about a page a day. The books themselves are works of art, with color and black and white photographs, pages Xeroxed or cut from magazines, color or black ink drawings and comments, collages of custom material from many sources. Although people seemed confused at first why Tyler would want to do this, they're now eager to sign his books.

This is a wonderful way to record local history of customs and the people involved. Every car organization should find someone to do a similar project in their area, although I suspect that this is not something that you can ask someone to do; you have to find someone who, like Tyler, is mildly obsessed with recording local history in this interesting and lively fashion. Tyler's plan is to donate the books to the University of California at Berkeley's library where they will be available to future generations.

Swap Meets

A big problem when building a hot rod during the Fifties was finding parts. There were no swap meets, no central place where rodders could buy, sell or trade. If you needed a used dropped axle or a decent T body, you made inquiries through a network of rodders, asking someone who might know someone who knew someone who had the part. You hung out at the local drive-in restaurant, asking questions or perhaps posting a list of what you wanted. Or you joined a club, and let the others know what you wanted.

You sometimes could find what you needed at the local junkyard. The early Fifties was a transitional period, with cars from the Twenties and Thirties being junked out along with then new cars. Engines, stock instruments, sheet metal and odd-ball parts, such as gauge clusters from a 1941 Buick or a 1950 Plymouth, were plentiful and cheap. An abundance of old cars sat in driveways, backyards and fields, seemingly without pressure from the city that they be removed, and there was no shortage of old metal.

Another source was the classified ad section in the newspaper. I've looked back at issues of the paper I read in those days, and I'm surprised at how few cars or parts were advertised. Our paper had a special section called the "Thrifties," for items priced under $15; I once saw a Thickstun or Tattersfield dual intake manifold for $10, but I can't remember ever having seen other speed equipment.

Certain things were always hard to find. For example, roadster bodies were scarce. In the early 1950s I used to lie awake at night, obsessed with the notion that soon there would be no more roadster bodies and I imagined that somehow that would be the end of hot rodding as we knew it. (Thank God for Wescott and the other glass body builders!)

Other parts that were hard to find were hydraulic brake systems, fifteen- (especially) or sixteen-inch disc wheels (to replace those outdated spoke wheels), column shift transmissions and the hot rod standards—'39 Ford taillights and the '32 Ford grille. I knew I wanted '39 Ford taillights and a '32 Ford grille on my rod because I'd seen them on nearly every car featured in *Hot Rod*. I could have substituted '39 Plymouth taillights, which were teardrop shaped, but they were just different enough to look dumb I thought, having seen a pair on a rod. Maybe they'd look good on an early *Plymouth* roadster — since they had the raised ship logo — but not on an early Ford. So my father and I began the great search for a pair of '39 Ford taillights, going from junkyard to junkyard. We finally found one on a '38 deluxe sedan in north Portland, where a junky cut it off the fender with a torch, and another in a junkyard in Gresham. The price was piddling—fifty cents, perhaps—the work, and the joy, was in the search. But those taillights were in such demand that I once bought a 1930 Ford roadster body because it had a pair; turned out the owner had bolted the rim and lens to the body, and there were no buckets!

Some parts were impossible to find. For example, '37 DeSoto bumpers, used aluminum finned heads and '32 roadster bodies were scarce as hen's teeth.

My father followed up an ad in the paper and we located a man who was wrecking out a '42 Mercury sedan, which was nearly a new car. We bought the complete front and rear ends to get the brakes for the roadster, and the column shift transmission for the heck of it. Just as we were leaving I noticed a Portland-made Lance dual manifold, which I wished we would have bought, and a pair of rare '37 DeSoto bumpers which we did buy for $10. To show how much these bumpers were coveted, like a fool I allowed a fellow Road Angel to temporarily put them on his '40 Merc coupe. He was also a Golden Gloves contender, and once the bumpers were on the car there was no way to get them off — or to get my money!

A few people had the bucks for new speed equipment. Although used dual intake manifolds turned up occasionally, I chose to spend $37.50 for a brand new Edmunds intake. I had what I described as a "three-quarter race" engine in my roadster because it lacked aluminum heads. I simply could not find a pair of used heads and I could not afford a new pair at $75.00; that was what I had paid for the entire roadster! I ran a set of stock heads milled .040, and it always irked me when someone, usually a kid my age who didn't even own a car, would ask when I was going to buy some "Offy" heads. Actually, finned aluminum heads were rare — most of the hot cars I saw had shaved cast iron heads. The owner of a sharp roadster in my town chrome plated his heads, because plating cost a fraction of the price of aluminum heads.

Often we found things through the grapevine. Someone told me about a '32 Ford roadster that was being junked out; I bought a perfect '32 radiator for only $5.00. I don't know why I didn't buy the body, or the entire car. A few months later I did buy a '32 roadster body and frame, complete with fenders, lacking only a deck lid and windshield, for only $5.00 from a farmer near Oregon City. So parts were around, and sometimes the price was right, but you had to really look.

One of the biggest boons to rodding — along with glass bodies and rod runs — is the swap meet. They began slowly in the late Sixties and mushroomed during the Seventies; today you see them almost every weekend on a vacant lot or in the local civic center.

This 1936 Ford 3-window was original and complete, very straight.

This nice '32 Ford 5-window coupe was available at Harrah's swap meet.

In the beginning, a swap meet was exactly that: People swapped parts. I'll trade you a mint '32 Ford bumper, even Steven, for those '32 Ford front fenders. The trading was done because each person *needed* the other person's parts.

Now parts have become so expensive that money talks. Rusty metal has become a big business! I go to swap meets looking for Fifties hot rod items, and the stuff is available I'm happy to report — if you have the money.

I recently attended the Portland (Oregon) Swap Meet, said to be the biggest meet west of Hershey. It extends over 26 acres and has 3,400 stalls — with six acres and 1,224 stalls under cover. It attracted 35,000 buyers, which, with the 10,000 vendor admissions, added up to a crowd.

Oldies 'n' goodies were available. A friend bought a like-new set of Kinnmont disc brakes for $500. Another friend, who flew in from Michigan, found a Vertex magneto, still in the box, for $50. A pair of brand new Harmon and Collins flat head mags sold for $100 each. Flathead speed equipment was fairly common and priced right: Offy heads for the 8BA at $40 a pair, a Fenton dual set-up with carbs, lines and fuel block was $45, a side mount generator bracket for $5, old chrome wire looms for $3. Those are just a few of the things I wish I had bought! A set of excellent 16-inch Kelsey-Hayes wires went for only $65. A full-race V-8 60 marine conversion in need of a rebuild, sold quickly for $875, and a new full-race Merc flathead went unsold at $1,000.

There were several hundred cars for sale, including some that were right out of the Fabulous Fifties. A full custom '46 Ford convertible was priced at $12,500, a full custom '53 Olds was priced at $14,500 and Tom McMullen's tub — a car we could only have dreamed about in the Fifties — was offered at $23,500. There were project cars that could have been built into Fifties dream cars. For example, there were two all-steel '33 Fords, a roadster for $10,000, and a cabriolet, ready for paint, at $16,500. And there were starter kits, such as the rough but complete 1929 A roadster that sold for $2,595 — that's $1000 less than what you'd pay for a glass body alone. We can only hope that a hot rodder got it and will do it good!

Odds and ends of old car parts can be found at swap meets.

ROAD ANGELS REDUX

During the 1950s, if you were even a casual hot rodder you probably belonged to a car club. Put duals and skirts on your '36 Ford sedan and you qualified as a member of the Road Knights, Gear Grinders, Hi-Revers or whatever your club was called. You got a nifty cast aluminum plaque with the club name to mount on the rear bumper, and the right to stand in the parking lot after a club meeting, kicking tires, listening to lies and telling a few yourself. It was great fun, and I'm reminded that the only organization I've ever joined was a hot rod club, the Road Angels.

That clubs exist is a paradox, because hot rodders by definition are individuals, mavericks, loners and sometimes outlaws; they would seem the least likely people to want to meld into an organized group. But it happened almost from the start with the Night Flyers of Fullerton, formed in 1932, and by 1941 there were dozens of clubs in the So-Cal area. By 1950 hotrodding had spread across the country and there were clubs in towns with only two or three rodders.

A car club gave one a sense of belonging and a sense of identity. The Road Angels might have been a typical club. It had been formed in 1950 by several guys who had gone to high school together. It was disbanded in December of that year when 17 of its 25 members were drafted in one week and sent to Korea. It was reorganized in June, 1951, and when I joined it two months later it again had about 25 members. They ranged in age from 16 (me) to perhaps mid-twenties. Several were married, three were in high school, one was in college, but most were working at auto-related or factory jobs. Most lived in southeast Portland (Oregon) and many had gone to the same high school, so the car club was in a way an extension of the high school social club. We met monthly in the banquet room of an Italian restaurant, conducted business, and then cruised to a drive-in, Barts, two blocks away, where we checked over each other's cars. The members over 21 then crossed the street to the Creston Tavern where they "consumed some suds."

Those were exciting times. Hot rodding was new, and things kept changing. The Road Angels joined forces with the Ramblers to form the Columbia Timing Association (CTA). They secured an airport near Portland for a drag strip, and a long airstrip in Eastern Oregon to use for one-mile timed runs. The club held reliability runs, beach trips, picnics, dances and a wild stag party with kegs and many risqué films!

The Road Angels was terminated around 1955, and so I was surprised recently to see the club banner flying over a group of cars at the Portland World of Wheels Show. Then I saw that each car had a Road Angels plaque! It turned out that over 30 years after its death the club had been resurrected. And, in fact, it even had a couple of members from the original club.

The prime mover was Gary Davis, a member of the Road Angels in the early Fifties. He had a super 1934 Ford roadster that he would race in a minute. His competitive spirit got him involved in professional motorcycle racing, where he earned a national number. Like a lot of hot rodders from the Fifties, he never lost interest in modified cars. Now he owns a pair of neat Ford delivery sedans, a '39 and a '54, both red with gold lettering to advertise his plating business, and he's building an old-style '35 Ford roadster.

Another Road Angel member from the Fifties is Roger Simonatti. He had a purple '38 Chev tudor when I met him in 1952 and, except for those years when he was raising a family and building fast ski boats, he has always had street rods. In recent years he's been building about two a year.

The club has a number of members who have been building and racing hot rods over 40 years. Ray Van Dorn got the bug in the 1940s, and was heavily into drag racing during the 1950s. Since his quarter mile days he's been heavily into street rodding, and recently built a new '32 roadster. His buddy, Bill Peterson, is a diehard hot rodder and one of the most skilled metal beaters in the Northwest; both Peterson and Van Dorn were members of the Ramblers during the Fifties. Another old-timer is Ken Jones, who raced a channeled '32 roadster at El Mirage in the 1940s when he was a member of the Pasadena Roadster Club.

I asked Gary Davis why a bunch of old hot rodders decided to revive the Road Angels club. He pointed out something that I hadn't noticed, that most rodders tend to go places in pairs—you like to have someone with you to talk to or to help carry the heavy parts from the swap meet area to the parking lot. So he was the catalyst that brought together the pairs of rodders. In fact, many of the members have known each other since year one, and they were already doing things together. They also know that they're comfortable with each other and enjoy each other's company.

Is the formation of the old club an attempt by members to relive their youth? Not exactly, although the excitement of being a young hot rodder can be felt in the air at the monthly meetings. What is different is that most are married, so spouses also attend meetings and club functions, and all are older, so they are interested in comfort. This means the functions often are built around runs to some pretty posh places, with deluxe accommodations.

It also means that the members now have big-buck machines, because they have the money to fulfill their desires. As a group they're successful business people. It's interesting to look back forty years to the people the club members were, and to see how many have done well. One of the members of the original Road Angel club was Danny Hanna, founder of Hanna Car Washes, who now has more Lear Jets than most of us have cars in the driveway. A lot of people back then were pretty certain that hot rodders were doomed to be bums. With the advantage of hindsight, we can see that the competitive spirit, coupled with mechanical ingenuity, enthusiasm and fortitude, drove a good many hot rodders to find the American Dream.

THE OUTSIDERS

Although the name suggests an outlaw motorcycle gang, it's an appropriate name for this informal club comprised of rodders from overseas. The members are primarily from England, Europe, Australia and New Zealand, and most of the expatriates have migrated to southern California where they work in the rod shops or within the rodding network. The average club member developed an interest in hot rodding as a teenager, eventually came to the United States for a vacation, saw the American Dream and managed to stay.

I found out about the club through Paul "House" Gilbert, a rodder from New Zealand. He emigrated to the States years ago, and worked at Magoo's shop when it was owned by Dick and Lois, then at Darrel Zipp's shop, and later at Jon Gumpton Restorations where he applied his metal-working skills to such exotics as Mercedes 300 SL gullwing coupes and pre–World War II Mercedes. He's now working with Donn Lowe in his shop, and they keep busy turning out some extremely fine customs and street rods.

Paul told me that the Outsiders get together three or four times a year, and all members try to attend the club's annual picnic, held this year December 10th, from which he'd just returned. Attending were Michael Wegner from Germany, Steve and Carol Dennish, Colin Dennis, Steve Ricketts and John "Biffo" West from England and Steve Dowsett and Pete Nash from Australia. Quite a number of New Zealand rodders now live in So-Cal, including Geoff Mitford Taylor, Mike and Judy Lawrence, Garry "Golliwog" Adams, Grant and Lynn Downing, Paul "House" Gilbert and Squeak Bell, who owns a rod shop in Bakersfield.

Perhaps typical of the group is Steve Dowsett, who works for Super Bell. His daily driver is a mildly customized, primered '57 Ford Ranchero, and he's saving his money to import his steel '32 Ford roadster with the Ardun that he left back in Australia. Like many of the Outsiders, he's nuts about the good old days the U.S. enjoyed and he owns, I'm told, every small rodding magazine ever printed plus tons of rodding memorabilia. He also has a large collection of Haywood-Wakefield furniture and rockabilly '78 records. A couple who brought a car with them is Mike and Judy Lawrence. They drive the '47 Ford convertible they've owned for twenty years here and in New Zealand. Mike works for "Frantic Fred" Badberg. Then there are Steve and Carol Dennish, who own an English-bodied right hand drive '32 Ford sedan, with purple flames done by New Zealander Craig Morrison, and a '32 Ford 5-window coupe with a 1933 Ford four-cylinder engine.

Sure, these folks could've stayed home and enjoyed rodding, but they took courage and made a big move to experience a new country and, some say, a new language. In So-Cal they're driving the same roads where hot rodding began, and they're able to attend the big rod runs, the car shows and bop off to Bonneville for Speed Week. But it's probably no accident that they're doing the kind of work they enjoy. It strikes me that these guys are able to find employment because they have the necessary skills, and that's the result of the education system in their respective countries. While I don't know the background of every member of the Outsiders, I do know that in many countries students receive an excellent basic education by age 15, then enter an apprenticeship program and learn a trade, eventually passing the trade qualification test. That's why they are excellent tradesmen, everything from mechanics to engineers, beaters, machinists, painters, wood workers, trimmers and engine builders when they land here and their skills are in demand. Similar programs were once standard in this country, and perhaps it's something schools here ought to reconsider.

A Letter to a Young Hot Rodder

Dear Albert Drake,
My name is Shane Atkinson, I met you at the '87 Nats North, where you signed one of your books for me. I'm writing to congratulate you on the best book I've ever read. Never before have I been able to relate to the feelings and things said in a book as I have yours.... I almost think I'm in the wrong decade.

Another reason for writing is I'm going to, despite 100 percent rejection in every direction, build a Model A channeled roadster, Fifties style. I already have two Model A frames and I'm looking for a body. But when I have the two, how do I go from there? How did you guys lower the original chassis? Did you guys box the frame? What kind of hydraulic brakes did you replace the mechanicals with? Can a banjo steering wheel be found? What year Ford wheels are on your roadster?

These questions must be terrible but I don't know who to ask, and I'm serious about building such a car.

A friend, Shane Atkinson

Dear Shane,
What a nice letter! Many thanks for letting me know that you liked *Street Was Fun in '51*.
I'm glad that you want to build an old time hot rod. Me too! I'm not the best person to ask because when it comes to hot rods I'm not very practical. Also, I'm hopelessly stuck in the Fifties. And I'm really limited in what I like. I like lots of things on old time hot rods, but sometimes I'm not sure why. I like the *shape* of Stromberg carbs, '39-'48 Ford hydraulic backing plates, flathead water hoses, etc. I first handled those parts when I was about your age, 15, putting together my first hot rod. I knew nothing about cars then, and handling them was my education.

So when I think of building a car today, I think of those parts. I think of old time rods, flathead and three-speed running through a banjo rear end. I *know* that flatheads overheat, that Ford gears are fragile, that axle keys shear like brittle taffy. I *know* that *new* stuff is better, costs less, runs cooler, lets you drive to rod runs hundreds of miles away, etc. But I tend to not listen to that practical side of my brain — do it the old way, I tell myself.

I still build lots of cars in my head — all old style! But there's one thing I never do that we did a lot of back then, and that's to channel the car. All it takes is a torch — just cut away the floor, let the body fall over the rails and build some brackets. Hey, you can lower the body from three inches to 12 inches in about 15 minutes! But then the fun begins! When you cut away the floor you lose rigidity. The body will always flex, the doors won't close if the car's on an incline and you'll suddenly develop a hundred rattles. Also, nothing lines up! You have to relocate the steering column, alter the dash, cut down the seats, chop a few inches out of the radiator and grille, build a new hood, etc., etc.

If you want to lower the chassis, leave the body where it is and step the frame about five inches in the rear. That'll get it down, but you'll still have lots of leg room.

You could build a fun car if you took your stock Model A frame, put '39-'48 Ford juice brakes on it, front and rear, put a dropped axle up front, stepped the frame, used old Ford 16-inch wire wheels with big 'n' littles. In fact, if you wanted to use the Model A engine and transmission, you could build the car easily — just mount the pedal assembly and split the wishbone. Use the A steering, or a 1950s Ford pickup unit. For a body you could buy a '23-'25 T bucket, or a '26-'27 T bucket — they're around for a couple hundred bucks. Mount it on the A frame, fashion a radiator, get a T windshield, perhaps a round gas tank, and you'd be on the road. With a stock A engine the whole rig couldn't cost much. It'd look like a real Fifties hot rod (a lot like the one on page 32 of *Street Was Fun in '51*—except I think that one had a stock front axle, and I know it had mechanical brakes!).

Or you could build that same car with a Ford flathead V-8 engine and transmission (and bigger radiator). Probably cost a little more because you'd have to fashion a crossmember, reshape some things. By the way, a *stock* flathead—even a *worn out* flathead—will make that light car scoot!

I've always thought it would be fun to build a rod that resembles Bud Parham's '23 T (page 51 of *Street*)—that car has a nice stance. It used a Model A frame, rear end, flathead V-8 and transmission. You can buy all the things he used, substituting a glass body for the steel one. That car had a stock flathead, simple flat vinyl interior, little chrome—it was a super car but not a high-buck machine.

You could build that same car with a T bucket now and, a couple years from now, if you have the money, you could remove the T bucket and mount an A roadster body. Whether you used the A engine or the flathead V-8, that'd be a cute rig.

That's my bag—I just finished building that car, once again, in my head. A more practical person might suggest that you build a car such as the one I just described but use, say, a modern V6 engine, automatic and a modern rear end. Then you could run disc brakes, late wheels and radial tires, etc. Probably not a bad idea. I have never done such a thing; I do not daydream of doing such a thing, but I'll bet it has its advantages. You could buy a rusted out 1970s car, of which there are many in Michigan thanks to the road salt, get the V6 and running gear to hook to the A frame and mount a T body on that. You could do things to make it look old-timey. A few years ago at Merced I saw a neat Model A roadster and it looked old; it had a four-barrel with a Fronty rocker cover, as if he'd converted his four-barrel A engine to an OHV set up. In fact, he was running a Chev II four barrel—only the valve cover was old!

Those are some of my ideas, and I hope they're somewhat helpful. Good luck on the project. You've got me dreaming of building something new—and even if I only build it in my head that's okay!

Hill Autotorium

While most of us have to be content with a room in the house, or at best a garage, in which to display our automotive memorabilia, Tom and Diana Liechty have a museum! It's called Hill Autotorium and it's "A Museum Dedicated to the '50s and 'Kustom' Cars," as seen on the sign by the front door. It's not nearly as big as most museums, but it's as interesting and it's run with the same kind of seriousness. Tom and Diana's lives revolve around custom cars. The museum sums up their lives, and they like to share their treasures with other dedicated custom car aficionados.

Tom has been into custom cars for over 50 years. He started the Style Rollers in Mt. Clemens, Michigan and the Auto Butchers club in Detroit in the 1950s. He's also owned a number of notable customs, including a radical 1948 Mercury built by ClarKaiser after World War II, "Forecasta," a bubble top Corvair built by Daryl Starbird and "Golden Penny," a 1954 Chevrolet hardtop that Tom built in the late 1950s. His wife, Diana, is equally enthusiastic, and drives a 1955 Pontiac hardtop that is a mild custom. When they were married, the service was conducted by an old friend, Father Larry Ernst—the same Larry Ernst who had Barris chop a new 1952 Chevrolet and thus create one of the decade's outstanding custom cars.

In 1987 Tom and Diana bought a stylish house, a sort of Frank Lloyd Wright chalet, deep in the hills of Michigan; it's situated halfway up a small mountain, and across the road from a lake. A great house in a great setting, but it lacked room for their stuff. In 1988, Tom designed a separate building, hired a firm to do the work and within months it was finished. A two-story building, it measures 62 feet by 30 feet. From the outside it's a plain, windowless structure, but when you enter you swear you're back in the Fifties.

Two things a person needs to know about Tom before entering the museum: he can't stand an empty space, and he's terribly inventive when making something to put in that space. Okay, a third quality is his vivid imagination. For example, he built the "Thunder Vac," which he describes as "a Eureka vacuum cleaner with a big block Hoover." It has a bolt-on carb, Hooker headers, Moroso air cleaner, Hurst shifter, Stewart-Warner tachometer, etc. He had several name car builders do the wheelie-bars, the flames, bellypan and upholstery. It's a conversation starter, a show winner and, Tom adds, "It's a working vacuum cleaner, and extremely good on long hallways!"

Another example is a down-sized custom car that resembles the Barris-built "Golden Sahara." This car, built for Iggy Bearis, is all steel, with the rear panels made from a 1949 Ford. Although it lacks an engine, it has elaborate custom features such as a hinged bubble top, a cocktail bar and a working color TV in the back seat. Tom also built a beautiful trailer for this car, and the whole works, car and trailer, fit in the back of a van.

Tom's latest creation is a chopped golf cart! It's difficult to describe, but it shows how Tom's imagination works. The rear fenders, for example, are two halves of a Sears rooftop car carrier, and the lakes pipes are Cool Flex radiator hose. The hand-built tail lights are 5½ feet long and they work! It has air suspension, a VCR and TV, a functional on board liquid system with dual spigots, a golf club floor shift, an overhead console that operates everything and other features too numerous to mention. Tom got the cart finished just hours before the doors opened on the 50th Detroit Autorama, where it won a first place award.

Those rigs might give you a sense of the museum, where there is so much to see. There's the reproduction A&W root beer drive-in, with a black and white checkered floor, 5 tables and 15 chairs and small lights that flicker and rotate on the sign. There are display cases with model cars, club plaques and trophies. Then there are things that dazzle the eye and the mind, such as the Egyptian sarcophagus, the "egg chair," the cryogenic chamber, the flying saucer and Iggy Bearis, a bear with a life of his own — but you need to have Tom and Diana tell those stories!

Iggy

On a recent trip to Michigan I stopped to see Iggy and his parents, Tom and Diana. When I last saw Iggy, in 1991, he was only four, but already working as a security guard in the Hilltop Museum and quite serious about his future education, for which he was taking donations. On this visit I was pleased to see that he's maturing into a handsome, enterprising and very active bear. He's been doing lots of writing about customs, he's formed his own TV production company and he now has his personal custom car. In fact, he even has a full-size eatery, called Iggy's Drive-In, decked out in a pure 1950s-style.

For those who may not know Iggy, I should explain that he was born in St. Ignace, Michigan, nearly ten years ago, but was really "conceived" in the back seat of a radical custom. After Tom and Diana got him, he was carefully placed on the rolled and pleated rear seat, and the car's heavy bubble skirts, placed on top of Iggy, activated his voice mechanism, and he felt compelled to sing all the songs he knows. This went on for 360 miles! As Tom put it, "Iggy had a lot to say!"

To describe Iggy in a brief space, I'd have to say that he's a product of these times but he

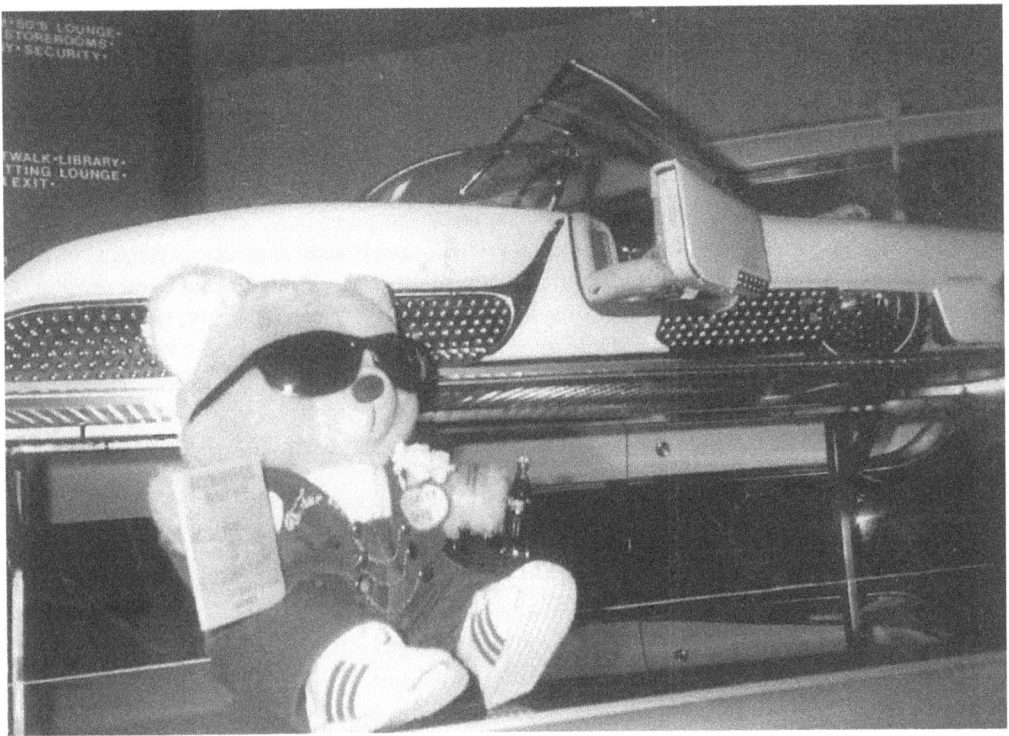

Iggy, looking cool, and his radical custom car, "Honeycomb," and a copy of *Hemmings*.

has a strong affection for the 1950s, because he digs the imagination and creativity displayed during that decade. For the past three years he's been writing a column called "Bear Facts" in *Styleline*, the magazine of Kustoms of America; the column bridges decades as he discusses customs, his friends in the hobby and his personal life. For example, he revealed his brief addiction to tobacco. Iggy thought that smoking was cool and Tom, concerned for the bear's health, had to convince him to stop. Then Bill Hines gave Iggy a cigar on the boat ride in St. Ignace and Iggy got very sick. He now has a nicotine patch, but has taken up chewing tobacco, complete with a brass spittoon.

Being a normal young bear, Iggy recently got a credit card in his name with a $5000 limit. This gives him a certain amount of independence, and last summer he took off for two weeks without telling anyone. It turns out that he went to the Olympics in Atlanta, where he won a gold medal—for bear-hugging—and was not involved, at all, in the explosion. His parents got a call from Dayton, Ohio, asking if they'd pick him up. He told them he'd hung around after the Games in order to sign some contracts; one got his photograph on Wheaties boxes! He later accompanied Tom and Diana to the Pigeon Forge, Tennessee, run wearing the gold medal around his neck and displaying the Wheaties box with his photograph. The public went nuts, flocking to shake his paw and to purchase, for $5, his lapel pin, "I know Iggy."

Iggy loves custom cars; he's met almost everyone in the hobby, and has sat in almost every notable custom car; he has a thick photograph album to prove it. Thanks to Tom, Iggy finally has his own custom. It's a radical rig, all steel, with a distinctive front and rear end. Finished in white pearl and gold plate, it's called "Honeycomb," and resembles the "Golden Sahara" that Barris built back in the Fifties. Both seats swivel to face the cocktail bar in back; it has a working color TV and uni-stick steering. Although Iggy would prefer to drive the car, Tom feels that it should be trailered to distant events and so he built a neat, four-foot covered trailer for "Honeycomb." It's all black, has three axles, a side door, awnings, roll-out steps and a cocktail bar (Iggy's going to be hitting the booze!). Everything on the trailer is functional, but scaled down. When he displays the car, Iggy employs a Barbie-style doll that's just his size; she wears a white pearl dress, holds a microphone and narrates the story of how "Honeycomb" evolved.

Some three years ago Iggy formed a TV production company, and his show, called "Automotive Lifestyles," is presented on six local channels, with plans for a broader audience. From spring to fall he travels extensively, attending rod runs and custom meets, riding in his own video rig with "Honeycomb" in the trailer. When he's not shooting, he's meeting people; he knows so many people that he's giving consideration for a run for public office, perhaps as president (he's certain to do better than Dole did).

Meanwhile, his personal life is one long adventure. Last year he got an ear pierced (left one) and got an earring; Tom and Diana were upset, but tried to be understanding. Shortly afterward Iggy said he couldn't stand the tension in the air, and said he'd give up the earring if Tom would put flamethrowers on Iggy's video cart. Tom did, and Iggy removed the earring. But now he's got a tattoo on his cheek (left one), a heart with Mom printed inside, and the folks are not too happy with that either!

In 1994 Iggy's car was the feature car at the St. Ignace Straits Show luncheon, a big event where all the notables gather. This was indeed an honor; marred only by the accident Iggy had the night before. He was on the cruise boat, meeting some of his heroes, and he took a tumble (after smoking Bill Hines' cigar?) and broke his leg. At the luncheon he had a big cast on the member, but was still able to get into his tuxedo. The notables felt so sorry for Iggy that they came over and began signing the cast. He still has the cast, signed by Joe Bailon, Linda Vaughn, Chuck Miller, Paul Hatton, Bob Kaiser and a bunch of other big names.

LIVING THE FABULOUS FIFTIES—AGAIN!

In my old roadster, finger hovering over the starter button, expectation filling the garage around me. *Should I or shouldn't I?* During the summer I'd rebuilt the brakes and engine; I'd started it for brief periods, but with the garage doors closed. I knew that the car would go, and I knew it'd stop. One part of me said drive it! Another part, the conservative side, said leave it in the garage where it had been sitting for twenty-eight years.

Twenty-eight years! Where'd time go, I wondered.

I'd bought the car thirty-five years earlier, on February 21, 1951. It was a 1929 Model A roadster; the title indicated that it had originated in California, where someone, at some time, had replaced the original four barrel engine with a stock 1936 Ford V-B. It was a good road car, with all road equipment, including full fenders, dual side-mount tires, a hood and top, and I could imagine it being driven up the coast to Oregon, where I bought it.

The modifications were minor: a reworked chrome grille that looked like a combination of 1933 Packard and Chrysler grilles, 16" General Jumbo wheels, dual pipes, chopped windshield, pleated genuine red leather interior and they looked somewhat like 1934 Ford fenders; this was trick, and nicely done. The work had been done years before—perhaps in the late 1940s, perhaps in the late 1930s. In many ways it was typical of the updated Model A Fords one saw with some frequency, but this car differed in a major way: it was *mine!*

Perhaps I had kept it all these years because it was my first car. I had bought and sold numerous cars during the time I had owned this one, and had never felt the urge to sell it. There were other reasons, all of them wrong. It was a matter of aesthetics and textures. I liked, and still do, the curved cowl, abrupt deck, the cute '32 grille. I love the sound of the old Ford starter, the ragged V-8 exhaust, the shape of the gear shift lever.

Most of the reasons make no sense to me. It's just a car, I tell myself — metal, upholstery, rubber. Sell it, get high-tech.

But it's more than the car; it's the memories. Imprinted by that baptism of dual exhausts, for thirty-five years I've been a hot rodder. Now I realize that I'm hot rodding in the world of thirty-five years ago. A world where traffic was minimal, pollution not a problem and bureaucracy hadn't yet passed a thousand laws legislating what and how you drove.

In short, a world where a fenderless, hopped-up roadster made sense.

Too young to drive, I sat for hours behind the wheel, aiming the car down the highways of my mind. I pulled knobs, stepped on pedals, steered. Occasionally, when my parents left, I started the engine, just to hear the dual pipes. Sometimes I backed it down the driveway, then went forward, a distance of thirty feet. A few times, after dark, the house empty, I backed it out and hurtled through carless streets for a couple of blocks and raced for home before the cops showed up.

With almost no money, I tried to work on the car. I had promised my father that I'd leave the fenders on, but the first day I didn't go to school I removed the fenders and running boards — also the hood, bumpers and grille. Suddenly, it was beginning to look like a real hot rod!

My father got a worn-out '49 Ford V-B engine, and together that spring we rebuilt it. By June the new engine was in, running, and equipped with an Edmunds dual intake manifold and some chrome goodies. We hung a '32 grille and a '40 Ford dash on it, and shot the car a fire engine red enamel right in the driveway.

The summer of 1951 was the best summer ever. I turned sixteen, got a driver's license and went cruising. I would often wake at dawn, back the roadster out of the garage, wipe it off and spend most of the day looking at it. Then I'd think of a reason to go somewhere — the store, library, the drug store, anywhere — and I'd cruise around in the cool of the evening.

For the next two years I drove it to high school, and the following year to work; it was exciting, dependable transportation. Nights found me competing in street races, all strictly illegal, on streets that were super smooth and devoid of traffic — at least in memory.

Those were the good old Fifties. On weekends I cruised the drive-ins, sitting for hours with a cup of coffee, listening to the radio in the next car pound out the rockabilly beat of the Big Bopper, Elvis, the Everly Brothers, Fats Domino.

Life was perfect!

Then I got into motorcycles, and parked the roadster for two years. When I got it out again I completely rebuilt it: new engine, interior, tires, paint, chrome — and put it in several shows.

But something had happened. I'd changed — I'd started college, and seemed to have little time to work on a souped-up car. While I loved the roadster it just didn't handle like a sports car. Finally, now that the roadster had achieved in my mind something close to perfection I found I didn't enjoy driving it. When it had been in primer or had had a highly imperfect red enamel paint job, I didn't worry about the car. I'd park it and leave it for hours. I'd go to a movie and leave it on a dark side street. Because no one ever messed with it, I never worried about it being stolen or vandalized. But. now I worried about the car when it was parked in my own driveway, and I didn't like to leave it unattended anywhere. I drove it less and less, and finally, after getting an undeserved speeding ticket that involved a huge fine, I put the roadster in the garage, where it sat for twenty-eight years.

I got married, finished college, had kids, made major moves around the country, advanced in my profession and lived my life. But I was always a hot rodder. I constantly read the rod magazines, drew pictures of rods, and dreamed about getting my roadster back on the road.

Then one day I was back home, back in the garage, looking at the roadster. Somehow, I felt, my life had fallen apart — the kids had grown up and moved away, my wife filed for divorce, and therefore I had lost interest in my work and just about everything else. When my mother died, I had to confront the past. The main reason I had been able to keep the roadster through all the years was because my mother allowed me to store it in her garage. Now everything had changed, and I was forced into a decision: keep it or sell it.

I had told myself that if I ever felt depressed I'd get busy and build a new rod, but depression is the great incapacitator. I remembered the fun I'd had building this roadster, and I opened the door to sit on thirty year old upholstery. I moved the wheel, worked the pedals, just as I had when I had first bought the car and was too young to drive. I looked at the pristine Sierra Gold paint, a Chev color that was new in 1956.

Suddenly, it was 1956! It was the Fabulous Fifties, a decade that was mildly neurotic but not nuts; perhaps the last decade when the world made sense. And I needed, once again, to dig James Dean, Marlon, Elvis, rock 'n' roll. Even the decade's absurdities, such as coonskin caps and Hoola-hoops, seemed worthwhile.

So I rebuilt the engine and brakes, and one day I sat in the garage with my finger poised over the starter button. *Should I or shouldn't I?* The car had been in the garage for so many years that none of the neighbors knew about it, and almost no one else. To take the car out would render it vulnerable. There would be no point in keeping it safe for twenty-eight years if something were to happen to it now.

But desire overcame caution. I hit the button, heard that familiar starter sound, heard that flathead catch, kick back, catch and roar to life! I smelled exhaust, the rich pungent odor that recalled a time years before when I had sat in this car in this garage running the engine.

I swung open the overhead door, got in the car and backed it from the same garage, down the same driveway and into the same street where I'd done all this thirty-five years earlier. As I cruised through the old neighborhood I felt dizzy thinking about the passing of time.

I cruised to a main street and waited for traffic to clear. Then I cranked the wheel and hit the gas—tires spun, exhausts roared and when I looked back I saw black streaks on the asphalt. Suddenly I remembered driving this same hot rod down this same street on my way to high school, driving on misty mornings when my adrenaline was so pumped I could barely keep my trembling foot on the gas, Suddenly, the troubles passed! I remembered how it felt to be alive, all my senses alert, and I let out a primal scream.

The roadster saved my life, and I'll keep it forever. In the year 2000 I plan to be an old codger, an anachronism like my car, and driving the roadster in the traffic of two cylinder unicars. I plan to be laying rubber, too! No doubt someone will remind me for the ten thousandth time that such behavior is childish, and I'll tell them, maybe so, but it's good for the soul.

Maybe, just maybe, it can keep you alive—like rock 'n' roll.

LINDA VAUGHN: FIRST LADY OF MOTORSPORTS

We've all heard Andy Warhol's famous quote about how, in the future, everyone will be "famous for fifteen minutes," and then decline into obscurity.

Politicians, actors, and public figures come and go, rarely enjoying enduring success. But Linda Vaughn has enjoyed the public spotlight for nearly forty years.

Times were different back in the late '50s ... it was a time of unabashed beauty contests and the assertion that sex sold cars to primarily male buyers.

Advertisements in print and commercials on television used beautiful women to complement the lovely curves and parts (such as Dagmar bumper guards) of automobiles.

Perhaps as a child growing up in Dalton, Georgia, Linda Vaughn saw the opportunity to use both her mind and her beauty to become a star in the automotive industry. As one of seven children, she had to think ahead about making a living. When she graduated from high school at age 17, she was already a certified dental technician. As Linda explained to us, "This occupation helped me achieve my goals of finishing school, having pretty clothes to wear, and a pretty smile with sparkling white teeth."

As a young girl, Linda possessed obvious physical beauty. A genetically inspired mix of German, Irish and Cree Indian, she was encouraged by friends and family to enter beauty contests.

In 1961 Linda was crowned Miss Dalton Georgia, and went on to become runner-up in the Miss Georgia contest. Both were precursors to the Miss America pageant. Linda's intelligence and charm caught the eye of a Miss America Pageant judge, Dorsh Wall. Dorsh instantly saw Linda's potential, took her under her wing and suggested she enter the Miss Atlanta International Raceway pageant.

Linda's career in auto racing promotions took off after she walked away with the Miss Atlanta International Raceway title. A true southern belle, Linda was already familiar with stock car racing. As part of her job, she got to know many racing officials and drivers. One of her favorites was "Fireball" Roberts. She became an instant celebrity when she and Roberts did the Twist on the track to promote its annual NASCAR race, and footage of the dance appeared in newspapers, magazines, and on television sets across the country.

At the suggestion of "Fireball" Roberts, the PR people at Pure Oil Company hired Linda Vaughn, named her "Miss Firebird" and had her ride on the "Firebird Float" as a pre-race event. She kept this position for three years, until Pure Oil was bought by Union Oil and the promotional program ended. What seemed to be bad luck was actually an opportunity. In 1966, just as her "Miss Firebird" job, ended, Linda began her long-time association with George Hurst.

Soon she was crowned Miss Firebird, and she was finally able to quit her job as a dental technician. She also won the Queen of Speed title, competing against beauty queens from other stock car tracks. As a result, she got to ride in the pace car at the Daytona 500, and became a familiar sight at the ever-growing NASCAR races, where her special combination of beauty and personality won the hearts of many NASCAR fans.

Hurst was a born promoter, and had used beauty queens in the past to promote his products. He had crowned several young women "Miss Golden Shifter." But in 1966, Hurst tried something new. In conjunction with *Hot Rod Magazine*, he ran a nation-wide contest to find the next "Miss Golden Shifter." Among the many candidates, Linda Vaughn was the overwhelming favorite.

To show the high esteem in which she was held, previous winners of the "Miss Golden Shifter" title held it for one year each; Linda held it continuously for thirteen years! She was allowed to choose a dozen other girls (The Hurstettes) to help with the promotional duties.

One of her first jobs was at the U.S. Nationals at Indianapolis Raceway Park, where Linda stood on the trunk lid platform next to a huge Hurst Competition-Plus Shifter. George Hurst drove the Pontiac before a packed house, and the crowd went wild! Linda repeated this performance numerous times, hanging onto the shifter while the car traveled at speed around the track, or down the drag strip. It was a demonstration of beauty and bravery. Later, Hurst developed the Hurst/Olds muscle car, which was selected as the Official Pace car for the Indianapolis 500 race in 1972 and 1974. Both years Linda Vaughn stood beside the 10-foot-tall shifter as the car raced around the track.

The publicity also impressed the name Hurst in the public mind. He made a good product, there was demand, and it sold like crazy. It was the mid–1960s, when Detroit made incredible cars; gas was cheap, insurance was available, and power was in the air. Guys wanted a fast car, with the shifter on the floor. You only had to say "Hurst" and everyone knew what you meant.

It was also a time of fighting in Vietnam. Linda Vaughn visited military bases and hospitals for four years with the Hurst Armed Forces Club, and toured Vietnam several times. The troops, naturally, went wild — not only because she was beautiful, but also because she reminded them of home. Linda also attended various racing events, trade shows and charity benefits throughout her career, which she continues to do today.

Although the times may have changed, Linda Vaughn remains eternally beautiful and upbeat, using her charm and personality to interest people in products and racing. Another great salesman, Ed Almquist, sums up Linda's success best, "Because of her knockout beauty, sparkling personality and marketing savvy, Linda Vaughn became the top sex symbol for racing ... and its greatest spokesperson."

My Brush with Greatness

A few years ago, I was at the Portland Roadster Show banquet, with one eye on my food and the other on the clock. I had heard that Linda Vaughn would arrive around 6:30 P.M. to sign autographs and meet the public. I had read about her for many years, but I had never seen her, and I was determined to be part of the public that she would meet.

At 6:15 I excused myself, said I'd be back for dessert and beat it downstairs to the show. A table and three chairs had been set up beside a 1933 roadster called "White Lightening" (sic), which, the sign said, was Linda Vaughn's personal hot rod. She was nowhere in sight, but already a line was forming near the table, a gathering of about twenty young men. I took my place at the end of the line. They were laughing and joking, but they weren't giggly high school kids. In their hands, ready for Linda's signature, were original Hurst brochures and boxes, GTO advertising, "Doc" Watson Hurst/Olds catalogs and a faded NHRA tee shirt with several autographs. These guys knew who she was and what she represented, and they were intent on getting her autograph on their treasured muscle car materials.

Then the line went silent, and I saw that Linda Vaughn had appeared, seemingly out of nowhere, and she greeted the group as she sat at the table. She was the same as she's been presented in photographs and print: blonde, voluptuous, trim, friendly, smiling, articulate. I later decided that she possessed an innate ability to meet a crowd of strangers and make each person feel special.

She greeted the first guy, smiled, asked his name, and as she spoke she began signing the brochure with a broad-tipped, black felt pen. Then she did something absolutely amazing: she continued the conversation with the first guy while greeting the second guy and signing his offering. She kept the line moving while managing to not cut anyone off, so that everyone left happily.

Except those guys did not leave. They hung around, a logjam of car guys. Each guy had a story to tell, and he was determined to tell it to someone! As the line inched forward, I was in a position to take some photographs, which I did. Then the person in the chair beside Linda Vaughn said something to her, and she said, loud enough for those close to her to hear, that she had just arrived from a show in Seattle, had not eaten and would have to leave for a bit.

I'm normally not a pushy guy, but I reached over and shoved my program toward her, with the hope she'd simply sign it and I could leave. She looked at me, still smiling, worked through the guys ahead of me, and signed the program when I stood before her. Then she asked my name, and personalized a publicity photograph for me.

Her writing is wildly cursive, the result of years of signing things. I can easily read my name, with a couple hearts floating above it. And there is a definite capital "L," which could be part of "Linda" or possibly "Love"?

Cruisin' the Neighborhood

Hey, know what's parked in that garage down the street — the one the owner never opens the door of? Or what's under the black vinyl tarp, or parked behind the garage? It could be interesting iron.

Ever since I got interested in cars many years ago I've kind of kept tabs on what's around. At one time I thought I knew where every hot rod was in the town where I grew up. And, having crossed the U.S. a number of times by car, I've prided myself on having kept a mental inventory of where the vintage tin is located. I don't want to own them but just know where they are. Keeping tabs on old iron.

But now I'm not so doggone sure I really know what's around. There could be a surprise in every garage. I'm learning there's more stuff around home than I could've imagined.

I got an order for a couple of books from a guy named Ken Powell, and since he lived only fifteen miles away I decided to drop the books off rather than mail them. That'd give me a chance to meet him, and talk cars for a while. We'd talked over the phone once, and I saw his car in the 1988 Lansing World of Wheels Show. I don't know why I hadn't seen it before; he'd had it on the street for some time, and he drives it 200 days a year.

I found the house, on the main street in Holt, Michigan, and went around to the garage where I met Ken and got a good look at his wheels. It's a 1951 Mercury coupe that's been given the full treatment: chopped a bunch, lowered front and rear, frenched headlights and taillights, nosed, decked, side trim removed, dual spots and the grille cavity filled with a '54 Chevy unit sporting extra teeth. It's painted a distinctive blue and silver-gray, with a tasteful stripe. This is a street-driven custom that's in show condition.

We bench raced a while, and then Ken asked if I'd be interested in seeing the car his neighbor was painting. You bet — this neighborhood looked like a bastion of hot rodding! We walked next door to Earl Hensley's house, stopped to admire his '59 Chevy and then entered the garage. Earl was shooting color on a chopped 1957 Chevy owned by his friend, Gary Felske. Gary, I'd met a couple of times — in fact, I had once helped to award him first place in a Fifties dance contest — but I had not seen the car. Or I didn't remember having seen it. But had I seen it I would've remembered, because it's distinctive. Chopped, dropped, louvered, lakers with some novel metalwork. The color I would describe as Black Cherry, and the car, even masked and being color sanded, looked good.

When Earl and Gary went back to painting, Ken and I stepped outside. We were just in time to see Terry Towers pull up in his '40 Dodge coupe. This car I'd seen for the first time at the Lansing car show a couple of months earlier. It's a sweet street rod, seemingly stock, with late model running gear, mag wheels and bright red paint. It was recently finished, which would explain why I hadn't seen it.

But Terry is a member of the very active SR Cruisers, and he'll be putting lots of miles on the car this summer. Terry went into the garage, and Ken I asked if I wanted to take a ride in the Merc. Did I? You bet! The day was cool, with some traces of winter still on the ground, but the sun was out and it was the first day of Michigan spring. The Merc fired instantly. Ken let it warm up, and we cruised two short blocks to a friend's house. No one was home, but Ken figured it was okay if we looked in the garage window. The garage was deceptive in size from the outside; through the window I saw a DeLorean, a couple of late model rigs, and as my eyes adjusted I saw a '50 Merc coupe with the lowered lid under construction. Then, at the back, I saw a chopped '53 Buick! It was finished, and I wondered why I'd never *heard* of this unusual car!

Then we drove a few blocks more to Mike North's house. I had met Mike some eighteen years before, when he was driving a channeled full-fendered '32 roadster, but I'd never been to his house. It's a big house with a big yard, a country-size yard right in the city, and a big garage. Mike has it filled with good stuff. In a smaller garage we found Mike cherrying out a '58 Ford truck to use as a daily driver. He had it completely disassembled, was doing a complete rebuild, and although it was in pieces he expected to have it on the road in a few weeks.

Mike is a perfectionist, and has built some cool machines, including a '50 Merc custom that was in *Hot Rod*. His current ride is a full-custom '54 Merc called "Yesterday's Dream," which has a chopped top that's half Sun Valley, half padded. Everything is frenched, and the car's painted a gorgeous Candy Apple.

He had a Chevelle parked beside it, with new paint and a fresh race engine, but I headed past it toward the rear of the garage. There, in pieces—but what beautiful pieces—was the 1956 Ford pickup that Mike has been working on for years. It's a wide window cab, neatly chopped, door handles shaved and all metal cherried out. To show you what kind of a guy Mike is, he once had the cab and box painted red—it was perfect, show shape—and then he had it done again in black.

Beside the cab was the chassis; the rails were painted black and everything that bolts to the rails was chrome plated—even parts that will not be seen when the cab, bed and fenders are assembled. In the corner, covered with plastic, was a fresh and very hot engine. Everything's ready to be bolted together, but what I was looking at was the result of years of work, and Mike will assemble it when he feels it's perfect.

As Ken and I drove back to his house, the Saturday afternoon traffic on Cedar Street going ga-ga over this outrageously gorgeous custom, I was eye-balling every garage, What kind of interesting iron could be in that garage, I wondered, or that one, or that one?

And what about the garages in *your* neighborhood?

CRUISING WITH THE NW SPEEDSTERS

When I got the call from "Rajo" Ed Gloss, asking if I wanted to take a tour with his speedster group, I didn't have to think twice. Ed is 85 years young, and the perennial hot rodder. He's been into rods since year one, or at least since 1924 when he got a 1919 Chevrolet that had been made into a speedster. His current ride, which he built from a pile of obsolete parts in 1980, is little more than a pair of bucket seats mounted on a chassis, with, of course, a rare Rajo OHV conversion on the Model T engine. I first saw this car a few years ago at the drag strip, where Ed hit 68 mph in the quarter.

So, on a recent Sunday morning, I fired up my roadster and eased it into a beautifully sunny day. As I cruised through the quiet neighborhood, I thought this is what Ed was doing for years before I was born. The route today would follow the route Ed and his hot rod buddies took over the famed "Woodland Dash" during the late 1920s and until the mid 1930s. A bunch of them hung around at Slim's Service Station in Portland, and occasionally, about midnight, they'd head north over the old bridge and drive into Washington to Woodland; then they'd go like blazes over the winding, narrow road to Castle Rock in their hopped-up Model T Fords, Model 77 Chrysler roadsters, maybe a new Model A. Yes, he had told me, there were accidents, some-

The restored custom body for this Model T has been narrowed and uses a clamshell deck.

times a bad one, but no one had been killed over the years and so the event had always been fun.

I zoomed down the freeway and turned off at Mall 205, where I saw several old cars and a bunch of people gathered. There were a couple original-looking Model T roadsters and an unrestored, rare 1930 Model A roadster pickup. There were also four speedsters, and before I got parked two more cruised across the tarmac. The speedster was a popular hot rod long before that term was coined. A young man in the 1920s could strip whatever he wanted from his car, giving it that race car look, or he could remove the body and replace it with one of the many aftermarket bodies that were available, such as Ames, Mercury or Morton and Brett.

A variety of speedsters soon gathered, some with fenders, some without; some with hopped-up T engines, some with stock mills. One new speedster had a sleek fiberglass reproduction body, while others were homemade. One thing that they all had in common were rusty water stains, oil leaks and the strong odor of gasoline; these cars lacked the show quality appearance of the cars seen at rod runs, and it was easy to see that they were driven!

Finally everyone was there and 14 Model T Fords and the Model A roadster pickup rolled out of the parking lot. I love the distinctive sound of the seemingly unmuffled T exhaust note; Ed Gloss took the lead and his exhaust barked through a long brass exhaust pipe. We hit the freeway and headed across the bridge into Washington. The Model Ts were cruising and had no trouble keeping up with freeway traffic. I followed a fenderless T with a narrowed, shortened body, reminiscent of the old SoCal dry lake cars called the modifieds. This car was so narrow that when the driver put his arm across the seat top his hand touched the right door!

We drove about 30 miles, then pulled off the freeway and parked at Paradise Point Park, a place where Ed Gloss had camped with his parents 80 years earlier. A truck had arrived earlier and the barbecue was already underway. Soon everyone was eating hot dogs, hamburgers and

Top: Members of Northwest Vintage Speedster Club cruising at freeway speeds. Except for the road, this could be a scene from the 1930s. *Bottom:* What the well-dressed pilot wears: Leather flying cap, goggles to keep the bugs out of your eyes, and perhaps a silk scarf.

potato salad and talking cars. Because of a retirement party that afternoon for a club member, the run had to be cut short, so everyone hung around the park and checked out the speedsters.

Later, I cruised alone across the bridge back to Portland, the sky clear and the sun warm, and I thought that I was doing exactly what I had planned to do for years—cruising in beautiful weather with rodding buddies—and I hope to be doing it when I turn 85 years young.

THE SPIRITS OF HOT RODDING

For three days the rain came down in sheets, and to emphasize my isolation the phone had not rung once. Now it was night, a tree branch scratched at the darkened kitchen window, the wind blew from the east; the mood was cast, but it was a stanza from a poem by Thackeray that sucked me in:

Ah me! how quick the days are flitting!
I mind me of a time that's gone,
When here I'd sit, as now I'm sitting,
In this same place — but not alone.
A fair young form was nestled near me,
A dear, dear face looked fondly up,
And sweetly spoke and smiled to cheer me
— There's no one now to share my cup.

The stanza struck a chord in my empty house; even my dog is gone. The empty house, the rain, the shadows in my bedroom, the footprints of ghosts. I should mention that the poem is not just about romantic love, as suggested by that dear face, it's about friendship, or more accurately lost friendships. The poet returns to a restaurant famous for its bouillabaisse, a rich fish soup, and he recalls old friends he used to eat and drink with, all dead.

I love the second stanza, which gives the ingredients for bouillabaisse, but it is the mixed sadness and joy for the past that overwhelmed me. When he recalls Jack, Tom and Augustus, and notes that "On Jame's head the grass is growing," I thought of car guys who are gone, and I miss them. I missed Bob DeFehr at the Portland Roadster Show; he was a big guy and he left a big void. For him the PRS combined Christmas and the Fourth of July, with a touch of Thanksgiving. He loved to show his 1954 Buick "Skylark," talk with anyone and everyone and eat hamburgers. Lots of hamburgers! I miss Bub Johnson; he made every rod run and show, offering advice, seeking trends, signing up members for his Lone Wolf car club. Fortunately, his wife, Joyce, and son, David, keep the red roadster pickup, Cherry Bomb, running.

Bruce Miller has also left a void; he was almost a legend, and he never got the full notice he deserved. Helped found the national rod run; started *Street Rod*; considered himself "Mr. 32." He also considered himself a super-salesman, which he was not, but he was a super guy. Another super guy was Jack Aiken, Mr. Congeniality. He had a movie star's looks, and a stable of rods and customs that might have been funded by Howard Hughes! I think he attended every rod run and show, driving a '50 Merc custom, or a '48 Ford woodie, or a gennie Cobra, or his '36 Ford roadster. I miss Reed Hall, gone ten years already. Reed started and sustained many of Portland's groups and events, including the Canby swap meet, and made dash plaques for every rod run. I yearned for the day when I could quit my job and return to Portland to sit in Roakes with Reed, Bub, Bruce and others, having a hamburger and watching interesting traffic on 82nd.

Where are you, old companions trusty
Of early days here met to dine?

I'd love to drink a beer with Norm Cahill, a guy who loved beer. "Chromehill" he called himself; he had one of the most beautiful, if not the fastest, flatheads in his '40 Merc convert. Tall, a smooth dresser, he truly had a gift for gab and could have made a million bucks if he'd taken a different path. What a session we could have if Cahill, Bud Parham and Don Moore gathered at the same table. Parham and Moore were the first and second presidents of the Columbia Timing Association and full of stories.

Another guy I really miss is Don "Duck" Collins, genius. Duck built race cars: the chassis, body, running gear, engine, upholstery — everything but paint. Give him a mallet, sand bag and some aluminum and he'd beat out a flawless body; he could weld anything and make anything in his machine shop. All his work was flawless. His memory too, and what stories! Another racer was Bob Scovell, who had raced at the old Ascot in the 1920s. I talked with him often; the talks were insightful but slow going since he believed in the Socratic method: if you asked him a question, he asked you one. He lived to be 93, and every talk we had began in 1905, the year of his birth. If I could just get Duck and Scovell together, differences aside, and Dick Goodfellow and Harold Langdon, and listen to them discuss the history of auto racing in the 20th century; oh yes, and argue too.

Other old timers also, guys like Hayden Waddington, Orville Withey, Gordie Youngstrom and Arden Enger. And some who left too soon, taking big chunks of history with them. I'm thinking of Tom Foster, co-host of the Goat Herd GTO gathering, one of the best events I've attended, and Stan Huntley, a sports car whiz who shortly before his death drove the Model A sedan he'd driven to high school decades earlier, and many others. I'd like to talk with guys I never knew, guys like Doc Howell, whose writings I read in ***CruZin'*** and other publications. It seemed like there was lots of time, and now there's none.

> *Good lord! the world has wagged apace*
> *Since here we set the claret flowing,*
> *And drank, and ate the Bouillabaisse.*

SUNRAYCERS

They are no doubt the collector cars of the future, these sleek, science fiction-looking machines with solar collectors on almost every inch of their bodies.

Thirty-two of the cars, built by college students, took 11 days to make the 1,600-mile trip from Florida to Michigan. And a crowd estimated at 10,000–15,000 spectators and an equal number representing pit crews, support people, race officials and General Motors representatives—waited on July 19 at the Ingham County Fairgrounds in Mason, Mich. for the Sunraycers to arrive.

The purpose of the journey was to give a demonstration of the practical application of solar power. "GM Sunraycer USA provides student engineers with a unique way to apply course work to solving real-life problems and challenges," Donald L. Runkle, vice president of the GM Advanced Engineering Staff had said earlier. "The rest of us will have a rare chance to see solar power in action and perhaps get a glimpse of future automotive technology."

The view on July 19 was only that — a glimpse. The cars had enjoyed good weather and plenty of energy-producing sun through half a dozen states. Then they got to Michigan. In the early afternoon dark clouds piled up, the wind began and it rained.

The crowd waited expectantly, but only six cars had arrived at the day's finish line by 6:30 P.M. The other cars had to be trucked to the fairground, to the disappointment of the fans who had gathered to view this historic moment.

First to arrive was a dark horse, the entry from Crowder College in Neosha, Mo., which had traveled at speeds nearing 50 mph. Local favorites were the University of Michigan's Sunrunner and Western Michigan University's Sunseeker. The UM entry was met at the state line by an enthusiastic crowd of well-wishers; although it arrived at the fairgrounds in fifth place, it actually had a three-hour lead.

Then the rains came. While most of the pit crews and race officials ate a free steak and lobster dinner in the large exhibit hall, and most of the spectators stood in the animal sheds, listening to hundreds of gallons of rain beating on the tin roofs, the lucky ones crowded into the pit area to talk with crew members and to check out solar innovations. They learned that the UM team had its own meteorologist who traveled with the car and tried to anticipate weather conditions, and that although the UM car weighed only 440 pounds, it had more than 14,000 solar cells. They viewed the innovative design of the Western Washington University car, which has a huge wing filled with solar collectors and a driver at each end; the canted wing collects the sun's rays in one direction until noon and then the car is turned around to get the afternoon sun.

They also heard about the accident suffered by the University of Waterloo car. In Ohio it was passed by a truck, but the curious truck driver wanted a better look at the car and side-swiped it, knocking it into a ditch. The driver wasn't hurt, but the car was damaged.

Thursday morning the sky was clear and the sun brilliant. Hundreds of people arrived at dawn to see the cars leave at nine, heading for Warren, Michigan, on the final leg of this solar car race. They might well have been looking at the hot rods of the future.

Index

Abee, John 133
Adams, Charles 82
Adams, Garry 177
Aiken, Jack 191
Aldrich, Multy 169
Allen, Duane 143
Almquist, Ed 21–32
American Graffiti 95
Ames, Geno 95
And Then There Were Four 62
Argosy 42
Armstrong, Louis 83
Ashby, Sterling 141
Astounding 42
Atkinson, Shane 178–79
Ayulo, Manuel 38

Baer, Bruce 77
Bailon, Joe 13, 136
Baker, Lavern 94
Ballard, John 135
Barlow, Roger 26
Barrie, James M. 19
Barris, George 13, 95, 102, 132, 171
Bartels, John 86–88
Baskerville, Gray 149
Batchelor, Dean 38
Baxter, Chuck 143–44
Bearis, Iggy 180
Belafonte, Harry 85
Bell, Dave 138–39
Bell, Squeak 177
Bennett, Tony 75
Bertrand, Pete 38
Best Hot Rods 42
Beston, Robert "Flash" 13–14
Beyond the Pavement 35
Binney, Bill 33–34
Biondi, Dick 139
Birner, Arnold 7
Blanchard, Chuck 77
Bliven, Red 127
Blossey, Otto 143–44
Bluebook 42
Bodet, Pascal 148
Brennan, Brian 150
Brewer, Teresa 57, 75
Brooks, Dan 99, 102
Brown, Johnny Mack 42

Brown, Ray 44
Buehrig, Gordon M. 14–16
Burger, Gerry 74
Burgess, John 41
Burns, Jack 84, 91
Burns, Jerry 84, 91
Butler, Bob 140

Cahill, Norm 191
Campbell, Homer 140
Campbell, Stewart 123
Canfield, Noah 142–43
Carson, Sunset 20, 42
Castera, George 42–44
Chrisman, Art 71–72
Clark, Ron 135
Cobbs, Tom 71
Collins, Don "Duck" 32, 192
Como, Perry 56
Connoly, Pat 71
Connors, Chuck 64
Cook, Terry 138
Coonrod, Jack "The Bear" 106
Cooper, Gary 89
Corno, John 97–99
Cosart, Lee 62
Costanzo Automotive 47
Cotton, David 65–67
Cotton, Dell 65–67
Courtney, Ron 95–96, 98–99
Crane, Richard 136
Creighton, "Junkyard Jim" 46, 166
Crisp, Gary 99
Cronin Auto Parts 85
Crowner, Dave 143
Cunningham, Roger 77
Cycle 42, 129

Dajon, Jean Michael 148
Dajon, Merve 148
Davis, Gary 176
Davis, Jim 73
Davis, Sammy, Jr. 65
Day, Bob 41
Dean, James 141
DeFehr, Bob 164–65, 191
Dennis, Colin 177
Dennisch, Steve 177
DeRosa, Frank 171

Deyoe, Larry 32, 59, 164–65
Dickerson, Marty 71
Dilday, Bob 143–44
Dillon, Suicide Bob 30
Dimmitt, Charles 114
Dr. Zhivago 84
Dove, Ronnie 138
Downing, Grant 177
Dowsett, Steve 177
Drake, Albert 36, 56–57, 60–61, 73, 75, 77, 79, 93
Drake, Albert Howard 1, 10–11, 58, 173
Drake, Bonnie 48–49, 74–75
Drake, Hildah 10–11
Drake, Monica 161
Drake, Moss 116, 161
Dry Lakes Pictorial 37
Duhenick, Dave 99
Dunlap, Bob 41
Durden, Tommy 138

Edelbrock, Vic 38
82nd Street Drive-In 88
Elliott, Wild Bill 20
Engemann, Dave 109–111
Enger, Arden 192
Ernst, Larry 179
Estes, Bob 41

Fancher, Don 95
Felsen, Henry Gregor 35–37, 138, 142
Felske, Gary 187
Fenical, Ken "Posie" 138–39
Ferrera, Don 28
Fisher, Bob 143
Fisher, "California Bill" 16, 30
Floyd, Doc 106
Ford, Dick 37–38
Ford, Edsel 5
Ford, William Clay 102
Foster, Mike 139
Foster, Tom 192
Francis, Connie 56
Fuller, Dana 73
Future Shock 44

Gallagher, Tom 143–44
Gardner, Virgil 71

Geisart, Eric 149
Geisler, Bruce 123–25
Gentle Persuasion 89
Gilbert, Fabrice 149
Gilbert, Paul 119, 177
Gloss, "Rajo" Ed 188–89
Gommi, Paul 115
Goodfellow, Dick 192
Goodman, Ray 142
Goody, Sam 84
Gratz, Carl 131
Griffin, Jim 5
Grubb, Roy 143–44
Guthrie, Gary 67–69
Guylas, Joe 143–44

Hahn, Frank 70–71
Hall, Reed 191
Hammel, Gina 40–41
Hammel, Robert 13, 16–17, 23–26, 33–35, 39–41
Haney, Doug 49–51
Haney, Harold 49–51
Hanna, Danny 176
Happy Days 56, 67, 95
Hardin, Drew 131
Hare, Bud 38, 71
Harrington, Dick 143–44
Harris, Julie 74
Harry, Wayne 106
Harvey, Jim 115
Hascall, Dr. Charles 41
Hatton, Paul 138
Haviland, George 102
Hebb, Paul 126
Hell's Highway 62–65
Henry, Jack 37–39
Hensley, Earl 187
Herbert, Chet 71
Hernandez, Joan 148
Hicks, Joe and Vera 51–53
Hill, Brian 115
Hill, Phil 26, 40
Hines, Bill 181–82
Hines, Ollie 103, 142
Hirohata, Bob 131
Hirschberger, Pete 140
Hoare, Tyler James 170
Hoffa, Jimmy 65
Holden-Higbee, Katherine 6
Hooper, Bob 77
Hot Rod 35–36
Hot Rod Magazine 1, 28, 42, 52, 58, 76, 96, 106, 129, 139, 150, 185
Hot Rodder! 36
Houle, Vern 37–39
How to Restyle Any Car 22
Howard, Johnny 77

Hunt, Don 143
Huntington, Roger 142
Huntley, Stan 192
Hurst, George 185–86
Hutchens, Hal 133
Hutchenson, Ben 143–44
Hyde, Wild Bill 30

Iandola, Dan 7–9, 119
Innes, Roger 143–44
Iskendarian, Ed 38

Jenkins, Andy 169
Jensen, Kermit 143–44
Johanson, Harold 71
Johnson, Bob 191
Johnson, Charles 142–44
Johnson, Glenn 129–32
Johnson, Ted 34
Jones, Ken 176
Jones, Stan 99
The Jungle 26
Junkins, Johnny 38
Juri, Leo 115

Kaiser, Bob 135
Kalitta, Connie 138
Klausing, Tim 41
Klibenski, Rick 136
Klotz, Gordon 143–44
Knight, Gary 143–44
Knowles, Bob 18, 95
Krueger, Bob 143–44
Krueger, Don 128
Kruger, Bill 166
Kruger, Jerry 166
Krupa, Gene 84
Kustom Kemps of America 93

Langdon, Harold 192
Larsen, Fred 71
Lawrence, Mike 177
Lea, Tory 106
Lewis, Jerry Lee 55
Liechty, Diana 179–80
Liechty, Tom 179–80
Liethold, Bert 72
Likes, Bill 67
Lindsley, Jim 169
Loewy, Raymond 15
Lowe, Donn 177
Luke the Drifter (Hank Williams) 55, 57
Lundberg, Jon 144
Lytle, Jim 111

Mabee, Joe 71
MacKinney, Roy "Mack" 115
MacMinn, Strother 34, 37–38

Mahaffey, Don 58
Mahaffey, Wayne 57–59
Marin, David 149
Marino, Tony 140
Martinez, Herb 171
Mauer, Gordie 144
McAfee, Ernie 7
McCarthy, Senator Joseph 27
McCormick, Bob 133
McGrath, Jack 38
McMullen, Tom 116
McMurtrie, Spike 138
McQueen, Steve 143–44
Meadors, Gary 118
Medley, Tom 58
Miller, Bruce 150, 191
Miller, Chuck 138
Milne, Norm 13
Moening, Bruce 143–44
Montgomery, Don 118
Moore, Don 191
Moreau, Dale 149–51
Morelli, Mike 21
Motor Trend 1, 101, 126
Motorsport 42
Mott, Stan 107–09
Munsford, Wayne 120–21

Nadeau, Ed 82
Nash, Pete 177
Nicholson, Don 138
Nicholson, Nick 106, 138
Nixon, President Richard 89
North, Mike 188
Nubback, Gary 115

Ochs, Stan 104–05, 145–46
O'Connor, Donald 26, 40
O'Kane, Neil 115
On the Road 80
Orr, Karl 37, 103
Orr, Veda 37, 103
Ory, Kid 83

Palmer, Jim 115
Parham, Bud 179, 191
Parks, Wally 38
Pauselius, Mike 115
Pawlowski, Elaine 138
Payne, Leon 57
Payne, Phil 26
Peck, Buz 106
Petersen, Roy 32, 142
Peterson, Bill 176
Phillips, Bunny 41
Phillips, Lucille 41
Philpot, Tom 135
Popular Mechanics 22
Porter, Chuck 71

Porter, Roger 106
Powell, Ken 187
Powell, Rod 171
Pratt, Tom 106
Presley, Elvis 94

Randol, Keith 66
Ray, Johnny 56
Rea, Geoff 119
Reason, Al 138
Reasoner, Bill 171
Reavie, Ed 36, 131
Rebel Without a Cause 141, 148
Reed, Brad 82
Rhoades, Randy 167
Rich, Buddy 84
Richard, Little 94
Rickerts, Joe 41
Ricketts, Steve 177
Riley, George 7–9
Road and Track 1
Roberts, "Fireball" 185
Robison, Earl 77
Rockwell, Norman 13
Rogers, Al 77
Roth, Ed "Big Daddy" 169, 171
Roth, Dr. Milton 41
Rufi, Bob 7
Runkle, Donald 192
Russell, Bruce 113

Santayana, George 11
Sauer, Steve 62, 129
Scace, Bill 73
Schaller, Bus 71
Scovell, Bob 192
Sharp, Chuck 170
Sherman, Alan 120
Shuman, Arnie 118
Shuman, Bernie 118

Silverstein, Marvin 130
Simmons, Jean 74
Simonatti, Roger 77, 176
Simpson, Joe 71
Slaughter, John 150
Smith, Clay 38
Smith, LeRoi "Tex" 114
Smith, Paul 167–68
Smothers Brothers 138
Snapp, Eldon 38
Snyder, Gary 75
Snyder, Tom 143–44
Southard, Andy, Jr. 118
Speed and Mileage Manual 22
Stanley, Chuck 41
Starbird, Daryl 65, 179
Starr, Kay 57
Steele, Tom 20
Stewart, James 64
Stockton, Jim 134
Stoesser, Rudi 34
Story, Ralph 41
Street Rod 150
Street Rodder 150
Strong, Emery 106
Stroppe, Bill 38
Styles, Dick 138
Sukalac, Pete 95
Sweet, Chuck 143–44

Talboy, Leonard 23
Tanzola, Warren 142
Taylor, Geoff Mitford 177
Telen, Don 77
Thocker, Marty 144
Towers, Terry 188
Treat, Fred 41
Turner, Kernan 82
Tyler, Tom 115

Vail, Gary 123
Van Dorn, Ray 30, 103, 155, 176
Van Dyck, Louis 26
Van Horn, Jim 142–43
Vaughn, Linda 184–87
Vetter, Craig 153
Von Arx, Eugene 8
Von Neuman, John 26
Vukovich, Billy 39

Waddill, Bill 143
Waddington, Hayden 192
Waight, David 161
Waite, Don 71
Walker, Jack 135
Waller, Fats 83
Walton, Harold 99
Walton, Kent 115
Weber, Harry 23
Wegner, Michael 177
Weidell, Connie 38
Weir, Chris 120
Weird Tales 42
Wescott, Dee 73, 140
Wescott, Kay 140
West, Jessamyn 89
West, John 177
Westergard, Harry 13
White, Vern 99
Wilburn, Kathy 150
Wilkerson, Dave 115
Will, Gary 150
Winiecki, Tad 152–54
Withey, Orville 192
Wolfe, Thomas 94

Youngstrom, Gordie 192

Zerbach, Bill 9–10
Zipp, Darrel 177

www.ingramcontent.com/pod-product-compliance
Ingram Content Group UK Ltd.
Pitfield, Milton Keynes, MK11 3LW, UK
UKHW050525150426
5217IPUK00026B/1807